There is absolutely no social criticism, of even the most implicit kind, in science fiction films. No criticism, for example, of the conditions of our society which create the impersonality and dehumanization which science fiction fantasies displace onto the influence of an alien It.

—*Susan Sontag*

Invasion of the Body Snatchers is perhaps the prime metaphor for the political paranoia of those years, while *Forbidden Planet* provides a more sophisticated analysis. In this latter film, the monsters are not insidious, implacable otherworldly beings against whom there is no defense short of complete mobilization, but rather creatures of our own ids, reflections of our own elemental fears.

—*James Monaco*

. . . we have yet to create our Gatsby, our Ahab, Emma Bovary, Huckleberry Finn. But *Charly* did that, both in the story and in the movie. That scene in which Cliff Robertson, after having had his intelligence upped, is standing before the conclave of the world's greatest scientists, and he's holding this dead mouse in his hand and he looks down at it and says, "Charly Gordon is a man who will very soon be what he was"—it wrenches your heart. I mean, I cry every time I see that scene. It's heartbreaking, and it's pure science fiction.

—*Harlan Ellison*

These opinions and more, on some of the finest science fiction films ever produced and some of the worst, square off within these pages, modified and flavored by the writing of one of the field's finest practitioners,

SCIENCE FICTION: STUDIES IN FILM

Science Fiction
Studies in Film

FREDERIK POHL & FREDERIK POHL IV

SF
ace books
A Division of Charter Communications Inc.
A GROSSET & DUNLAP COMPANY
51 Madison Avenue
New York, New York 10010

SCIENCE FICTION:
STUDIES IN FILM

Copyright © 1981 by Frederik Pohl and Frederik Pohl IV

An ACE Book

First Ace printing: January 1981
Published Simultaneously in Canada

2 4 6 8 0 9 7 5 3 1
Manufactured in the United States of America

TABLE OF CONTENTS

Introduction 1:
SCI-FI AND SF: EXPLORING THE BRIGHT CONTINENT

When Gary Kurtz appeared before two thousand science-fiction fans at the banquet of the 1977 World Science Fiction Convention, he was booed.

It wasn't that the fans hated him. Indeed, he was there to be honored—to receive an award, in fact, as producer of the madly popular Star Wars. *What got him the raspberry was a slip of the tongue. Intending only politeness, he began by saying, "I'm glad to be here with all you other sci-fi fans." And the effect on the audience was almost as though he had said to an NAACP dinner, "I'm glad to be here with all you niggers."*

"Sci-fi" was not intended to be a race name. It was invented in all geniality, a couple of decades ago, by the world's number-one science fiction fan, Forrest J. Ackerman. It caught on at once, with almost everybody. It became the standard shorthand term for science fiction with Time *and* Newsweek, *with* Variety *and the entire film and TV industry, with almost everybody who had ever heard of science fiction but did not know very much about it. The only major bodies of people with whom it did not catch on were those who loved science fiction best—its writers, its editors and, above all, its fans. With them "sci-fi" is a pejorative. The good stuff is "sf". "Sci-fi" is the junk.*

Still, the term "sci-fi" does have some well informed defenders. After all, its coiner, Forrest J. Ackerman, is not only an author and editor but has even earned the appellation of "Mr. Science Fiction", and if 4sj Ackerman lends his mana to a coinage what lesser person can quarrel? And scholars like Elizabeth Anne Hull reason that "sci-fi" is an appropriate term for that different, but not necessarily worse, kind of speculative imagining that films typically bring us. Star Wars is fairly sci-fi, according to Dr. Hull, while Robert A. Heinlein, for instance, is surely sf.

This is a useful distinction, but one with a few problems. Before we can distinguish between the terms we ought to define what at least one of them is, and oh! how hard that can be!

Science fiction is difficult to define, but usually possible to diagnose. You examine the body of the work in question. You look for certain symptoms. Is it about the future? Then it is probably science fiction. Does it take place on another planet? Then probably yes. Is the core of the story a significant new invention or discovery or event which changes the lives of persons around it? That's harder to decide. Like a temperature reading in the diagnosis of disease, it depends on degree. The Alec Guinness movie, The Man in the White Suit, shows that trait. Indeed, it fits quite comfortably into the science fiction canon, if one wants to put it there. But it is not what most people mean by "a sci-fi flick" at all. It has no spaceship, no Black Monolith, no disaster.

What is wrong with the diagnostic approach to science fiction is that it rests on analyzing content. It looks to see what the story is about, and that doesn't really solve the problem. The late English science fiction writer J. T. Phillifent (he wrote under the pseudonym "John Rackham") said that attempting to define sf in terms of content is wrong to begin with, since what distinguishes sf from competing creative genres is not content at all, but "method".

It is a loss to all of us that Phillifent died without saying just how he defined "the science fiction method". But that such a thing, analogous to the more famous "scientific method", does exist seems not arguable.

All creative works begin in the minds of their creators. When a science fiction writer constructs a novel or a film, he begins by asking himself a specific question. The question is, "What if—?", and the answer is the work. Question: "What if chemists invent a fabric that will never wear out?" Answer: The Man in the White Suit. *Question: "What if human evolution has been inspired by some outside force, instead of blindly obeying Darwin?" Answer:* 2001: A Space Odyssey. *Question: "What if creatures from another planet come to our own?" Answer:* The War of the Worlds, The Invasion of the Body Snatchers, The Thing from Outer Space. *Question: "What if some present social trend continues to its logical extrapolative conclusion?" Answer:* Brave New World, 1984, Just Imagine, The Time Machine.

The answer to the "What if—" question is sometimes called the "one big lie" that is permitted science fiction writers, and to the extent that it can be made to seem plausible, the story is science fiction rather than fantasy. To the extent that that answer is logically and dramatically satisfying, the story is good. But those are the parts of the process that constitutes the science fiction method, and the important observation to be made about that is that the process works on any raw materials at all. Not just spaceships, mutants or Martians. It works when applied to social phenomena like kid gangs (A Clockwork Orange), or to alternative possibilities in the prehistoric struggle for the survival of the fittest (The Planet of the Apes) or to engineering (Transatlantic Tunnel).

We are not yet home free, however, because defining something in terms of method implies that to be absolutely certain you need to be able to read the mind of the person who did it. The good sign of the coin is that we don't really need to define a thing in order to explore it. Marco Polo could not have drawn a map of the continent of Asia before he trudged to China, but he learned a lot about it on the way.

There is a clue to what sf is all about in the very fact that maps of it are so hard to draw. Arthur C. Clarke was once asked why he wrote the stuff, and he replied, "Because most other literature isn't concerned with reality." (1) Science fiction concerns itself with that greatest of realities confronting us all—change—constant, accelerating, sometimes even overwhelming change—in a way that no other literature does. In a similar vein, an Oxford don named Tom Shippey says, "Science fiction is hard to define because it is the literature of change, and it changes while you are trying to define it." (2)

If we have not yet managed much of a definition, take comfort from the fact that there is no very good definition of a continent, either. Look in your dictionary. You will find it says something like, "A continent is that body of land which competent geographers have agreed to term a continent."

So what is science fiction? It is that thing that people who understand science fiction point to, when they point to something and say, "That's science fiction!"

The importance of science fiction, really, doesn't lie so much in what it is as in what it does.

At its best, it does a great deal. Among other things:

It stretches the imagination.

It stimulates thinking about the future consequences of present actions.

It serves as a technology-transfer medium, telling its audiences what the state of the art is in many different disciplines.

It provides insights into our own world from outside— what Harlow Shapley called "The View from a Distant Star".

And, finally, it is the sovereign prophylactic against future shock. If you read enough science fiction, nothing ever takes you unaware.

Not much science fiction does all of these things. There is a lot that does none of them, lacks redeeming social value entirely, offers its audience nothing but pleasure and does not always deliver that.

But the best of science fiction does deliver in many or most of these areas; and maybe there is the difference between sf and sci-fi.

There is absolutely no social criticism, of even the most implicit kind, in science fiction films. No criticism, for example, of the conditions of our society which create the impersonality and dehumanization which science fiction fantasies displace onto the influence of an alien It.

—Susan Sontag (3)

When a critic like Susan Sontag said, even though it was a quarter of a century ago, that she could find no criticism of our society in science-fiction films, it was not malicious bigotry speaking. It was simply that she was looking in the wrong place. She was looking at The Mysterians *and* Rodan—*at sci-fi. She was managing not to notice, for instance,* The Time Machine *or even hoary old*

Metropolis, *to name but two of the films that would have blown her thesis out of the water at once.*

The sci-fi boom of the '50s was based partly (as we shall argue when we come to that chapter) on the political paranoia of the time, but it was also based on considerations of money. Sci-fi was cheap. The boom rested on three discoveries:

That you could photograph bugs and mat them in at super-heroic size to films of actors and sets;

That you could pull a toy rocket against a black backdrop and make it look reasonably like spaceflight; and

That if you put a space helmet on an actor, you could pretend that a horrendously inhuman alien being was inside.

In the 1920s the Westerns were the films of the possible. California desert was cheaper than a set, and you could always rent a horse. In the 1950s the film of the possible was sci-fi. They did not have to be very successful to succeed, because they were cheap. They did not need name actors. They did not need expensive new special effects, because they mostly used the ones that had been developed for something else. They did not even need expensive (much less talented) script writers—one of the sci-fi producers, J. Fred Gebhart, proudly boasted that he wrote his own. (It showed.) Hardly any of these people knew anything about science fiction . . . or needed to.

Sontag says that the dominant mode of these films was not really "science" fiction but disaster, and in that she is dead on target for most of them. The rest were The Man from Planet X. *With a few exceptions, they were made for exactly the same reasons, and often by exactly the same producers, as the beach-bunny films that came along a couple of years later. They could be made both cheaply and quickly—some were shot in a week!*

*That is where, as well as when, the term "sci-fi" began. There have been far more splendiferous exemplars later—*Superman *is sci-fi both* King Kongs *are sci-fi,* Star Wars *and* The Empire Strikes Back *are superlatively and delightfully sci-fi. What they have in common is that none of them says anything. What science fiction in print some-times does, sci-fi does not bother to. No sci-fi film (or novel) has ever troubled its reader's intellect.*

That's why people like Sontag can dismiss science-fiction films with so much contempt. Kingsley Amis pointed out that science fiction is usually recognized by the ninety per cent which is crud, and when some specimen of the worthwhile ten per cent shows up critics say, "Ah, but that isn't really science fiction."

But it is. What it isn't is sci-fi.

I grew up with science fiction, began reading it around 1930 at the age of ten, never stopped. All through my childhood and adolescence I read everything I could get my hands on, but science fiction by first choice. And my hunger for books was matched by my thirst for films.

In the decade of the Thirties, which were the years of my teens, I must have averaged three or four movies a week, not counting repeats. (A good movie was worth staying to see over again, and at least once my mother sent the police to scour the theater where I was watching a film for the fourth consecutive time.)

This was not just me. Movies were America's central anodyne in the 1930s and thereabouts. They were the most convenient and inexpensive pleasure anyone could buy. Going to the movies was a sort of McLuhanite syn-thesis of pleasure. The medium was as important as the message, especially in the Twenties and Thirties, when the marble palaces bloomed, all gilt and tapestry and densely carpeted floors, niches with statuary, tinkling fountains, crystal chandeliers. Before the theater chains were through there was not a community in the United States that did not have its stunning palace of film. The first-run theaters had orchestras and stage shows, and to clear the house an organist would roll out of concealment at the console of his mighty instrument. Even in the nabes there was a kind of luxury most people never saw anywhere else in their lives—perhaps in their churches, a few of them; never in their homes. To enter the Brooklyn Paramount or the Radio City Music Hall was to come into a richer and better world. (By the mid-Thirties it was usually even an air-conditioned one.) People behaved better at the movies. They were wittier as they waited in lines, more good-humored as they held doors for each other, more courteous and graceful as they intersected with strangers.

In the movies you were at your best, and what did your best behavior consist of? Why, exactly what you saw modeled before you on the screen. There was an approved behavior pattern for every sex, age and condition. The best behavior for a maiden was to be witty, kind, reverential toward culture and unquestionably an intact virgin. The best behavior for a youth was to be strong, courageous and, on first sight, aflame with ardor. The best behavior for a mother was to be self-effacing and always loving; for a father to be undemanding and wise; for a child to be ignorant, loving and cheerful. It is my opinion that half the social and sexual confusions of mid-Twentieth Century Americans came from unresolved dichotomies, as the models on the screens failed to match against the imperfect realities outside. But it is also my opinion that the civilizing screen taught graces and concerns to people who might have found no other place to learn them.

Except of course for books, but not everyone reads books. I did. I did both. Books were the meat that taxed the mind and stimulated thought. But films were the drink that slaked the thirst for experience.

Both experiences are often worth having. Either can, on occasion, be of transcendental delight. But they are not the same. There is a difference between them, and the exploration of that difference is what this book is about.

—Frederik Pohl

New York City
July 1980

Introduction 2:
CATCHING UP

I was born the year Forbidden Planet *was released. By the time I became aware that there were such things as science fiction films, over three quarters of them were already history. From this, I know, I get a different view of films than one would who had seen them all as they came out. I can never know the effect that Méliès'* A Trip to the Moon *had on its contemporary audiences, or, for that matter, what* The Day the Earth Stood Still *had on its. I wasn't there. My mother wasn't there for most of these events, even; she was far too young for film-going when, say,* Just Imagine *initiated, and instantly killed off, the science-fiction musical. But I think there are advantages to this accident of the calendar as well as limitations. I get the opportunity to judge each film on its merits, rather than in the context of expectation in which it was first viewed.*

Although they wouldn't show Forbidden Planet *for me in the maternity ward, it was still my first science fiction film. Seven or eight years after its release (and mine), it became WOR-TV's "Million Dollar Movie" for a whole week. WOR's custom was to show its features three times a day, just like a regular movie theater, and as a result of this (combined with a babysitter who didn't enforce bedtime rules, as long as he was left alone to do his homework) I managed to see* Forbidden Planet *four or five times during its run. I was hooked.*

By the time of the next truly significant film, 2001: A Space Odyssey, *I was pretty well able to catch up. The older films I saw on television; the newer ones mostly turned up as quadruple features (with fireworks, no less) at the drive-in, courtesy of monster-mad friends and their amazingly agreeable parents.*

In high school I was able to keep up my education by getting a job as usher, in Walter Reade's Mayfair Theater, in Asbury Park, New Jersey. It looked good to begin with. All the movies were mine, free, over and over again. It had its drawbacks, though, particularly when I learned the full power of the medium as I watched an audience of crazed Kung Fu'ers tearing up my theater. As time went on I got raised to projectionist, and finally manager, in college summer vacations; and along about then is when I decided I might as well formalize my relationship with film by getting a degree in it.

The place to do this was Syracuse University's S. I. Newhouse School of Public Communications. Mr. Newhouse, who had made his pile in newspapers, had put together a complex of studios, classrooms, laboratories and lecture halls for the University. Film majors were not supposed to just watch films, or even to study books about them. We made them. Tiny ones, to be sure; but after you have written, cast, set, lighted, photographed, directed and edited even a tiny film you develop a certain amount of respect for the people who make the big ones. And for the film people I consider the big ones—the ones who understand the grammar of film, who are capable of taking a script and transmuting it into a hundred and twenty good minutes on the screen—I have a great deal of respect. The courses were not all hands-on; we studied the arid wastes of semiotic analysis and memorized the "Wilson's Law" of Professor Tim Wilson. ("All films are too long.") I don't think a Syracuse film degree can turn your average college student into a Kubrick or a Lang, but it certainly helps understand what they do.

And so this book.

It seemed to us that there was a need to take a hard look at science fiction films, both as films and as science fiction. There are a great many picture books on the market, and some of them are really beautiful; there are a good many books about the making of individual films—most of them puff pieces, to be sure, but some not; and there is a substantial library of critical works, mostly academic in tone. But there did not seem to us to be a book that did full justice to both the film and the science fiction aspects of the sf film. In the course of the two years the writing of this book has entailed, we spent a great deal of time in Hollywood and other film centers, talking to people who were actually involved in making some of the great films, as well as endless library research and, of course, several thousand hours devoted to watching the films themselves.

I hope you will think it was all worth it.

—Frederik Pohl IV

New York City
June 1980

SOURCES

1.   Clarke, Arthur C. From *The Double: Bill Symposium*, Bill Bowers and Bill Mallardi, eds. privately published, 1969.
2.   Shippey, Tom. Keynote address, First World SF Conference, Dublin, 1977.
3.   Sontag, Susan. *The Imagination of Disaster*. Farrar, Strauss & Giroux.

Science Fiction
Studies in Film

———————————

Chapter 1

From Méliès to *Metropolis:* the Silents

Who invented the science fiction film?

It is almost as bad a question as asking who discovered America, since the answer depends greatly on what you consider to be "science fiction". There is certainly not much "science" in the earliest examples. (But then there is not much more science in some of today's science fiction best-sellers.)

You can even play word tricks, and say that "the science fiction film" existed before film itself did in the real world . . . at least in the sense that many things "existed" in science fiction (television, atomic power, space travel) before they had any real-life counterparts. In the early science fiction story *L'Eve Future,* author Villiers de L'Isle-Adam wrote a description of a motion picture—and a talkie at that!—long before Thomas Edison began his experiments with capturing motion in a camera. De L'Isle-Adam describes a kind of dramatic performance in which a vision of a woman,

> its transparent flesh miraculously photographed in color and wearing a spangled costume, danced a kind of popular Mexican dance. Her movements had the flow of life itself, thanks to the process of successive photography which can retain six minutes of movement on microscopic glass, which is subsequently reflected by means of a powerful lampascope. Suddenly was heard a flat and unnatural voice, dull-sounding and harsh. The dancer was singing the *alza* and the *olé* that went with her *fandango.* (1)

Patents have been granted on less. In fact, there is a story that at least one was granted and to a science fiction writer at that. In H. G. Wells's *The Time Machine,* as the Time Traveler returns from the future, he sees his landlady walking backward across a room. One of the early film pioneers read the passage and sought an interview with Wells to discuss the possibility of making such a sight possible with the motion-picture camera, and a joint patent was applied for.

Word games aside, there remain the questions of who made the first science fiction film and what it was. One thing we know for sure. It was a silent, and it happened very early.

The physical evidence exists, although seldom in the form in which the original makers delivered it to the projectors. No silent film, especially no silent science fiction film, survives in its precise original form. The closest we have are films recopied from paper prints (made in the first place for copyright reasons; film could not be copyrighted, but prints of films could). The physical films themselves do not survive at all, because the film base in use at the turn of the century does not live that long. It crumbles into powder in a few decades with even the best of handling. Most early films, in fact, received the worst. Master prints were burned or blown up in one war or another, when they were not simply thrown into the trash to clean house. Miles of film were sold for whatever money reclaiming the silver salts would bring.

So what we have are at best duplicates, printed from whatever version of the original was at hand when someone belatedly realized that they represented something worth saving. Some of the Méliès films were copied only in black and white, so the original color is forever gone. Even

Metropolis, as we see it today, represents only a little more than half of the seventeen-reel epic Fritz Lang shot in the mid-1920s, as little as seventy-five minutes instead of several hours. And they are not always the same seventy-five minutes, because the current prints were made from a variety of second-generation originals, each a little different due to the accidents of film breaks and splices, or of cutting to fit a time slot, or to suit some exhibitor's notion of what was worth showing. That master curator of sf film memorabilia, Forrest J. Ackerman, has for years been haunting showings of the film with a photographer next to him, catching stills that do not exist in the usual prints. There is even some faint hope that something close to the original seventeen reels, or at least the German version's twelve, can be reconstituted by matching all the present prints. But that's *Metropolis.* For lesser films, often only fragments remain and some—like the 1920 *Algol,* by Hans Werkmeister—are lost forever, barring a miracle.

Still, the big ones and the significant ones mostly survive, in some form or other, and on the question of priorities the evidence exists. It is only a question of interpretation. James Baxter, for instance, says that the first science fiction motion picture is a sixty-five foot strip of film from 1899—the scene from H. Rider Haggard's *She* in which Ayesha is transformed from eternal beauty to hag in a pillar of flame. Most students put it three years later, with *A Trip to the Moon* in 1902. That argument is only a quibble about dates. The man behind the camera was the same in both cases, and his name was Georges Méliès.

Of all the claims to fame Georges Méliès might have advanced for himself, the honor of making the first science fiction film is among the least. (Even assuming he had understood what the term "science fiction" meant, since it would not be invented for another quarter of a century.) Méliès was film's first and greatest pioneer of almost everything. Or else Louis Lumière was; both men have their partisans, and each was a very vocal partisan of himself. Méliès and Lumière occupied the same decades of film history, and those were the very decades in which film history began. They did many of the same things, quite independently often enough, because each had to invent what he did as he went along. (But they also avidly watched each others' films, and learned from them.) They did a number of quite different things, and there the argument was not about which of them had done them first but about which thing was better. Lumière was the first to capture reality in a film. Méliès was the first to invent it.

There is a parallel between their film rivalry and the concurrent one-upping between H.G. Wells and Jules Verne over the science fiction novel. Verne prided himself on his exact adherence to known science. Wells prided himself on his extrapolative imagination. The dichotomy between the Wells school and the Verne still exists in science fiction, most of a century later; and so does that between Lumière and Méliès in film.

What Lumière did was to open his shutters on the world around him, the readily visible world of Paris streets and factories. To recapture for his audiences on a screen what they could have seen merely by looking through a window was marvel enough for him. It was that for the audiences, too, since no one had ever done it for them before. What Méliès did was to trick his audiences by showing things that had never existed anywhere: a familiar practice for him, since he had had a career as a stage magician and knew the fun of the impossible.

One showed what was. The other gave form and color to what was not. Lumière put a camera in a French railway station, to show what it was like. Méliès (in *An Impossible Voyage*) showed a toy train taking off into space. When Lumière's camera showed a locomotive charging toward the audience women screamed. Méliès made them scream, too, but by stopping the camera while filming a pretty woman and substituting a skeleton, so that before the viewers' very eyes beauty turned to decay. Lumière was literal, and his tradition still lingers—*Fahrenheit 451,* even though it was filmed by one of the waviest of France's *Nouvelle vague* moviemakers, is in debt to Lumière. Méliès was figurative and fanciful; *Superman* is Méliès.

Marie-Georges-Jean Méliès made *A Trip to the Moon* in August, 1902, in between *The Catastrophe of the Balloon La Pax,* a sort of reconstructed newsreel, and *La Clownesse Fantôme,* one of his many conjuring films. In all, Méliès made 23 films that year, but *A Trip to the Moon* was almost the longest of them, 845 feet against his *Robinson Crusoe*'s 910, and certainly the one that has best survived. (Clips from it appeared as a prologue to *Around the World in 80 Days* half a century later.) The film was heavily borrowed. H. G. Wells's *The First Men in the Moon* had been published the year before, and the monstrous, lobster-clawed Selenites were Méliès's notion of what Wells's creatures would look like. Méliès' astronauts travel in an immense cannon-shell, straight out of Jules Verne's *From the Earth to the Moon,* forty years earlier. (Wells used the same Space Gun for his *Things to Come* in 1936). But the "plot" is Méliès's own. It is comedy, and would have been musical comedy if he had had a way to put sound on film—the pretty "stars" are dancers from the Théâtre Chatelet; the acrobats who played the Selenites were borrowed from the Folies-Bergère. The girl sitting on the Moon is one of Méliès's stable of stars of a different kind, Bleuette Bernon. By night, when Méliès could not film, she was a music-hall singer.

Georges Méliès was born in Paris on December 8, 1861, to a wealthy shoe manufacturer. The boy was not a good student, except in drawing; his best artistic works were painting sets for his toy puppet theater. Méliès wanted to become an artist, but his father put him to work in the family shoe factory. It was not a loss. The factory machines taught him how to handle hardware, and how to improvise. As a young man he became interested in magic, and that was a gain, too; his films show the effects of all his life interests: art, machinery, magic and theater.

As soon as he was able, Méliès quit the shoe business and bought the Theatre Robert-Houdin from the great magician's widow. There he produced spectacular shows for the Parisian public, magical illusions combined with adventuresome plots—many of them later redone as films—but the theater was not profitable and, in 1895, Méliès looked for something new. He had seen the Lumière brothers' films and tried to buy one of their cameras. They were too shrewd to sell to a possible competitor, but Méliès was shrewd, too. He built his own, which he called a "Kinetograph". He began using it at once—for newsreels, advertising films, documentaries, travelogues. Most of his early films were about 60 feet long, running one minute—as much film as the Kinetograph would hold.

Story has it that Méliès was filming a Paris street scene when his camera jammed. Méliès untangled the film and resumed shooting; when he developed the film he found that where a bus had been before the jam a hearse had "miraculously" appeared. It was the first stop-action photography, and Méliès saw its possibilities. He was off and running.

His specialty became the trick film, combining photographic novelties with bits of stage magic. He made hundreds of them. His favorite themes were: fairies; the temptation of Man by devils; and the removal and restoration of living animals and humans (or often just parts of their bodies). Méliès looked at the cinema primarily as a method for presenting his stage productions to a wider audience, and as a means for doing tricks over and over until they were just right, without having the audience see his failures. His usual procedure was to work out a collection of tricks, then invent a story to tie them together. It served him well. He had produced more than 400 successful films by the time he made *A Trip to the Moon.*

Because Méliès had been a magician, he saw film as a way of magicking audiences with "dreams" or "nightmares"—one or the other of those two words appear in many of his titles. Because he had been a cartoonist, he supplemented his live action with animation. Because he had been a stage director, he never thought of moving the camera—and in *A Trip to the Moon* his actors bowed to the audience as they finished their turns. And because he had been a manufacturer, he knew the value of mass-producing goods. In his life he made more than 800 films! Most were short, some were mere scraps,—but what a total!

All the films were, of course, shot in black and white, since color photography had not been invented, but often they were shown in color. The color was laboriously painted in, frame by frame, in transparent aniline tints and alcohol, by a Mme. Thuillier and the other Parisian ladies in her studio. More than 15,000 frames had to be painted for each copy of a film like *A Trip to the Moon,* and the colorists were not always accurate—clothes, for instance, would sometimes lag behind the characters who wore them. Coloring more than doubled the cost of a print, but also increased receipts at the box office even more.

> I made myself the model sculptured terra cotta and the plaster moldings. . . . The entire cost was about 10,000 francs, a sum relatively high for the time, caused especially by the mechanical sceneries and principally by the cost of the cardboard and canvas costumes made for the Selenites.
> —Georges Méliès (2)

When *A Trip to the Moon* was released, the film audience was very different from today's, nor was it even homogeneous. Some of those first viewers might have seen the film in Méliès's own Theatre Robert-Houdin, as a part of a program including stage illusions and musical turns. Others would have seen it in a converted store-front theater, as part of a collection of short subjects.

For a modern viewer, *A Trip to the Moon* is nostalgically moving. We know more about science, and we have seen the effects of post-Griffith film structure, so we see the film's faults at once. We notice immediately that all the scenery is painted flats. We watch the action run off the edges of the frame, and wonder why the camera does not pan to follow it. The reason is very simple. Méliès didn't know any better. He was inventing the medium as he went along.

It is not certain that *A Trip to the Moon* is actually the

first science-fiction film. Apart from Méliès's own earlier *She,* there was the British *The X-Ray Fiend* in 1897, Ferdinand Zecca's 1901 *The Conquest of the Air* and several other claimants; but Méliès gets the title, if for no other reasons than that *A Trip to the Moon* was seminal, and survived.

A Trip to the Moon runs fourteen minutes. Its scenario of thirty "scenes", each one a little skit, was written by Méliès, who also acted in the film, designed the sets and costumes, directed, photographed and produced it. We begin by seeing a "scientific congress at the Astronomic Club", the planning of the trip, the recruitment of the explorers (and, of course, their body servants), the workshops where the shell is built, the foundries where the space-gun is cast, the astronomers entering the shell and the shell being loaded into the cannon, a parade, the firing of the gun, a salute to the flag: the voyage is launched. The shell flies through space, approaches its destination and lands right in the eye of the Man in the Moon. We look back to see the Earth, then visit "the plain of craters" and see a volcanic eruption. There is a dream, then a snowstorm, then a descent into one of the craters at 40° below zero, where the explorers pass through a grotto filled with giant mushrooms, encounter the Selenites, battle, are captured, escape to their shell, "drop" into space, wind up at the bottom of the sea and are rescued. The closing scenes are:

26. The great fete and triumphal march.
27. Crowning and decorating the heroes of the trip.
28. Procession of the Marines and the Fire Brigade.
29. Inauguration of the commemorative statue by the manager and the council.
30. Public rejoicings.

∿∿∿∿∿∿∿∿∿∿∿∿∿∿∿∿∿∿∿∿∿∿∿∿∿∿∿∿∿∿

FILMOGRAPHY
LE VOYAGE DANS LA LUNE (A Trip to the Moon)
(Star, 1902, French) 825 ft.

Producer/director/writer/costumes/sets, Georges
Méliès; suggested by Jules Verne's *From the Earth to
the Moon* and H.G. Wells's *The First Men in the
Moon;* camera, Lucien Tainguy.

Georges Méliès (Leader of Expedition); Bleuette
Bernon (The Woman in the Crescent); Victor André;
Delpierre; Farjaux-Kelm-Brunnet; Ballet Girls of the
Théâtre du Chatelet (Stars); Acrobats of the Folies
Bergère (Sélenites).

∿∿∿∿∿∿∿∿∿∿∿∿∿∿∿∿∿∿∿∿∿∿∿∿∿∿∿∿∿∿

Space travel was more interesting in those days; no
spacesuit was required, and the trip took just a few minutes. Moreover, each star—and there are quite a few
between Earth and Moon in the film—is a beautiful woman; and, finally, the Selenites' method of waging war is
more concerned with turning cartwheels and disappearing
than with doing harm to anyone.

After *A Trip to the Moon* Méliès was at the height of his
powers, but they had only about another decade to run. In
1905 he made *An Impossible Voyage,* in which a train
travels so fast that it flies off into space, taking its occupants
through the aurora borealis, through a solar flare and back
to Earth. In 1907 he borrowed again (and again, pretty
loosely) from Jules Verne, with *20,000 Leagues Under the
Sea, or, a Fisherman's Nightmare.* His pace slowed. In
1912 he made *The Conquest of the Pole* and three other
films, and he never made another.

Méliès was not a businessman, or at least not of the
stamp of the film giants already growing all over the world.

His films were very popular throughout Europe and America because they were high in production values, compared to the competition, but they were also more expensive to produce. Anyone with a printer could duplicate them, and they were bootlegged extensively. His New York office was robbed. The U.S.A. imposed an import duty on motion-picture prints, so Méliès shipped duplicate negatives across the water to save money. No special laboratory work was needed to make the duplicate; he simply shot each scene with two simultaneous cameras. But it meant more cost. Finally, he could not meet the payments on his loans, was foreclosed; and World War I put him out of business. The French government requisitioned his theater for a fraction of its value. Four hundred of his films were melted down to become French army bootheels, Méliès set fire to hundreds more in despair, and he was reduced to running a sweets shop by the Gare Montparnasse with his ex-mistress, now bride, Jehanne d'Alcy. He was discovered, as a living fossil of film, in the early 1920s and had a brief moment of revived fame, with talk of "consultancies" and honors. Then that bubble burst, too. He lived the rest of his long life in a home for destitute actors.

Over the next couple of decades there were scores of what could be called science fiction films that are worthy of mention, worthy of study—worthy, in fact, of almost anything but being sat through. It was twenty years before anyone did much better than Méliès in sf film; but film itself was growing huge. The tiny minutes-long scraps of Méliès and Lumière were growing into the standard Hollywood seven-reelers. Stars were born. Audiences swelled to the tens of millions. The new cinema royalty drove their Stutz

Bear-Cats and were photographed by their swimming pools, and many a millionaire was made overnight.

The part of all this that could be called science fiction was tiny, and very far from being self-aware; but it was there. There were even stories, and personalities, that remain recognizable today. The first version of *Frankenstein* was made in 1910 by the mighty Edison studios, and pirated in 1915 by Ocean Film Corp. as *Life without Soul.* In 1913, H. G. Wells was plagarized again (counting Méliès as the pioneer in that, too) with *The Island of Terror,* a thinly disguised version of *The Island of Dr. Moreau.* A silly little puppet film made in 1917, *The Dinosaur and the Baboon,* was the great model-maker Willis O'Brien's first experiment in animating prehistoric animals; eight years later he got his chance to do bigger and better tricks with rubber and wire in making the prehistoric beasts for the 1925 production of A. Conan Doyle's *The Lost World.* There was a film that had everything! Stampeding animals, erupting volcanos, a foot-high brontosaurus knocking down a scale-model Tower Bridge— and Bessie Love to play the female lead. The great René Clair tried his hand at genuine, if rather simple-minded, sf in the 1923 *Paris Qui Dort,* released in English as *The Crazy Ray.* The Clair film constitutes a significant first. In it, Albert Prejean, playing the part of the night watchman at the Eiffel Tower, wakes up to find that only he and a handful of other Parisians have escaped the effects of a mad scientist's experiment with a paralyzing ray, and joins with the scientist's daughter to deal with the consequences. That's the first: the triad of mad scientist, pretty daughter and hard-handed hero who repairs the scientist's blunders and carries the girl away. Half the science-fiction pulp writers of the 20s, 30s and 40s plugged the durable trio into their stories.

As early as 1913, J. Wallett Waller made *Message from Mars*, filming a successful London play about a Martian who comes to Earth to help pitiful humanity with its problems, and in 1924 Soviet director turned the idea around, when Jacob Protazanov made the greatest Russian science-fiction film of the time, *Aelita: The Revolt of the Robots.* Like *Message from Mars, Aelita* was also taken from a play, this one by no less a writer than Alexei Tolstoy. The film made by Mezrabom-Russ was a surreal, or a cubist, or an expressionist, but anyway a daringly designed epic of the interplanetary romance between the Queen of Mars (played by Yulia Salontsena) and a Russian cosmonaut who comes from the fledgling U.S.S.R. to bring Red socialist harmony to the Red Planet. It is meant as comedy. The laughs come from the Queen of Mars's reactions to being introduced to such fleshly Earth amusements as kissing (they don't do that on Mars) and from the comic adventures of two stowaways; but in the savagely cut version that appeared in the United States (and much more so in the battered prints that now survive) the comedy is badly bruised. One can only guess what it might have been like in the original. Still, the settings, designed by two experts from the Kamerny Theater in Moscow, Isaac Rabinovitch and Alexandra Exter, look nicely fanciful, more like curious previsions of Buckminster Fuller than anything in the real world, especially the Soviet world of 1924. *Aelita,* with all its faults, is one of the best science-fiction films from the days of the silents. It would be half a century (until *Solaris*) before anything as impressive came from the Soviet Union again.

かんかんかんかんかんかんかんかんかんかんかんかんかんかんかんかん

(*Aelita*) is far more interesting to read about than to gaze upon. The producers had quite a good if a none too fresh idea, but it is worked out with a certain apathy, possibly because the Russians did not detect an opportunity to spread a little propaganda. The very passages that one conjures up in one's imagination are not in the film. Instead there are many scenes with queer settings and Martians sparsely costumed in spiked hats and celluloid or metal garments. . . . The film is short, for which one feels thankful, but, short as it is, it seems too long.

—Mordaunt Hall (3)

かんかんかんかんかんかんかんかんかんかんかんかんかんかんかんかん

FILMOGRAPHY
AELITA: THE REVOLT OF THE ROBOTS (Mezrabom/Amkino, 1924, Soviet) 6050 ft.

Director, Yakov A. Protazanov; script, Fyodor Otzep and Alexei Faiko from the play by Alexei Tolstoy; art directors, Issac Rabinovitch, Alexandra Exter, Viktor Simov, and Sergei Kozlovski; camera, Yuri A. Zhelyabuzhsky and Emil Schuneman.

Cast: Nikolai Tseretelli, Igor Ilinski, Konstantin Eggert, Nikolai Batalov, Yuri Zavadsky, Valentina Kuinzhi.

かんかんかんかんかんかんかんかんかんかんかんかんかんかんかんかん

Probably *Aelita's* design and sets were influenced by an even more famous silent film, *The Cabinet of Dr. Caligari* (1919).

Is *Caligari* science fiction? It is hard to say so with a straight face. Read the essentials of the story and see for yourself: A certain Dr. Sonnow, operating under the stage name of "Dr. Caligari", runs a carnival attraction. His main freak is a sleeping man, Cesare, whom Caligari commands to awaken and perform somnambulistic displays for the audiences. Between performances, Caligari gives Cesare an after-hours job: he sends the sleeper out to commit murders.

It is not the story that interests *Caligari*'s viewers. What gives the film its vast importance, so much that no writer on film since 1919 has failed to give us his comments on it, is its technique. *The Cabinet of Dr. Caligari* appeared in the middle of and was part of, the revolution in modern art. Its sets and backdrops were foreshortened and distorted. The acting, even in the context of the universal mugging of the early silents, was highly stylized. Contemporary reviewers agreed that *Caligari* was a revolutionary film, differing only on what name to give to the revolution. "It is not Cubism," *Life* decided, but *Exceptional Photoplays* thought it was—or else Dadaist—or else, perhaps, "a sort of reflection in the world of plastic representation of the conceptions of relativity which are agitating mathematicians and astronomers." Time has not quieted that quarrel.

Caligari was made in Germany, just after the 1918 defeat. The United States had not quite recovered from the anti-Germanism of World War I, and it took a year or two to be imported (by Samuel Goldwyn) for American audiences. A considered opinion came a decade later from Erwin Panofsky, who declared, in the exact tradition of Louis Lumière, "The medium of the movies is physical reality." That being so, "it becomes evident that an attempt at subjecting the world to artistic prestyling, as in (*Caligari*), could be no more than an exciting experiment that could exert but little influence upon the general course of events. To prestylize reality prior to tackling it amounts to dodging the problem. The problem is to manipulate and shoot unstylized reality in such a way that the result has style."

A decade later still, in *Film Form,* Serge Eisenstein called *Caligari* a "barbaric carnival of the destruction of the healthy human infancy of our art." Eisenstein might not have been wholly dispassionate. When he wrote those lines the *Wehrmacht,* under Adolph Hitler, was practicing its own barbaric carnivals of destruction all across the Western U.S.S.R. Even Jean Cocteau complained that what was most interesting about *Caligari* was not cinematic: it was settings, rather than camera effects—this from the man who went on to make *The Blood of a Poet!*

Really, one can qualify *Caligari* as science fiction only if one is prepared to believe that "the secrets of somnambulism" represent some sort of yet undiscovered scientific reality. But there is a better reason for mentioning the film. The director for *Caligari* was Robert Wiene. The producing company was the German giant, UFA. To translate the scenario of Hans Janowitz and Carl Meyer into acceptable form they brought in a script doctor. His name was Fritz Lang.

So, in the history of science fiction film *Caligari*'s influence was far from "little". Whatever else it might have been or done, it brought together Wiene, Lang and UFA, the team that collaborated on the biggest blockbuster of the genre, the most expensive film ever made in Germany till that time, the first big-budget and fully aware science fiction film: *Metropolis.*

What a wonder film was! And still is, to be sure—but it's not quite the same. After nearly a century of life it has powerful competitors for the public's leisure time: television; tape cassettes; interactive electronic gaming; and a host of other marvels. But in those days—for half a cen-

THE CABINET OF DR. CALIGARI (UFA, 1919)
The doctor goes for a stroll among the 'cubist' sets.

FILMOGRAPHY
DAS KABINETT DES DR. CALIGARI (The Cabinet of Dr. Caligari) (UFA, 1919, German) six reels.

Producer, Erich Pommer; director, Robert Wiene; script, Karl Mayer and Hans Janowitz from a story by Hans Janowitz; art directors, Walter Reimann, Walter Röhrig, and Hermann Warm; camera, Willy Hameister.

Cast: Werner Krauss, Conrad Veidt, Lil Dagover, Rudolf Lettinger, Friedrich Feher, Rudolf Klein-Rogge.

tury, nearly, from just before the First World War to just after the Second—movies were almost the only game in town. Radio could not make as much happen for its mass audiences. Perhaps books could, but only at the expenditure of the effort to read and imagine. The neighborhood film palace was where the action was. The flappers and the doughboys, the bonus marchers and the migrant farmers, the draftees and the returned veterans on the GI Bill—and their parents and their children, too—all went to the movies for pleasure, because that was where pleasure could most cheaply and effectively be bought. If there ever was a mass art form, it was "The Movies."

Most people went to The Movies purely for fun, and the early critics reflected that. Serials were better than feature films, one reviewer announced, because audiences "want variety and won't stand being wearied." Another revealed that the best foreign films were from the Latin countries, because "the French and Italian performers are more adept than any other nationality in talking with their hands." But even in the earliest silent days, there were those students who saw the "art" in the mass art form, and felt the awesome responsibility of film's power.

Yet that responsibility was not, all in all, very well met. Today's observers get an inflated notion of the merit of early films, because it is only the ones that were in some way special that survived. The great bulk of the "product" was—product.

Why is this so? Apologists for the film industry say that the producers could not, after all, sell what the customers were unwilling to buy. Until audiences evolved who were capable of appreciating masterpieces, masterpieces could not be made.

Bearing in mind the film's monopoly on the world's

recreation, this is hardly true. Audiences took what they got. They did have the limited franchise of the box office. But their votes, in the long run, were almost always "aye"; you can count on your fingers the major film studios that managed to lose money during Hollywood's long reign over the world's culture. Audiences did not go to a movie as much as they went to "the movies", and, particularly after the rise of the double feature, their votes were no more than 50% effective at best. Hollywood knew this well. It used the second half of the double feature to fob off its most meaningless and meretricious works. It could have used it for its most aspirant.

The history of England's BBC gives evidence that audiences will accept even culture, at least in limited amounts, if that is what they are offered. The Beeb developed audiences for serious music and history, on both radio and television, while America's commercial networks developed knee-jerk consumers instead. Hollywood could have done something of the same, but did not bother.

In Germany, UFA bothered. James Monaco says, "UFA set about consciously raising the esthetic standards of German film. The result was one of the major efflorescences of talent in cinema history: German Expressionism." And a grand and lasting result of that was *Metropolis*.

Erich Pommer produced *Metropolis*. Robert Wiene was associated with it. The script was by Thea von Harbou. But the brain behind it was Fritz Lang. He carried the seed of the story around for a couple of years, and what inspired it was that futuristic city of slaves to the machine, New York. He came in to the port from postwar Berlin, a former enemy alien, not allowed at once to land, and gazed out at the skyline. It would be half a century before every city in

the world had one just like it, and it was a picture Lang wanted to get on a screen. He did not yet have a story, but that came shortly later, when he saw Broadway and Times Square, advertising signs, neon lights and traffic. He brought back the notion to his wife, von Harbou, worked with her on the script, and *Metropolis* was the result.

The story of *Metropolis* is complex. We are in the city of Metropolis in the year 2000 AD. The city is run by an industrial titan, John Masterman, who lives with his son, Freder, and the other wealthy aristocrats, in skyscraper penthouses. The workers live far below in squalor. Freder falls in love with a beautiful and spiritual girl of the working class, Maria; in order to break up the romance (and take the steam out of the workers' attempts to better their condition) Masterman orders his pet mad scientist, Rotwang, to construct a robot duplicate of Maria. Something goes wrong—the robot leads the workers to riot; the city is damaged; its waterworks are destroyed, and the lower levels are flooded. Maria rescues trapped children and leads the others to safety; boy gets girl, and Masterman shakes hands with the leader of the workers' revolt. Rotwang and his robot are disposed of, and everybody, we are led to believe, lives happily ever after. But it is not the plot that makes *Metropolis* great; it is the spectacle. UFA claimed to have used more than 30,000 extras in the mob scenes (eleven thousand had to shave their heads). The machines looked like Frank R. Paul drawings; the laboratory scenes were copied in a dozen subsequent sf films. Even today, the effect is impressive. In the mid 1920s it was astonishing.

When Lang began *Metropolis* he was still a young man, but not an inexperienced one. He had already fought and been wounded in World War I; while ex-*Leutnant* Lang was convalescing he first tried writing film scenarios. In 1917 *Hilde Warren and Death* was produced, with Lang himself playing Death. With his aid and occasional collaboration, Lang's wife, Thea von Harbou, turned her hand to writing novels about the future. The war made Lang think about his personal future. Postwar Germany, with the mark rapidly descending to the value of used Kleenex, taught him concern about social catastrophes. New York showed him a vision of physical things to come. With his rapidly growing experience in film—he had already completed several successful films, including the *Siegfried* for which von Harbou had also done the screenplay—*Metropolis* was inevitable.

I have my own ideas regarding the trend of civilization and the state it will have reached when our great-great-grandchildren are adults. You also have your opinion. No doubt it differs from mine. Erich Pommer has his, and it may differ from both yours and mine. He puts his in a picture and asks you and me to accept it. I, for one, will do no such thing. I refuse to believe that a century hence workingmen will be slaves who live underground. If Pommer wished to produce a story laid in a mythical country, and showed me bullfrogs driving rabbits tandem, I would not quarrel with him, for it is his own mythical country and I must accept all that his brain people it with; but when he says, "This is what your descendants will be doing one or two hundred years hence," I refuse to follow him, for definite knowledge on the matter being unobtainable, I do not see why I should dismiss my own opinion and accept his.
—Welford Beaton (5)

It was Lang's intention in the film to show what the world *might* come to in another century or so. (He thought of the movie's action taking place in the year 2000, but when *Metropolis* was imported to the United States Paramount's flacks did not think that adventurous enough; they advertised the film as a preview of a thousand years in the future.) Like any good science fiction writer, Lang did not pretend to show *the* future. *Metropolis* is a caution, not a forecast. But, as with all science fiction, some audiences, and many critics, took the warning for the belief, and bitterly resented being told that this was what future generations were condemned to.

But resentment was balanced by a thrill of startled delight. For a film's success the next best thing to unanimous adulation is sharply divided opinion—sometimes *even* better, because controversy starts people talking. *Metropolis* was a great success. It needed to be, since it was so terribly expensive. America beckoned. Paramount hired Channing Pollock to write English-language titles and cut a "tiresome" twelve reels (already reduced from the original seventeen) down to an American audience-sized seven (Pollock did so by cutting out most of the human relationships, shrewdly saving all the crowds and shock and special effects. He was paid $20,000 for the job.). In 1927 *Metropolis* opened in New York, to a drum-roll of reviews studded with words like "stupendous", "sardonic", "overwhelming", "unique", "an eye-crasher." "On Saturday night, after the first view of *Metropolis*," said the New York *Telegram*'s critic, Frank Vreeland, "I picked myself up out of my seat at the Rialto feeling like a limp rag. . . . Here at last the movies have truly and immemorially justified themselves, with a smashing, reverberant idea that might have swept, all glowing and palpitating, out of the boldest pages of H. G. Wells."

Wells himself was the first to disagree. Perhaps thinking darkly of the probable debt Lang owed to his own novel, *When the Sleeper Awakes,* published a quarter of a century before, he dismissed *Metropolis* as "quite a silly film".

A Technical Marvel

Nothing like *Metropolis,* the ambitious UFA production that has created wide international comment, has been seen on the screen. It, therefore, stands alone, in some respects, as a remarkable achievement. It is a technical marvel with feet of clay, a picture as soulless as the manufactured woman of its story. Its scenes bristle with cinematic imagination, with hordes of men and women and astounding stage settings. It is hardly a film to be judged by its narrative, for despite the fantastic nature of the story, it is, on the whole, unconvincing, lacking in suspense and at times extravagantly theatric. It suggests a combination of a preachment on capital and labor in a city of the future, an R.U.R. idea and something of Mrs. Shelley's *Frankenstein.* . . . But at the same time the various ideas have been spliced together quite adroitly. It is a subject on which an adverse comment has to be taken from the perspective of the enormity of the task, as most other pictures would fade into insignificance if compared to it.

—Mordaunt Hall (6)

What stupendously and immemorially crashed the eye was the spectacle and concept in *Metropolis.* Audiences and many critics were overwhelmed. Perhaps due to Pollock's drastic cutting, the more personal elements of the film hardly whelmed anyone at all. Welford Beaton wished that there had been two directors—Lang for spectacle, someone like Lubitsch for "making the characters human." In *The Nation,* Evelyn Gerstein thought that "*Metropolis* lacks cinematic subtlety. It is only in the shots of the machinery in motion and in the surge of the revolutionists that it is dynamic. . . . It is Metropolis itself, the city of domed basements and curving machine-rooms, of massed buildings that conceal the sky, of aeroplanes that ply their corner-to-corner traffic, or trains that seem to shoot into unmeasured and untracked space, that makes Fritz Lang's film so significant."

For Lang and his co-workers, such criticisms could not have been hard to take. They knew what they had done, and the reviews proved that they had succeeded. They had produced a dystopia, a "comic inferno" long before Kingsley Amis invented the term, and they had conveyed to their audiences exactly what they had wanted them to see. The greatest risk had not been that audiences might be shaken up and disturbed, but that they might laugh in the wrong places. Disbelief = resentment = contempt = angry laughter. In the event, there was little disbelieving laughter, though Frank Vreeland noted that, "One has the feeling that these devouring industrial dinosaurs, wreathed in cruel gusts of steam like Moloch, grind out collarbuttons."

After *Metropolis*, Lang went on to make *The Girl in the Moon* (again with Thea von Harbou writing the script) in 1929, and the memorable crime and suspense thrillers, *M* and *The Testament of Dr. Mabuse* a couple of years later. The Nazis gave him trouble, and he left wife and country to wind up in Hollywood where, over nearly thirty years, he was responsible for a great many films, mostly low budget, mostly trivial. Lang's is one of the case histories which

have given Hollywood its bad name as a profligate dissipa-
tor of talent.

But *Metropolis* remains a triumph. It is more than half a
century old, and pieces of it have cropped up in science
fiction films (and novels and TV programs) ever since. The
floating bands of light that animated Lang's robot also
brought El Brendel back to life in *Just Imagine* in 1930 and
awakened Boris Karloff in his first *Frankenstein.* The de-
formed and black-gloved right hand of Rotwang is echoed
in Peter Sellers' Dr. Strangelove. The model of the robot
might have been the model for Jack Williamson's *The
Humanoids.* "This bizarre film," Frank Vreeland said,
"may bewilder some at first, because it is frankly a story of
the future, without any modern trick framework to make
the usual puerile connection with the average subway
straphanger." He put his finger on it exactly. *Metropolis*
did not cop out. It did not kid its subject, or pretend it was
all a dream. Thus, it is the first of the serious and self-aware
science fiction films.

While *Metropolis* was being made in Germany, *Amazing Stories*, the first science fiction magazine, was being
made in America. The two together constitute a
watershed. They set the pattern for what science fiction
could be in their media. There have been many better
films and better magazines since, but those two defined the
field.

SOURCES

1. de L'Isle-Adam, Villiers. From the story *L'Eve Future.*
2. Melies, George. Quoted by Lewis Jacobs in *The Rise of the American Film,* 1939.
3. Hall, Mordaunt. *The New York Times,* Mar. 26, 1929, 34:1.
4. Unsigned article in *The New York Dramatic Mirror,* Nov. 14,
1908.
5. Beaton, Welford. *The Film Spectator,* Sept. 3, 1927.
6. Hall, Mordaunt. *The New York Times,* Mar. 7, 1927, 16:3.

A decade ago I spent three days as Fritz Lang's neighbor in a Rio de Janeiro beachfront hotel. The master was old, tottering and nearly entirely blind. He spoke softly and seldom, and made his way around the Copacabana on the arm of his disciple and friend, Bob Bloch. He was eighty, but his mind was clear. He remembered making *Metropolis* and all the others in detail. I asked him if he would like to make something as ambitious and revolutionary as *Metropolis* again. Considering the state of his eyes and his health it was not a sensible question, but he gave me a sensible answer. "I can't," he said, "but you can be sure I *would*."

—FP

METROPOLIS (UFA, 1927)
Fritz Lang (to right of camera) directing a scene from the first sf block-buster.

FILMOGRAPHY
METROPOLIS (UFA, 1927, German) seventeen reels.

Producer, Erich Pommer; director, Fritz Lang; script, Fritz Lang and Thea von Harbou from a novel by Thea von Harbou; art directors, Otto Hunte, Rich Kettelhut, and Karl Vollbrecht; special effects, Eugen Shuften; music, Konrad Elfers and Gottfried Happertz; camera, Karl Freud and Günther Rittau.

Cast: Brigit Helm (Maria/Mary); Alfred Abel (Jon Frederson/John Masterman); Gustav Fröhlich (Freder/Eric); Rudolf Klein-Rogge (Rotwang); Theodor Loos; Heinrich George; Erwin Biswanger; Fritz Rasp.

Chapter 2

Imagining Things: The Thirties

From *Just Imagine* to *Things to Come*—and beyond—the decade of the 1930s was full of the real stuff.

It was a time of ferment. Along with the birth of the first science fiction magazine and the first triumphant science fiction film, the end of the Twenties had seen the first all-talking motion pictures. The world, especially Hollywood, was changed forever. Western civilization was stumbling blindfold through the beginnings of the Great Depression, and all the crystal balls had gone to black, but Hollywood thrived. Nothing succeeds so well in hard times as a nice, cheap luxury. You could go to the neighborhood film palace for a quarter if you were a grownup, for a dime if you were a kid, and for a can of beans to donate to the local unemployed on Tuesdays. You could laugh and forget your troubles at a comedy, the farther out the better—the mad Marx Brothers began their fantastic rise in the year of the Crash, 1929, and were on the decline by the mid-1930s, as the Depression began to ease. And in 1930 the first full-scale, all-talking science fiction comedy ever made appeared. It was called *Just Imagine*.

Just Imagine was made in 1930, about 1980. There was not much precedent for science-fiction films in America in 1930. The major genre films had been made abroad, and even the label of "science fiction" itself was still newborn. The producers must have regarded it as a gamble, and not a cheap one, either. In order to secure that willing suspension of disbelief that even a slapstick musical comedy needs, they resorted to making "the usual puerile connection with the subway straphangers'' that Frank Vreeland had decried three years earlier. They attempted to validate its "predictions" by prefacing it with a sort of comic-documentary which showed the New York of 1880, leaped to the New York of 1930 and then invited the audience to "just imagine" what an equal jump into the future might produce. What it produced was baggy-pants comedy, a couple of extremely forgettable songs, some surprisingly elaborate dance production numbers, a vision of a world in which skyscrapers had scraped right through the top of the sky and city traffic jams were made up of airplanes and autogyros and a—well—a plot.

> Fantasy, fun and melody are shrewdly linked in *Just Imagine,* the current attraction at the Roxy. . . . In the Gotham of the future there are all manner of novel ideas, including a city with nine levels, landing places for dirigibles and airplanes, which rise and descend like helicopters. It is a poor man, indeed, who cannot afford an airplane. The television works to perfection, even to discovering D-6 (Marjorie White) in her boudoir. She is able to dart out of vision, however, to add to her momentarily inextensive attire. Then there are strange circles of light instead of doorbells, and elevators that shoot up or down in the 200-story structures with amazing rapidity.
>
> —Mordaunt Hall (1)

This is the plot: A boy and a girl are in love, but Society, which regulates all marriages, has determined to give her to someone else. For the hero to overturn the ruling and win her, he must prove himself a success. An opportunity to do so appears when a sorcerer's-apprentice to a "scientist" offers him a chance to fly to Mars in order to test the scientist's newest invention, a spaceship. Meanwhile, other scientists have resurrected a man from 1930, who becomes the hero's chum. They, with the second lead, fly to Mars, have adventures there and return to claim the girl just as she is about to be irrevocably wed to the other guy.

The rest is all jokes and pratfalls. Single-O, the man from the past, is played by a Swedish-dialect vaudeville comedian named El Brendel. It is his comedic role to punch up all the funny differences between 1930 and 1980. He discovers that food now comes in the form of pills, and sighs, "Give me the good old days." So does drink. He downs a couple of bourbon tablets (which are still bootlegged; Prohibition has survived, though one of the characters says they expect to have light wines and beer legalized in a year or two), and repeats his litany. They then observe a young married couple hovering in delighted indecision before a vending machine. They make up their minds and put a coin in the slot. Out comes a newborn baby, and Brendel, with real passion in his voice, completes the Rule of Three and declaims, "Ah, give me the *good* old days!" The scientist's apprentice is played by an incredibly young Mischa Auer, and The Girl is an incredibly young, and lovely, Maureen O'Sullivan, later Tarzan's favorite Jane. O'Sullivan made her first four films in 1930, when she was all of 19. *Just Imagine* was one of them.

As part of the dehumanizing process of advanced urban civilization, on which the film relies for its more intellectual jokes, people no longer have names, only numbers. El Brendel becomes "Single-O". (None of the characters have more than two letters of the alphabet in the first part of their names, or two digits in the remainder. Quick arithmetic reveals that this implies a world population not in excess of 67,600.) Mars, when they reach it, turns out to be a curious place. On Mars everyone is born as an identical twin; of each pair one member is Good and the other Evil. (No attempt is made to explain how they reproduce, or why this is so—of course.) This is a vehicle for endless mistaken-identity jokes, most of which cause El Brendel to be hit on the head. Architecture on Mars consists largely of prismatic shapes of glassy stone, and what the Martians do with their time other than sit around and wait for Earthmen to visit them is not even suggested. But the jokes are at least up to the standard of an average 1930 movie musical (for what that is worth), and Maureen O'Sullivan is simply adorable. Not beautiful. She is too young for that. But you want to cuddle her forever.

Technically, *Just Imagine* is a strange mixture of the primitive and the opulent. When the rocket leaves for Mars it rises like a Fokker triplane—or like a model being pulled by a string. Newton's laws of action and reaction are confounded by the fact that the exhaust is no more than a balmy breeze—must be, since Maureen O'Sullivan takes no harm from stumbling into it in tears as her lover goes away. The sets are interesting, but there aren't very many of them. And they are mixed. The scale model of 1980 New York City is reported to have cost a quarter of a million dollars, but in some of the others the camera never follows anyone out of one scene and into another because the painted canvas stops six inches outside its field of view.

JUST IMAGINE (Fox, 1930)
Much of the film's budget went to build this $250,000 model of 1980 New York.

The acting, of course, is Something Else. Silent-film mugging was not yet extinct in 1930. O'Sullivan has only two expressions; one is melting innocence, the other a Theda Bara grimace of ultimate misery. Mischa Auer plays the same part he played all through his film career, namely Mischa Auer; Brendel does his vaudeville routines, including the obligatory drunk scene; and the two juveniles achieve such a high in empty-faced callowness as to make Dagwood Bumstead seem like Shaw.

What *Just Imagine* was not was a box-office success. It played its obligatory tours through the studio's outlets and was gone. It may be that the combination of science fiction and musical comedy is bad chemistry. With only one or two possible exceptions (*The Rocky Horror Picture Show*, and what else?) it is hard to think of any real successes of that kind. A year or two later the trick was tried again, with *It's Great to Be Alive.* The thesis of that was that all the men in the world were gone but one, and that one was sought by every female. Apart from some pretty bad tunes—

We are the girls from Czechoslovakia.

We are strong, and how we can socky-ya.

—not much of it is memorable.

Just Imagine was the work of the musical-comedy team of DeSylva, Brown and Henderson, who had already been responsible for the very successful non-sf film, *Sunny Side Up.* Something went wrong. The title song from *Sunny Side Up* was on every radio station for years, and is still heard once in a while. None of the songs from *Just Imagine* (they had titles like *I'm Only the Words, You Are the Melody* and *Never Swat the Fly*) was ever heard again.

Just Imagine was the first science-fiction film I ever saw. I had barely discovered science fiction itself, and the revelation that it existed even in the movie theaters blew my mind. So did the film, when I finally got my mother to take me to it. I immediately perceived that the picture could be a kind of validation test of sf itself; if I could only manage to survive to the year 1980 I could see for myself if aircraft would replace cars, names would be replaced by numbers, babies would come out of a vending machine and food would be taken as pills. At ten, I was not entirely sure how seriously to take science fiction's wide-ranging predictions. I'm a little more sure now, at least as far as *Just Imagine* is concerned, since it turns out to have a perfect batting average. Perfectly zero.

—FP

FILMOGRAPHY
JUST IMAGINE (Fox, 1930, U.S.A.) 113 mins.

Director, David Butler; script, David Butler, Ray Henderson, G.G. DeSylva, and Lew Brown; songs, DeSylva, Henderson, Brown; art directors, Stephen Goosson and Ralph Hammeras.

Cast: El Brendel (Single O); Maureen O'Sullivan (LN-18); John Garrick (J-21); Marjorie White (D-6); Frank Albertson; Hobart Bosworth; Kenneth Thomson; Misha Auer; Joseph Girard; Sidney De Gray; Joyzelle.

The musical-sf hybrid seemed to be sterile at the box office. But a year later another crossbreed came along that was fecund indeed: it was the marriage between science fiction and horror, and its name was *Frankenstein*.

No matter what one may say about the melo-dramatic ideas (in *Frankenstein*), there is no denying that it is far and away the most effective thing of its kind. Beside it *Dracula* is tame. . . . As a concession to the motion picture audience, Frankenstein is not killed, but he is badly injured. Two endings were made for the production, and at the eleventh hour it was decided to put in the one in which Frankenstein lives, because it was explained that sympathy is elicited for the young scientist and that the spectators would leave disappointed if the author's last chapter was adhered to.

—Mordaunt Hall (2)

Mary Wollstonecraft Shelley's novel was a natural for film. The Edison Studio's first version of it, in 1910, had had Charles Ogle as the monster, stewed up out of chemicals blazing in a huge cooking-pot. His makeup was a white, masklike face in a flyaway swirl of feathery hair. The 1915 Ocean Film adaptation (or theft) of the same theme dragged in settings in Colorado and on an ocean liner; their Monster (they called him "The Creation") was played by Percy Darrell Standing. Obviously the Monster was the most important part of the film, and when James Whale decided to make it his first priority was to find the right two people. More important of the two was the makeup man, and Whale found Jack R. Pierce, who studied anatomy and brain surgery for the purpose—or at least enough of each to make some interesting assumptions about how a mad surgeon might go about sticking a new brain into a skull. Then Whale began hunting for the right person to wear makeup. Bela Lugosi had been tried for the part, even before Whale took the project over. Lugosi hated it. (Years later Lugosi came down in the world and did play the Monster in Universal's *Frankenstein Meets the Wolf Man* of 1943.) Whale was not displeased when Lugosi turned it down. He had another image in mind. He finally saw the image eating quietly in the Universal commissary—its name was Boris Karloff.

Whale did not offer the part to Karloff at once. He sat making sketches of the plain, strong face, and showed the sketches to the makeup people before he approached the actor. It was not only necessary to find someone who could play the part; the final choice had to be willing (and physically strong enough) to wear forty-eight pounds of gear that took three hours and thirty minutes to put on in the morning, and an hour and a half to take off at night. Karloff was willing. To preserve secrecy (and perhaps Karloff's vanity), the actor was led to and from the stage with a cloth over his head and ate his lunch, as best he could, alone. He wore double thicknesses of pants, and the film was shot in the heat of the summer of 1931. Whale was delighted. The expression Karloff wore all that summer, he said, was the exact look of patient misery he wanted.

Mary Shelley wrote her novel in 1816, to break up the tedium of a long visit with Lord Byron. Byron, she and her husband, Percy Bysshe Shelley, each undertook to write a scary story. Not much has been heard of the tales produced by the two celebrated poets, but Mary Shelley's *Frankenstein* entered the collective mind of the world as a legend. Like all legends, the details vary with the re-teller, and the James Whale film took its story line from a play by John Balderston.

∽∽∽∽∽∽∽∽∽∽∽∽∽∽∽∽∽∽∽∽∽∽∽∽∽∽∽∽∽∽∽∽

FILMOGRAPHY

FRANKENSTEIN (Universal, 1931, U.S.A.) 71 mins.

Producer, Carl Laemmle Jr.; director, James Whate; adaptation, Robert Florey and John Balderston; script, Garrett Fort, Robert Florey, and Francis Edward Faragoh; art director, Charles D. Hall; make-up, Jack Pierce; special effects, John P. Fulton; special electrical effects, Kenneth Strickfaden; camera, Arthur Edeson.

Cast: Colin Clive (Frankenstein); Mae Clark (Elizabeth); John Boles (Victor); Boris Karloff (Monster); Dwight Frye (Dwarf); Edward Van Sloan (Dr. Waldman); Frederick Kerr; Lionel Belmore; Michael Mark; Marilyn Harris.

∽∽∽∽∽∽∽∽∽∽∽∽∽∽∽∽∽∽∽∽∽∽∽∽∽∽∽∽∽∽∽∽

In this version, Dr. Henry Frankenstein, off somewhere in Eastern Europe, sends his assistant out to salvage spare parts from corpses. He assembles the scraps into a complete body and animates it with the power of lightning. (Those studs at the Monster's neck aren't the bolts that hold his head on. They are terminals for electricity.) The Monster is too strong to be confined. It breaks the chains, kills the assistant, terrifies the countryside, drowns a little girl (in all good will, thinking she would float like a flower petal) and is finally captured and "destroyed". (But the Monster does not stay destroyed for long. It comes back again four years later in *The Bride of Frankenstein,* scarred from the fire that was supposed to have killed it, but still deadly.)

Boris Karloff wore perhaps the most famous facial makeup ever devised. At this moment that face is seen around the world on Halloween masks and breakfast cereals. It has been worn by a thousand actors in film, stage and television plays. Political cartoonists draw the neck bolts and the high, bulging skull on their targets. It is so familiar that it has become quite safe and mostly funny; but to see that face on Boris Karloff, as the Monster made his first stirrings of mortality was not funny at all. It was terrifying. Audiences loved it. With the release of *Frankenstein* in 1931 the sf-horror genre became instantly established as a crowd pleaser, and has been pulling in millions for the movie-makers ever since.

James Whale had known what good theater was since his young years in England's provincial playhouses, and he had no doubts about what he had. However, at a sneak preview in Santa Barbara the audiences seemed more puzzled and disturbed than pleased, so Whale recut the film to eliminate some of the more gut-wrenching parts.

Once in full release the customers lined up in full expectation of delicious terror, got what they paid for and wanted more. Whale understood the message of the box office and tooled up for a sequel. In *Bride of Frankenstein* (1935) he added Elsa Lanchester to play the Monster's mate, as well as Mary Shelley. He added fourteen pounds to Karloff's burden of makeup, and more than a foot of stilts to Lanchester's height. How many times has *Frankenstein* been made since, in one variation or another? Add on *Son of—, House of—, Ghost of—*and *Evil of Frankenstein; Frankenstein Meets the Wolf Man, Franken-*

∽∿∽∿∽∿∽∿∽∿∽∿∽∿∽∿∽∿∽∿∽∿∽∿∽∿∽∿∽∿

FILMOGRAPHY
BRIDE OF FRANKENSTEIN (Universal, 1935,
U.S.A.) 80 mins.

Producer, Carl Laemmle Jr.; director, James
Whale; script, John Balderston and William Hurlbut;
art director, Charles D. Hall; make-up, Jack Pierce;
special effects, John P. Fulton; special electrical effects, Kenneth Strickfaden; camera, John J. Mescall;
music, Franz Waxman.

Cast: Colin Clive (Frankenstein); Boris Karloff
(Monster); Elsa Lanchester (Bride of Frankenstein/
Mary Shelley); Ernest Thesiger (Dr. Praetorius); Lu-
cien Prival; Una O'Connor; Valery Hobson; Dwight
Frye; Walter Brennan; John Carradine; Billy Barty.

∽∿∽∿∽∿∽∿∽∿∽∿∽∿∽∿∽∿∽∿∽∿∽∿∽∿∽∿∽∿

*stein Meets the Space Monster; Abbott and Costello
Meet Frankenstein; Frankenstein's Daughter; I Was a
Teenage Frankenstein* . . . not to mention all the even
lesser ones, and the TV ones, and the borrowed ones.
. . . The mind boggles.

Across town at RKO-Radio the competition saw what
was happening, and learned, and acted.

The famous mystery writer, Edgar Wallace, had been
under contract to RKO for some time, working on a story
about a big ape. RKO called it *The Beast.* Under producer
Merian C. Cooper, the screenplay was finally written by
"Ruth Rose"—Cooper's wife. Willis O'Brien did the
model work and supervised the animation. Ever since *The
Dinosaur and the Baboon* O'Brien had been film's
Number One "prehistoric" models animator, and now he
was turned loose to do his finest work. In January, 1931,
Wallace changed the title of the project to *King Ape.* Three

years later the film was still in production and Wallace never lived to see a third title change, in January, 1933, to *Kong*. The publicity drums began beating. "The Greatest Film the World Will Ever See!" screamed RKO's flacks, who still weren't sure of the title; two months later the film was released as, at last, *King Kong*.

Everything about *King Kong* was big, starting with Kong himself. How big? Well, it depends on who you listened to. Or which section of the film you saw. Reviewers guessed anywhere from thirty feet to more than a hundred. Measured against human figures in the same scene, say as Kong bursts through the gates on Skull Island, he looks perhaps thirty-five feet tall; in long shots as he climbs up the Empire State Building, more like seventy. The various Kongs (and parts of Kongs) Willis O'Brien built ranged from the tiny sixteen-inch model that fought the dinosaurs up to the immense hand in which Fay Wray writhed. Had Kong been to that scale, he would have been perhaps eighty feet tall. He felt taller to Wray. Every morning she had to climb up into that hand; the grips would cinch the big fingers around her and seesaw her ten feet off the floor for a day's wriggling and screaming. The hard part was to keep from slipping through the fingers to a compound fracture on the floor below—half a century later, Wray said that was the most danger she faced during the filming. Bigness extended to the building Kong climbed. Merian Cooper originally intended to end the film on the brand-new Chrysler Building in New York City. But the canny builders of the Empire State Building waited until the Chrysler was irrevocably committed to its design, then added a few stories and a mooring mast to become the world's tallest. In mid-production Cooper switched.

FILMOGRAPHY
KING KONG (RKO, 1933, U.S.A.) 100 mins.

Producer/director, Merian C. Cooper and Ernest B. Schoedsack; story, Edgar Wallace and Merian C. Cooper; script, James A. Creelman and Ruth Rose; camera, Edward Linden; special effects, Willis O'Brien; editor, Ted Chessman; music, Max Steiner.

Cast: Fay Wray (Ann Redman); Robert Armstrong (Carl Denham); Bruce Cabot (Jack Driscoll); Frank Reicher (Engelhorn); Sam Hardy (Weston); Noble Johnson (Cief); Victor Wong (Cook); James Flavin; Steve Clemento.

King Kong opened in two New York theaters at once. One was the brand-new Radio City Music Hall, a theater as full of extremes and superlatives as the film itself. Being inside the Music Hall was like being inside an immense golden clam. Everything about it was the biggest and newest and the most advanced. All of Radio City—or Rockefeller Center, as it is more properly called now—was shiny and new. The Rockefellers had shamed New York City into shining up the pretty tacky neighborhood around it, even repainting the very Elevated lines that King Kong "ravaged" in his carouse across Manhattan. (Reviewer Richard Watts thought that scene was "a trifle ungrateful to the elevated lines.") The other theater was the equally pristine New Roxy (later changed to the Center Theater when the original Roxy's owners took it to court). Together the two had some ten thousand seats, which were filled ten times a day. Oh, yes. Big!

King Kong begins as a shoestring film producer named Carl Denham rescues a broke and jobless girl, Ann Darrow, by offering her the starring part in a movie he is about to make. Denham has learned of the existence of a great prehistoric creature which inhabits a little-known place called Skull Island; the film crew sail there and find that the creature is Kong. Natives who worship the huge ape kidnap Ann and leave her as a sacrifice. Kong comes to take her and bears her away through the jungle, fighting a tyrannosaurus, a pterodactyl, and all sorts of other monsters. They are pursued by Ann's lover, Jack Driscoll, who finally saves her. Denham uses Ann for bait. Kong follows, is gassed unconscious and transported to New York. There Denham puts him on show, but the flash-guns of newspaper photographers rile the ape enough to break his chains. He smashes elevated trains and climbs skyscrapers until he captures Ann again, and carries her to the top of the Empire State Building, where he is ultimately killed by U.S. Army Air Corps pursuit planes. He falls to the ground; Driscoll rescues Ann; Denham surveys the huge corpse and remarks, "Oh no, it wasn't the airplanes. It was Beauty killed the Beast."

They failed to realize that such a union was possible only by straining our powers of credulity and perhaps also one or two fundamental laws of nature. For if the love that Kong felt for the heroine was sacred, it suggests a weakness that hardly fits in with his other actions; and if it was, after all, merely profane, it proposes problems to the imagination that are not the less real for being crude.

—William Troy (3)

Fay Wray played Ann Darrow mostly by screaming; Bruce Cabot played Jack Driscoll principally by flexing his muscles; only Robert Armstrong, as Carl Denham, had any memorable lines, and perhaps only the last one, at that. It was not the acting that made *King Kong* a hit. It was mostly Willis O'Brien. Much of the three years' work on *King Kong* was spent in the painstaking, inch-by-inch movement and photography of his models (originally designed, many of them, for an unmade project of O'Brien's called *Creation.*) The models were marvelous little structures, some of which still exist in Forrest J. Ackerman's astonishing collection. The sponge rubber has dried to powder and the leathery reptilian skins have peeled off, but the ingenious articulation of the joints still works. The single scene between Kong and the pterodactyl took seven weeks to shoot. Twenty-three hours were necessary to make Kong peel off Ann Darrow's clothes, a scene which ran only thirty seconds on screen, and was almost immediately cut out anyway by the censors. O'Brien clearly deserved, but didn't receive, an Academy Award for *King Kong.* (He finally collected one, years later, for Kong's remote and tinier relative, *Mighty Joe Young.*)

There is something about Miss Wray that appeals to "movie" monsters. It was not more than a few weeks ago that she was being pursued by Lionel Atwill as a mad waxworks proprietor with a detachable face, and not long before that an insane scientist was planning to drain her blood for one of his experiments.

—Richard Watts, Jr. (4)

KING KONG (RKO, 1933)
The full-scale Kong bust.

Like James Whale with *Frankenstein,* Merian Cooper knew a good thing when he had it. Unlike Whale, Cooper reacted at once. *King Kong* premiered in March, 1933; before the end of the year *Son of Kong* was pulling in Christmas audiences. The son of Kong was far less fearsome than his dad, a blonde stripling off the old dark monster, and he was a lot more noble—when Skull Island is at last destroyed in a volcanic upheaval, the son sacrifices his own life to hold his discoverer above the tidal wave. *Son of Kong* was smaller in many ways—perhaps eighteen feet tall to Kong's forty or fifty or whatever; 70 minutes running time instead of 100; and a whole lot cheaper. *King Kong* had cost $650,000 to make—a large enough sum for 1933. When, decades later, Dinosaur de Laurentiis stomped his great heel on the remake, the tab was some thirty times as much, and the end result was, characteristically, about a tenth as good. Gone were the dinosaurs and most of Kong's animation; apart from two scenes, the ape was played by a man in a monkey suit. The only real improvement was in the Ann Darrow part which, as played by Jessica Lange, was sexier and less passive.

Boris Karloff's big boost to stardom came in a science fiction film in which he was buried under a half a hundredweight of makeup and steel supports; it was hard to see Karloff under the Monster. A quarter of a century later James Arness got *his* first big break even better disguised wearing the animated carrot suit in *The Thing.* It is interesting to note that science fiction films have propelled to stardom actors who were seen only in grossly distorted form—but in *The Invisible Man,* Claude Rains set an all-time record. Until the last half of the seventy-first minute of the 71-minute film, he wasn't seen at all.

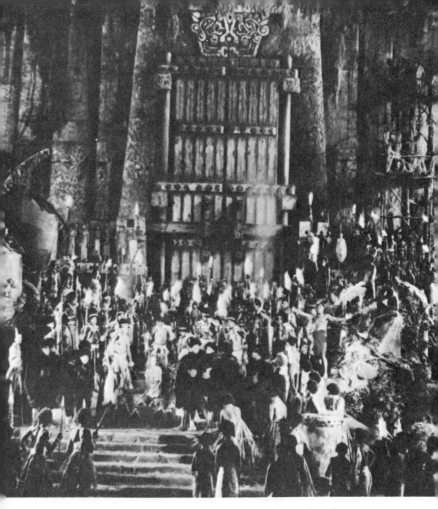

KING KONG (RKO, 1933)
The people of Skull Island make ready for Kong's visit.

Needless to say that this picture was received by many a giggle to cover up fright. Constant exclamations issued from the Radio City Music Hall yesterday. "What a man!" observed one youth when the ape forced down the great oaken door on the island.
—Mordaunt Hall (5)

The last time I had the pleasure of visiting with the late great Boris Karloff, we discussed the amazing longevity of the "Frankenstein" monster—who died, time and again, only to be resurrected. I spoke of my theory concerning the popular appeal of the monster: that audiences consciously and unconsciously identified with this creature, particularly the adolescent members of the audiences. Growing up is always an ordeal in our society, and there are times when most young people think of *themselves* as monsters—they feel themselves to be clumsy, inarticulate, unable to communicate with the adult community. They often consider themselves to be ugly, and rejected. They regard themselves as misunderstood, at the mercy of forces beyond their control, at odds with authority. For generation after generation, the "Frankenstein" monster has served as a self-image to youth.

Mr. Karloff agreed, but wondered aloud why a more modern symbol had not come to supplant the monster for the young people of today. He suggested, in his gentle way, that perhaps his monster was just a trifle old-fashioned. Whereupon I reminded him that his was a very modern monster, not only in attitude but even in physical appearance. Consider the shapeless garments, the sweater or the shaggy coat, the drooping lids and the slow movements so similar to those of one in a drugged state, observe the untrimmed hair and the bangs—is not yesterday's monster the very prototype of today's (1969) hippie?

—Robert Bloch (6)

The H. G. Wells novel was a natural for filming, and R. C. Sherriff's script followed the book with understanding. A Dr. Griffen (Claude Rains) discovers a drug that makes human tissue transparent, but which also causes brain damage. Griffen retreats to a country inn to wait for the drug to wear off, but the townspeople discover his secret and react with terror. *He* reacts with drug-induced fury; he is pursued, tracked by his footprints in the snow, and shot. As he dies his body finally materializes.

Making the film only awaited a time when the technical problems could be solved, and by 1933 Universal's John P. Fulton had done so with wires, double-printing and an army of retouchers who painted out the hardware that was not meant to be seen on the negatives. The director was James Whale, fresh from *Frankenstein.*

The Invisible Man did not spark its audiences to terror. Wells's gently Fabian style seldom displayed violence, and poor Griffen, freezing in the slush and hunted by everyone around, was as much to be pitied as feared. Whale was up to the challenge of making audiences feel what he wanted them to feel. He did not risk the angry laugh of incredulous tension; he eased the strain by planting little comic bits to trigger laughter where he wanted it, not where it might destroy his effect, as mountaineers bring down a controlled snowslide to prevent an avalanche.

The Invisible Man is about as close to perfection—that is, to the successful realization of its creators' aims—as a film ever gets. Of the three great blockbusters of the Thirties sf films, it may well be the best. But it is also the least. Although it was a great success, critically and at the box office, it has not sparked the infinite remakes and variations of *Frankenstein* or *King Kong*, has not become a household word, is seldom seen even on late night television, never acquired its cult coterie.

It was a great success but not *as* great, and that was the lesson the moviemakers remembered. *The Invisible Man* was a human-sized story, whose principal thrills were of the intellect. It *could* have happened, one thinks; what if it truly had? This is a quality of great written science fiction, causing the reader to write sequels in his mind long after he has finished the book. "Ordinarily we are precipitated abruptly and without warning into the strange and violent world of the scientific romancer's imagination," William Troy said, but added that in *The Invisible Man* both author and director had "taken a great deal of pains" to lead gently into the science fiction part. It was Wellsian rather than socko; but at the box office socko was bigger.

The Invisible Man . . . happens to be ideally suited to the talking screen insofar as it is impossible to imagine it being equally well treated in any other medium. . . . In Wells's novel the sight of the printed words on the page cannot be so disturbingly eerie as the actual sound of Claude Rains's voice issuing from empty chairs and unoccupied rooms.

—William Troy (7)

FILMOGRAPHY
THE INVISIBLE MAN (Universal, 1933, U.S.A.) 71 mins.

Director, James Whale; script, R.C. Sherriff, based on H.G. Wells's novel; special effects, James P. Fulton; camera, Arthur Edeson.

Cast: Claude Rains (Jack Griffin); Gloria Stuart (Flora Cranley); Henry Travers (Dr. Cranley); William Harrigan (Dr. Kemp); Una O'Connor (Mrs. Hall); Forrester Harvey (Mr. Hall); Merle Tottenham (Milly); E.E. Clive (Jaffers); Holmes Herbert (Chief of Police); Dudley Diggs; Harry Stubbs; Donald Stuart.

FILMOGRAPHY
ISLAND OF LOST SOULS (Paramount, 1932, U.S.A.) 72 mins.

Director, Erle Kenton; script, Waldemar Young and Philip Wylie from the novel by H.G. Wells.

Cast: Charles Laughton (Moreau); Richard Arlen (Parker); Arthur Hohl (Montgomery); Kathleen Burke (Lota); Stanley Fields (Davies); Bela Lugosi (Leader of the Ape-Men); Leia Hyams; Robert Kortman; Tetsu Komai; Hans Steinke.

Wells had two other major films in the Thirties; one of which was released a few months before *The Invisible Man*, in January, 1933: *The Island of Dr. Moreau*, retitled as the *The Island of Lost Souls*. Paramount was less faithful to Wells than Universal had been; even so the story followed Wells's original closely enough. Mad scientist Charles Laughton has learned how to remake animals into human shape by surgery—a slow and painful process. An uninvited castaway, Richard Arlen, gives Dr. Moreau a chance to show off his best work, a lovely woman (Kathleen Burke) rebuilt from a panther, and to demonstrate his mastery over the ex-animal subjects. With whip and threat of return to the House of Pain for more rearrangement, Moreau compels them to repeat the Law:

"Not to eat meat; that is the Law. Are we not Men?

"Not to go on all fours; that is the Law. Are we not Men?

"Not to gnaw the bark off trees; that is the Law. Are we not Men?

"Not to spill blood; that is the Law. Are we not Men?"

But the Panther Woman begins to revert to the beast; the animal-men catch Dr. Moreau acting in an un-Manlike

way, and take him to the House of Pain for some rear-
rangements of their own; only Richard Arlen escapes.
Philip Wylie was one of the collaborators on the
screenplay, but there is not much of either the excitement
of *When Worlds Collide* or the harsh irony of *Generation
of Vipers* in the film. It seems to go through the motions
adequately, and not much more.

There were two other significant science-fiction films in
the early 1930s. Viewed as prediction, they fell down
rather badly. Both concerned themselves with transatlantic transportation, a topic much on the world's mind in the
decade when bigger and faster superliners were trying to
set new records each year. *Transatlantic Tunnel* showed
how the problem might be solved by running railroads
under the sea bottom. *F P 1 Does Not Reply* proposed
setting up floating airports spotted across the ocean for
airplanes to land on and refuel, for passengers to stretch
their legs or even get a night's sleep before taking off on the
next lap. That suggestion was not wholly silly; crossing the
United States "by air" at the time involved flying a few
hundred miles at a time, then shifting to an overnight
Pullman berth in order to catch another plane farther
along in the morning. Of course, neither film prediction
came to pass. Within a decade the long-distance airplane
had made the one unnecessary and the other ridiculous.

The two films have much in common. Both were the
work of Kurt Siodmak, though from different studios—*F P
1 Does Not Answer* (1932) from UFA, *Transatlantic Tunnel* (1933—or 1935, depending on which language you
see it in) from Bavarian Films. Both had the unusual
distinction of being made three times, in three languages; *F
P 1* was shot simultaneously in French, German and English, with cast changes; *Tunnel* in French and German at

once, in English two years later, with almost entirely different casts. The casts were not important, nor were the
words. Both *Transatlantic Tunnel* and *F P 1 Does Not
Reply* were pure technology fiction. The conquest of
technology is the whole story of each—heightened, of
course, by a few saboteurs and accidents along the way.
The films required technical expertise, but the results no
longer seem very impressive. *Transatlantic Tunnel* is
mostly models; *F P 1* borrowed a floating drydock for its
biggest effects. They are seldom shown any more, even in
the film programs at science-fiction conventions, though in
the early 1930s they were greeted with delight by the fans.

THE TRANS-ATLANTIC TUNNEL (Gaumont-British, 1935)
Far under the Atlantic Ocean's seabed, Richard Dix spurs on his sandhogs.

(*F.P. 1 Does Not Answer*) is an ingeniously worked out tale, which captivates one's attention, notwithstanding a vagueness regarding nationalities and certain lurid features. The monster platform at sea, with its line of offices and huts and its immense landing space, is alone extraordinarily interesting. The structure is supposed to be 1,500 feet long and 400 feet wide. . . . Not the least interesting aspects of this novel piece of work are the glimpses of persons at a telephone, both aboard the platform and in the distant Lennartz shipyards.

—Mordaunt Hall (8)

An imaginative drama in the best Jules Verne tradition, *Transatlantic Tunnel* forges on through the years with such desperate courage that it enlists the spectator as an ally in the great enterprise. Sometimes the drama grows soft-headed, as when it obliges the charming Helen Vinson to sacrifice her virtue to the sinister financier who plans to halt work on the project. But when at last the whirling radium-drills are silent and the American and British crews meet halfway under the Atlantic, you want to go out and blow horns for the heroes of the adventure.

—Andre Sennwald (9)

FILMOGRAPHY
THE TRANS-ATLANTIC TUNNEL (Gaumont-British, 1935, British) 94 mins.

Producer, Michael Balcon; director, Maurice Elvey; adaptation, Kurt Siodmak from Bernhard Kellermann's novel; script, Kurt Siodmak, Clemence Dane, and L. du Garde Peach; editor, Charles Frend; camera, Günther Krampf.

Cast: Richard Dix (McAllen); C. Aubrey Smith (Lloyd); Helen Vinson (Varlia Lloyd); Madge Evans (Ruth McAllen); Leslie Banks (Robbie); Walter Huston (President of U.S.); George Arliss (Prime Minister of England); Basil Sidney; Henry Oscar; Jimmy Hanley.

F.P. 1 DOES NOT ANSWER (UFA-Fox-Gaumont, 1932)
The view from the floating platform with its attendant seaplanes.

F.P. 1 ANTWORTET NICHT (F.P. 1 Does Not Answer) (UFA-Fox-Gaumont, 1932, German) 90 mins.

Producer, Erich Pommer; director, Karl Hartl; script, Walter Reisch and Kurt Siodmak; English dialogue, Robert Stevenson and Peter MacFarland; camera, Günther Rittau and Konstantin Tschet.

Cast (English version): Leslie Fenton (Captain Droste); Conrad Veidt (Major Ellissen); Jill Esmond (Claire Lennartz); George Merritt (Lubin); Donald Calthrop (Photographer); Nicholas Hannen; Warwick Ward; William Freshman; Dr. Philip Manning.

Cast (German version): Hans Albers; Sybille Schmitz; Paul Hartmann; Peter Lorre; Rudolf Platte; Hermann Speelmans.

Cast (French version): Charles Boyer; Jean Murat; Pierre Brasseur; Danielle Parola; Marcel Vallée; Ernest Ferny.

But then came the real one, H. G. Wells's latest and by far the most ambitious effort. In 1936 Alexander Korda produced *Things to Come*.

> I think films back in the Twenties and Thirties were infinitely better than today. *Things to Come* is still an amazing film. It's about the whole panoply of history, the whole sense of the progression of time, of humanity having to come to grips with major questions. It was the first time, I think, that anybody really talked about what rampant technology was going to do. The technocrats had been beyond reproach for thirty-five or forty years, and suddenly here is this movie that says, "Hey, maybe we're moving too fast. Let's see what sort of effect this is all having!" The look of it! The whole look is so rich, and there's a *probable* thing about it. Just last night, Walter Koenig said the walking sickness section scared him more than *The Exorcist*. And it's an *intelligent* film.
> —Harlan Ellison (10)

When Harlan Ellison's best word for *Things to Come* is "intelligent", he puts his finger on the film's outstanding quality. *Things to Come* is an intelligent film, which plays to the intelligence of the audience.

What madman dared this terrifying experiment?

It was Alexander Korda, who hired William Cameron Menzies to direct it and gave him the freedom to give freedom to H. G. Wells. From then on it was all Wells. Wells wrote the script, and hung around the set to see that it was performed as he wrote it. Wells interviewed the actors, and explained his purposes to the set and costume designer. Wells even picked out the composer of the incidental music, Arthur Bliss.

Wells was the first of the modern science fiction writers, the one who freed the genre from the literal tyranny of Verne, and he knew what science fiction could be. He knew, for instance, how to achieve that great feature of outstanding science fiction—Robert A. Heinlein, for instance, is particularly good at it—which leads you, as you read the story or see the film, to think, "Ah, yes, of course; that's the way it would be." It is a question of visualization in depth. Wells had started with his "future history", the non-fiction book *The Shape of Things to Come*, for broad outlines. For the film he merely needed to invent incident and plot.

Things to Come is a "generations" film of two families, the Passworthys and the Cabals, and their lives through the next century, starting from 1936, (the year the film was made). We meet them at Christmas in "Everytown" (which looks a lot like London, specifically Piccadilly Circus). As the families are gathered together, the children playing with their new toys, strange sounds and sights outside bring them to the door; "Searchlights! What are searchlights doing on Christmas Eve?" What they are doing is seeking out enemy aircraft, because World War II, has, without warning begun. In montage the children's toy guns are transformed into real ones, into futuristic tanks and aircraft; we follow the interminable war through scraps of newspaper tossed on the breeze. Stalemate after stalemate, and endless destruction; at last there comes the "Wandering Sickness", a worldwide plague that decimates the human race and completes the destruction.

The second major sequence takes place in 1970—Wells's parallel time 1970, not the one our world lived through. We return Everytown, but it is ruined, a peasant village with the wreckage of buildings around Piccadilly barely recognizable. A strong man, Rudolph the "Boss" (Ralph Richardson), has imposed despotism on the survivors, readying them for another war against "the Hill People" for control of the enemy's oil reserves. A strange aircraft appears; from it steps black-clad John Cabal (Raymond Massey) in an immense glass helmet; he represents "Wings Over the World", the surviving technological base of humanity, located in Basra, Iraq. Cabal has left Iraq to survey conditions in England. The Boss seizes him, determined to get the secrets of new aircraft and weapons from him to finish off the Hill People; but after a time the immense, stately aircraft of Wings Over the World appear in the sky, dropping glass spheres of tranquilizing "Peace Gas". The Boss tries to rally his ragged troops to fight them off, running from one to another. "Shoot, shoot!" he cries. "We've never shot enough!" Then the anaesthetic overcomes him, and Wings Over the World has added one more cluster of humanity to its worldwide alliance of technocrats and airmen. The scene shifts to great machines building the hillside Everytown of 2036, a city of crystal towers, vast open spaces, looped bridges and walkways. Everytown is utopia, or close enough. The greatest popular concern is whether or not Man should go to the Moon via an experimental Space Gun, ready to fire. A luddite sculptor, Theotocopulos (Sir Cedric Hardwicke), leads a mob to destroy the Space Gun, but the mob fails and the capsule is off to the Moon. The film ends with a dialogue between Raymond Passworthy and Oswald Cabal. We are such little animals, moans Passworthy, gazing at the space shell that contains his son and Cabal's daughter; can't we ever rest? Rest? asks Cabal, while Arthur Bliss's magnificent music rises under his voice. We'll die soon enough, and that's rest. Meanwhile we can remain animals or we can grow and evolve. All the universe—or nothingness. *Which shall it be?*

Things to Come is another of the films that gave star status to struggling actors, and it did it with three of them. Ralph Richardson was perfect as the scruffy, earthy Boss; Raymond Massey glacially just as all of the Cabals; Cedric Hardwicke bullheadedly righteous as the epicene sculptor who revolts against the march of technology. (Ann Todd and George Sanders also appear in small roles, but you've got to look quick to find them.) The film ran long (two hours), and cost $1,400,000, the most ever spent for an English film up to that time. Alexander Korda was one of the few producers who could command that sort of money for a speculative venture, but then Korda was an unusual man. Born in Hungary, he had spent several years in Hollywood, making the very successful silent film *The Private Life of Helen of Troy;* then, reversing the usual migration pattern, spent the greater part of his career to England. His *The Private Life of Henry VIII* made Charles Laughton a star and his studio a fortune. So when Korda demanded the funds to build immense outdoor sets and even more expensive models—a 20-foot Space Gun, with moving, puppet bearing, sidewalks—the funds appeared. His "Special Effects Department" under Ned Mann listened to Wells's visions, and gave them reality.

The attention to detail that makes *Things to Come* an intellectual treat is epitomized in the building of the city of 2036.

How do you decide what a future city will look like? You can simply look out the window to what exists now, and decide those trends will continue for the next century or so. Which is what *Just Imagine* did. 1930 saw the flowering of the skyscraper; the Chrysler Building and the Empire State

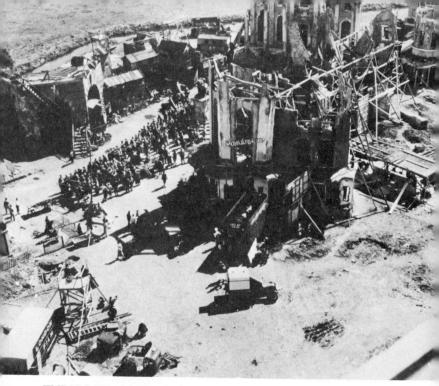

THINGS TO COME (London Films, 1936)
Aerial view of the Everytown set after World War II has turned it to rubble.

were racing each other in competition for the notoriety of being the world's tallest. *Just Imagine* simply multiplied everything by ten and came up with Super Skyscraper City.

But the history of architecture shows that no one style continues forever. Each era creates its own ideal structure, out of the tools, the materials and the strictures of its own time: For the Egyptians, the Pyramids; for the Romans, the arched aqueducts and the great vault of the Pantheon. The Middle Ages produced "mountains in stone" like the Chartres cathedral. The Eads Bridge over the Mississippi and the Flatiron Building in New York showed what structural steel skeletons could do; but all of the steel monsters, with or without their curtain walls, represent less than a

THINGS TO COME (London Films, 1936)
The inhabitants of Everytown await Theotocopulos's message.

century's style. Wells knew that, and he and his set designers considered the implications.

Why build cities *up*? Why not *down* or *in*? So the metropolis of 2036 Everytown goes into the side of the mountain.

Digging in is a near-perfect solution to problems that hardly anyone knew existed when *Things to Come* was made; an example of the intuitive leaps that science fiction writers sometimes make. There is no weather underground. There is little need for heating in the winter or cooling in the summer—the earth holds its heat year round. Buckminster Fuller tells us that an enclosed city can save as much as eight-ninths of its energy budget—he tells us that now, but Fuller was not around when H. G. Wells was planning the film. Ecologists now point out the dire necessity for energy conservation in the 1930s, but no one was worrying about energy, and the word "ecology" had not been coined. *Things to Come* does not spell out the reasons for the city being built. The film just shows us the city, shows us the building of Everytown by great semi-automatic machines blasting into the rock and lining its face with on-site manufactured slabs of plastic.

If the conception was all Wells, much of the detail was William Cameron Menzies. Once an illustrator of children's books, Menzies was a pictorial thinker. He planned his films by sketching every scene and set, was known for utilizing the full width of the screen, composing his picture right up to the edges of the film, as well as for the tightest of closeups. (According to Ezra Goodman, one of Menzies's cameramen once suggested, "Let's pull back to a long shot now and show the chin and hair."). And over it all, involving himself in every step, was Alexander Korda. He put his brother, Vincent, in charge of set design, and provided Wells (who had only once before written a screenplay, never produced and by all accounts bad) with Korda's favorite scriptwriter, Lajos Biro, who had written *The Private Life of Henry VIII*.

Even so, *Things to Come* was not entirely a success. It took a long time to recover the million-four production cost, and many of the reviews were hostile. The notion of turning world government over to airplane pilots struck many as preposterous, and perhaps still does. For all of Wells' vision, there are serious failures of logic and fact—the Space Gun, borrowed from Verne (and in part suggested by Willy Ley), is an impossibility. A few minutes' calculation should have convinced Wells that any space-farer headed for the Moon via cannon would leave the muzzle as a thin film of jelly crushed to the bottom of the capsule (His imagination was more than sixty years off in predicting the date of the first lunar spaceflight, too.). And the film suffered from the major criticism against almost all science fiction of the Thirties: the imagination was grand, but the people were one-dimensional. There is marvelous spectacle and thought in *Things to Come*, not much insight into the frail and corruptible human condition. Nearly everyone in it is incessantly *noble*. Raymond Massey gives a virtuoso performance as various Cabal, delivering his lines with great control and sometimes majesty. However, the lines themselves are preachments. Perhaps Lajos Biro could have helped here, but didn't. Wells's World War II (the dates very nearly right) is fought with King Arthur gallantry. The only enemy aviator we see donates his gas mask to save a little girl. The climactic storming of the Space Gun shows a frenzied mob (borrowings from Fritz Lang?) waving rods and rocks. But they do not think to riot until the arrogant Theotocopulos extorts them, whereupon they riot precisely according to his directions. The characters are the personified abstractions of a morality play. They speak to each other from prepared position papers. As a result, it is difficult to watch the film without praying for one of them to stammer, or pick his nose. Only Ralph Richardson's earthy Boss Rudolph comes truly alive, but even he is neither mean nor wicked, merely old-fashioned.

Possibly Wells intended some thoughtful comments on humanity, as subtle as his placement of the future Everytown. The 1936 Passworthy and his 2036 descendant are played by the same actor, Edward Chapman, in exactly the same style; Rudolph's 1970 mistress and World President Oswald Cabal's 2036 wife were played by the same actress, Margaretta Scott; Wells appears to have meant to comment on human nature, sometimes persisting even though environments change, sometimes changing to fit. Whatever the message was, it disappeared from the final film, because most of Scott's second role was left on the cutting-room floor.

Nevertheless—what glory! There are moments in *Things to Come* when the soul soars, and a large part of it is the music. Arthur Bliss was knighted for his excellence as a composer, and the *Things to Come* suite (conducted brilliantly for the film by Muir Matheson) is perhaps his best music. It is, perhaps, a little derivative of early Prokofiev, but valid enough to remain in existence on records and still played from time to time on the FM classical music stations. His score for the building of Everytown is a near-perfect *ballet mecanique*; the churchly tones of his choir, as Cabal and Passworthy gaze into the cathedral sky above the observatory to see their Moon-bound children, exalt the heart.

> Such Wellsian concepts as the World State are now abhorrent to us because we have learned sadly that we foster inside us tyrannies undreamed by rational Fabian Mr. Wells and those Victorians who saw mankind as readily educable. . . . Then again, we were told we were going to live in hygienic glass cities, wear tin togas, travel a lot (and in consequence all be a pleasing light bronze color), actually enjoy TV and all be sane and happy. It didn't work out that way. Here is the future, and our few palaces are built on rubbish dumps. Behind every beautiful new building lie seamy backwaters where human derelicts hide their wounds away. Even worse, we see that every scientific advance advances us merely a shade nearer some ultimate confusion.
>
> —Brian W. Aldiss (11)

If *Things to Come* had lowered its sights, it might have given us a more personal story, with a few fallible and appealing human beings to root for. Both Wells and Korda must have known that, for they turned at once to making a quite different film, *The Man Who Could Work Miracles.* It is pure fantasy, rather than science fiction, although Wells's logic-oriented brain worked out the physical consequences of miraculous power with scientific rigor. (A couple of years later John Campbell imposed the same formula on the writers for his fantasy magazine, *Unknown.*)

The Man Who Could Work Miracles is the story of a clothing-store clerk (Wells himself had been one in his youth) who, through the idle impulse of immortal gods, is given the power to pass miracles. Of course, he screws it up. His climactic miracle is to stop the Sun in its tracks, and as a result the Earth stops rotating, every thing on its surface flies off and, in the split-second before inevitable death, the clerk works the final miracle of ending his powers and putting everything back the way it was. Roland Young gives a marvelous performance as the bumbling haberdasher. But there is not much contrast in the film. Everyone in it is corruptible and confused, except perhaps the gods in the prologue—and how smart could they be to do a thing like that? *The Man Who Could Work Miracles* is the exact negative of *Things to Come,* and it was at best marginally successful, too. Wells never wrote another film (though any number of people wrote them from his novels), and indeed wrote little more through the rest of his increasingly bitter and pessimistic life.

Nevertheless *Things to Come* remains—a flawed masterpiece, but a masterpiece all the same.

Things to Come . . . tells an extraordinary story which, while it may not convince cinemaddicts, is likely to captivate them.

Since what happens 100 years hence is of no consequence to anyone now old enough to enjoy the cinema, the notion of producing a film of which the longest and most spectacular portions deal with 2036 seems, at first glance, daringly original. Original it is. It is daring only by contrast with Hollywood's timid preference for doing, insofar as possible, only what has been done before. Actually, nothing interests people more than matters which do not concern them. *Things to Come* is therefore magnificent entertainment and a tribute to the sound showmanship that has made Producer Korda the kingpin in England's booming cinema industry. . . . *Things to Come* may or may not entrance U.S. cinemaddicts but it is likely to make bigwigs in Hollywood scratch their heads about a future much more immediate than 2036.

—*Time* (12)

(*Things to Come*'s vision of future civilization) consists of beehive cities built into monster excavations—whether underground or in the sides of mountains I cannot say, since the photography at this point becomes very trick. The point is that the cities lie somewhere out of the sun, which according to one of the wise men is a poor thing at best, shining as it does intermittently through contaminated air. Down there or in there, wherever it is, the people of the future manufacture their own light rays as we do our central heat; and bask athletically in glass houses. . . . Try as I did to think otherwise, I could only think that living there would be like living in an electric ice box, you on your tray and I on mine. The whole picture was for me intolerably prosy and grotesquely unconvincing. I was confirmed in a former suspicion, namely, that the future is the dullest subject on earth.

—*The Nation* (13)

H. G. Wells, the eminent fortune teller, has painted a pessimistic, frightening, yet inspiring picture of our next 100 years in his first film, *Things to Come*, which had its local premiere at the Rivoli last night. Typical Wellsian conjecture, it ranges from the reasonably possible to the reasonably fantastic; but true or false, fanciful or logical, it is an absorbing, provocative and impressively staged production which does credit to its maker, Alexander Korda. . . . *Things to Come* is an unusual picture, a fantasy, if you will, with overtones of the Buck Rogers and Flash Gordon comic strips. But it is, as well, a picture with ideas which have been expressed dramatically and with visual fascination. There's nothing we can do now but sit back and wait for the holocaust. If Mr. Wells is right, we are in for an interesting century.

—Frank S. Nugent (14)

FILMOGRAPHY

THINGS TO COME (London Films, 1936, British) 130 mins.

Producer, Alexander Korda; director, William Cameron Menzies; script, H.G. Wells and Lajos Biro based on the book *The Shape of Things to Come* by H.G. Wells; art director, Vincent Korda; costumes, John Armstrong; special effects, Ned Mann, Edward Cohen, and Harry Zech; editor, Charles Crichton; camera, George Perinal; music, Arthur Bliss.

Cast: Raymond Massey (John Cabal/Oswald Cabal); Ralph Richardson (The Boss); Cedric Hardwicke (Theotocopulos); Margaretta Scott (Roxana); Edward Chapman (Pippa Passworthy/Raymond); Maurice Braddell (Dr. Harding); Sophie Stewart (Mrs. Cabal); Derrick de Marney (Richard Gordon); Pickles Livingstone (Horrie Passworthy); Pearl Argyle (Catherine Cabal); Alan Jeayes (Grandfather Cabal); Anthony Holles; Patricia Hilliard.

THINGS TO COME (London Films, 1936)
Raymond Massey comes from Wings Over the World headquarters in Basra to bring civilization to Everytown.

SOURCES
1. Hall, Mordaunt. *The New York Times,* Nov. 23, 1930.
2. Hall, Mordaunt. *The New York Times,* Dec. 5, 1931.
3. Troy, William. *The Nation,* Mar. 22, 1933.
4. Watts, Richard, Jr. *The New York Herald Tribune.*
5. Hall, Mordaunt. *The New York Times,* Mar. 3, 1933.
6. Bloch, Robert. From *SF Symposium* edited by Jose Sanz, Instituto Nacional do Cinema, Brazil, 1969.
7. Troy, William. *The Nation,* Dec. 13, 1933.
8. Hall, Mordaunt. *The New York Times,* Sept. 16, 1933.
9. Sennwald, Andre. *The New York Times,* Oct. 28, 1935.
10. Ellison, Harlan. From a taped interview with the authors, 1979.
11. Aldiss, Brian W. From address given in Nagoya, Japan, 1970.
12. *Time,* April 6, 1936.
13. *The Nation,* April 29, 1936.
14. Nugent, Frank S. From *The Nation.*

Chapter 3

The Fearful and Fecund Fifties

From *Things to Come* in 1936 to *Destination Moon* in 1950—fourteen years—there is hardly a pure science fiction film anywhere in the world. There were a few good fantasies, and all the deteriorating spinoffs of *Frankenstein* et al that anyone could want—a lot more than the audiences wanted, in fact, as they became progressively more dim-witted and threadbare. But no true sf worth mentioning until the year 1950 arrived. Then there was an explosion.

Why the hiatus? Probably because the world had had a war on its mind for a large part of those years. The technological terror of the *Luftwaffe* and Hiroshima took the steam out of scientific imagining. It was much the same in printed science fiction. The efflorescence of magazines in the late 1930s and early 1940s were swept away by the pressures of the war, so that by 1945 only a handful survived.

Then why the explosion?

There were at least two sets of reasons. One was dark and psychological, and did not show itself at first. The other, perhaps, was as simple as the laws of supply and demand.

Printed science fiction led the way. After the low point at the end of World War II, the sf magazines were some time getting their feet under them again. But *Astounding* survived; *Amazing,* with a strange mixture of deranged robots and sophomoric stories, boomed; the big slicks (*The Saturday Evening Post* and *Collier's*) began to take an

Tales of Tomorrow was the first pure science-fiction series on American television, and in some ways it was the best. For one thing, it was an anthology series—each week's story was independent of the ones before and after it—so that the full range of sf could be exploited. (As could never be done in, for instance, *Star Trek*, which was always limited to the specified imaginary future of the starship *Enterprise*.) For another, producer Mort Abrahams had the revolutionary notion of involving actual sf writers in the writing and even production of the series. He organized a semi-commercial corporation called The Science Fiction League (Hugo Gernsback would have complained, if he had ever known). About a dozen major sf writers of the time were members, and each undertook to make his stories available for adaptation to the screen. Long before the first episode was broadcast there were meetings, at Fletcher Pratt's apartment or Horace Gold's, to discuss each writer's contribution.

In the event, most of the stories were adapted by professional script writers and some were originals, but the series was nevertheless brilliantly conceived and intelligently produced—on a budget which would not now pay for the titles on *Battlestar Galactica*. Technology did *Tales of Tomorrow* in. When it was on the air (live!) there was no good way of filming a TV show and television tape had not been invented. All that remains are kinescopes, pretty poor in quality. It is a great pity, because some fine stories are on those flickering films.

—FP

interest in science fiction; and at the end of the decade of the 1940s the boom in science-fiction book publishing had begun. New magazines, like *Galaxy* and *The Magazine of Fantasy and Science Fiction,* were on the drawing boards. Even fledgling TV was mounting successful shows like the kiddy *Captain Video* and the astonishingly well done *Tales of Tomorrow.*

It was coming to be science-fiction time again. The movie-makers could feel the vibrations in the ground. In June of 1950 the first effects appeared. The title of the film was *Destination Moon.* It premiered at a private showing in New York's Hayden Planetarium—a gala science-fiction event, with most of the available science-fiction writers, editors and even fans rounded up for drinks and the viewing of the new production. It was a blue-chip operation, and it marked the beginning of the ten-year sf career of George Pal.

Destination Moon was a million-dollar film when a million dollars was *money.* "If I had a million dollars," Robert A. Heinlein reflected when it was all over, "I would sit on it and shoot the first six science fiction writers who came my way with screenplays." (1) George Pal was more adventurous. He read Heinlein's scripts, pondered the costs, made his decision and turned the taps on the money-barrels to start the machinery in motion.

The script of *Destination Moon* was not commissioned by Pal. It came to him over the transom. It had been written as a speculation by Heinlein (in collaboration with Alford van Ronkel), based rather loosely on his juvenile novel, *Rocketship Galileo.* Pal was not wholly satisfied with the script and so he put another writer on it (James O'Hanlon). But it was Heinlein's story all the same, from the first conception of the novel to the party for the film's release . . . which makes a puzzle.

Robert A. Heinlein is the Compleat Science-Fiction Writer. He has the credentials to prove it: four consecutive decades at the top of his field, so that when the Science Fiction Writers of America resolved to give its first "Grand Master" award, no other writer was even considered.

Heinlein is not a perfect writer. There are a dozen in science fiction who use language far more gracefully than he, and almost as many who are better able to weave known science in with speculation. He has shown little of the capacity for great imaginative leaps of a Delany, a Cordwainer Smith—of a Wells or a Verne, for that matter, considering how little they had before them to build on. Heinlein's greatest strength is his human plausibility. When he says this is how it might be, one sees at once that indeed it might; and when the people within his stories respond to the new environments, changed societies or strange technology their responses are both believable and fresh. Heinlein's stories are always told in terms of people. And that is the puzzle of *Destination Moon,* for there isn't a person in it. It has a few scientists and generals, pontificating their roles; one or two obligatory villains, all soon foiled; and four astronauts as plastic as their real-life counterparts were made to seem by NASA's flacks nineteen years later. The master story-teller did not give us a story.

But *Destination Moon* gives everything else. It was not just Heinlein, or even George Pal accepting his script and encouraging him to stay on the set while it was filmed—an act of daring unmatched since the days of H. G. Wells and William Cameron Menzies. It was an immense team effort. *Astounding*'s No. 1 cover artist, Chesley Bonestell, was hired to paint the backdrops and design the sets. Willy Ley, about to become *Galaxy*'s favorite columnist, was retained as the final authority on rockets and space ships in general. The actual orbit the film's ship followed to the Moon was calculated by real-life astronomer Robert S. Richardson of Mount Palomar—better known to some of us at the time as the science-fiction writer Philip Latham. Nothing was spared. When Pal put his bet on science fiction he went all out.

Destination Moon is beautifully done. Sets, models, process work and animation all fit together, as Lee Zavitz made filmable whatever Heinlein and the experts wanted to show. In order to make the astronauts seem to float in space, they had to be hung from wires—not just once; there were different hitching points for different camera angles. The actors were helpless as they hung from their off-screen gallows, and puppeteers had to move them around with iron pipes. The wires had to be strong, therefore were made of metal. Therefore they shone. A special crew member spent his days dabbing at them with black paint to kill the shine. Free fall was a new concept for mundanes in those days (even Bosley Crowther's review in the New York *Times* referred to it as "a 'free orbit,' whatever that means"), and the episodes that showed the astronauts floating weightlessly were the hits of the show. But all of the effects were visually satisfying. The film magic was so well done, Heinlein boasted, that "I'll warrant you won't notice it, save by logical deduction; i.e., since no one has been to the Moon yet, the shots showing the approach for landing on the Moon *must* be animation—and they are." (2) Audiences granted him the point. If *Destination Moon* is not a great deal of fun to watch any more it is largely because it looks so much like the actual Apollo films that it has become routine . . . and that, when you think of it, is not a bad triumph for the movie-maker's art.

Destination Moon paid its bills, but it was not a big box-office bonanza. For one thing, it was ripped off. Lippert Films, scenting a free ride on big promotion money, pushed a quickie called *Rocketship XM* before the cameras just in time to take the new off the idea of space travel. It is a dreadful film, scientifically preposterous and loaded with every pulp-sf cliche that can be crammed into 78 minutes, but it returned a far bigger percentage profit on dollars invested than *Destination Moon*, and some fraction of its grosses no doubt came right out of the pocket of George Pal.

Pal was not discouraged. Even before *Destination Moon* opened he had made up his mind to keep on with sf.

FILMOGRAPHY
DESTINATION MOON (Eagle-Lion, 1950, U.S.A.)
91 mins.

Producer, George Pal; director, Irving Pichel; script, Rip Van Ronkel, Robert A. Heinlein, and James O'Hanlon from a story by Robert A. Heinlein; art director, Ernst Fegte; animation sequence, Walter Lantz; special effects, Lee Zavitz; editor, Duke Goldstone; music, Leigh Stevens; camera, Lionel Lindon.

Cast: John Archer (Barnes); Warner Anderson (Cargraves); Tom Powers (General Thayer); Dick Wesson (Sweeney); Erin O'Brein Moore (Mrs. Cargraves).

ᵕᏕᵕᏕᵕᏕᵕᏕᵕᏕᵕᏕᵕᏕᵕᏕᵕᏕᵕᏕᵕᏕᵕᏕᵕᏕᵕᏕᵕᏕᵕᏕᵕᏕᵕᏕᵕ

ᵕᏕᵕᏕᵕᏕᵕᏕᵕᏕᵕᏕᵕᏕᵕᏕᵕᏕᵕᏕᵕᏕᵕᏕᵕᏕᵕᏕᵕᏕᵕᏕᵕᏕᵕ

Moon. It begins and ends in the present—i.e., 1964. It shows the first Moon landing by conventional NASA-type rockets (but filmed five years before Apollo landed there). The astronauts discover a Union Jack and a note attached to, by the sheer luck of it, the first rock they look at. This is the script writer's invention, not Wells's, and not much of an improvement.

In between the scenes of the "frame", however, Wells's story is moderately faithfully adapted, and quite well acted by England's leading filmic police inspector, Lionel Jeffries, as Cavor. Cavor is a mad scientist who invents a metal which cuts off the force of gravity as a window-shade cuts off light. He paints a sort of enlarged Christmas-tree ornament with Cavorite, climbs in with his bird-brained assistant and the assistant's only slightly less incompetent girl friend, and they are off to visit Ray Harryhausen's antlike Selenites.

It is unfortunately not a very good film. Jeffries plays the full range of his part well enough: in the building of his ship, a standard absent-minded professor; but in the later stages, as he deplores his assistant's unhappy practice of murdering every Selenite he gets close to, a kind, fearful, disappointed human being. He elects to stay behind and try to patch things up when the other two escape. He does not succeed very well (we find in the last installment of the frame), because he has given the Selenites a bad cold and the race has died of it. The same cold virus also caused their machines and buildings to rot away. (Now, that's what you call a *cold!*)

The cold germs represent a pretty cynical borrowing from Wells's use of the same device in *The War of the Worlds,* and not the only one. The explorers are marooned on the Moon, for a time, because the Selenites have stolen their space ship—exactly as the Morlocks swiped the Time Traveler's machine.

Even Harryhausen's usually marvelous animation is below par. There are obviously two kinds of Selenites in the film, the Harryhausen animations, and a bunch of little people in ant suits, and it is dismayingly easy to see which is which. Juran's 1964 version is no doubt an advance over Méliès's turn-of-the-century production. But it is not sixty years' worth of advance.

By the mid-1950s most of the main sf-film trends of the decade were already well established, and the existence of a market, some kind of a market, was no longer in question. Space technology had been tried, and many monsters, and exciting interplanetary adventure, and comic touches. It was time for a fusion of them all, and it came in the form of *Forbidden Planet.*

FILMOGRAPHY
FORBIDDEN PLANET (MGM, 1956, U.S.A.) 98 mins.

Producer, Nicholas Nayfack; director, Fred McLeod Wilcox; script, Cyril Hume from a story by Irving Block and Allen Adler; art directors, Arthur Lonergan and Cedric Gibbons; editor, Ferris Webster; special effects, A. Arnold Gillespie, Warren Newcombe, Irving G. Ries, and Joshua Meador; electric tonalities, Louis and Bebe Barron; camera, George Folsey.

Cast: Walter Pidgeon (Dr. Morbius); Anne Francis (Altaira Morbius); Leslie Nielsen (Commander Adams); Warren Stevens (Lieutenant Ostrow); Jack Kelly (Lieutenant Farman); Earl Holliman (Cook); Richard Anderson; George Wallace; Bob Dix.

In the mid-1950s my publisher, Ian Ballantine, took me to lunch and offered a proposition. Would I like to write the novel version of an upcoming sci-fi flick on which he owned the book rights? Tell me what it's about, I said. Well, said Ian, there's this spaceship that visits a planet inhabited by a mad scientist and his beautiful daughter, only there's a monster that kills everything. Forget it, I said wisely, looking at the press releases he had handed me; I never heard of the producer or director; the writers have never had anything to do with science fiction, so they can't possibly know what they're doing; the plot stinks; and, all in all, I advise you to walk away from this turkey.

Then the film came out and I saw it. The first shock was that the "electronic tonalities" were by Louis and Bebe Barron, old poker companions from Horace Gold's Friday-night parties, and it penetrated my mind that they, at least, knew quite a lot about science fiction. Then the film itself was, by God, thrilling. Lester del Rey was with me, along with our wives. As we left the theater, Lester said, "That's the first original science-fiction film I've seen that could have made a fine novelette for *Astounding*." He was on target. It was the supreme accolade of science-fiction rightness. I kicked myself all the way home.

—FP

The first conception of *Forbidden Planet* (only it was then called *Fatal Planet*) came from Irving Block, a painter who had done special effects for *Rocketship XM*. His was not exactly an original story. He proposed to lift the plot from William Shakespeare's *The Tempest,* and did. Translated into the science-fiction terms of 2200 A.D., the island of Bermuda became the planet Altair IV; Prospero became

Dr. Morbius; Miranda, Altaira; and Ariel turned into Robby the Robot. As in Shakespeare, the scene is visited by a group of travelers from outside, in this case the crew of a United Planets space cruiser.

There is no exact equivalent to Caliban in *Forbidden Planet,* but in the hole where Shakespeare had plugged Caliban *Forbidden Planet* inserts the Id-beast. This may be the film's greatest original invention; certainly it is the one that professional science-fiction writers most respected. According to the story, long and long ago Altair IV was inhabited by a highly intelligent and cultured race called the Krell. In their researches, they learned how to tap the basic power of human thought, and to give tangible form

FORBIDDEN PLANET (MGM, 1956)
Robby greets the expedition from Earth on their landing on Altair IV.

to emotions, even the deepest, most repressed parts of the subconscious. There, underneath culture and wisdom, lay the primitive, mindless Id. When they gave it form it destroyed them.

When the crew of the space cruiser arrives, Dr. Morbius welcomes them to what seems to be Paradise. His lovely daughter frolics with a tame tiger, the landscape is luxuriant Hawaii under a pale green sky, and all is peace. He shows them the majestic technology left by the Krell: immense banks of machines, filling hollowed-out galleries of generators and instruments many miles in extent. All seems well—well enough, even, for the captain of the space cruiser to fall in love with beautiful Altaira, and give her her first kiss.

Then the Id-beast returns to life. It attacks, at first tentatively and then with increasing frequency and force. It penetrates electronic force fields and crumples thick steel walls, and it kills. It cannot be resisted. It is the deepest primitive part of Morbius's own mind that is animating it, amplified by the old Krell machines, and it is only when it kills Morbius himself that it disappears.

Invisible menaces were nothing new to science fiction, or even to sf film. But this one had been thought out with care. It is visualized on the screen with great skill and cunning. Through most of the film it is unseen. That was one of the points that helped sell the film to MGM. "The great thing about this," Block explained to the producers, "is that it won't cost you a cent to make the monsters!"

Actually it did cost, and rather heavily—the special effects budget alone on *Forbidden Planet* ran over a million dollars. MGM called in Walt Disney's animators to give the Id-beast form. They earned their money. It is scary, especially in the attack on the ship itself, where it becomes visible as a series of electrical flares where it touches the force-screen. The beast's face is never seen clearly, but if you look closely enough perhaps you can see that it does in fact have some resemblance to a terribly distorted, bestial version of Walter Pidgeon's face, which is what the designers intended. It actually looks about as much like MGM's own Leo the Lion gone berserk. Mostly it looks *mean.*

If the Id-beast was frightening, *Forbidden Planet*'s other non-human was lovable. Robby the Robot cooked, cleaned, bootlegged bourbon for the ship's crew and spoke 187 languages, and charmed his associates while he did it. The idea of a lovable robot was nothing new for science fiction in print form—Asimov and Kuttner had been creating them for decades—but he was the first film robot of any importance since *Metropolis*'s Maria, and the only one to get laughs. He was too good to use up on a single film; MGM put together *The Invisible Boy* a couple of years later just to find a spot for him, and his copies decorated any number of other films and television programs. (The original robot itself appeared at a science fiction convention in Southern California in 1975 to hand out awards.)

Animating Robby wasn't a job for Disney. It took a live actor, small enough to fit inside the suit. Frankie Darro, grown up kid star, was one of several who blackened their faces and crawled inside to sweat through his scenes.

Forbidden Planet's score also developed a life of its own. Well, not its "score"—you are not allowed to call it that, because of jurisdictional questions with the muscians' union; it is called "electronic tonalities" in the credits. The creators were the husband-and-wife team of Louis and Bebe Barron. The "tonalities" became a successful record album and, for many years, the theme music for Long

John Nebel's all-night talk show on New York radio. But the picture was not a financial success. The special effects pushed the costs way over the budget and, although the money was well spent, the bottom line was bad news.

When I was assigned to direct the photography of Metro-Goldwyn-Mayer's *Forbidden Planet*, I was faced with . . . unique problems . . . (but) *Forbidden Planet* is not my first encounter with a science-fiction production. "Way back" in 1922 I photographed a thriller for Biograph Studios in New York titled *The Man from Mars*, featuring unearthly creatures with huge heads and gleaming talons. I shot the production in black-and-white in a "new" process they called 3-D! I recall that most of the picture was shot at a stop of f/8 and without the benefit of an exposure meter. *Forbidden Planet* in color and CinemaScope is a far cry from this.

—George Folsey, A.S.C. (15)

Altaira and Adams watch Dr. Morbius die

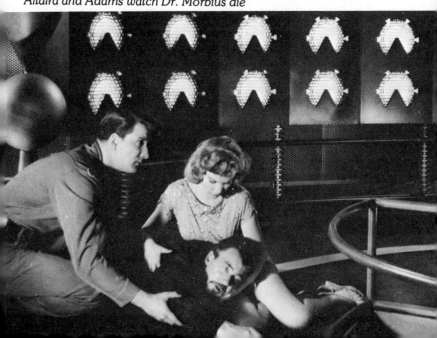

Before *Forbidden Planet*, Bebe and I had been doing experimental film scores, and we were getting a very good response. We thought we should try to see if we could work on a feature film. We followed the trade papers and knew that Dore Schary was the biggest man in Hollywood—he was the voice of the industry—and we also heard that he was a very nice guy. His wife was having a one-woman art show in New York. We knew he'd be there. We crashed the thing and looked around for the guy who looked least important—he wouldn't want to crowd his wife's show, so he would be that guy. And we went up to talk to him. We told him we'd been doing some interesting things with electronic music. He didn't say, "What's electronic music?" He just said, "If you're ever in California, give me a call. I'd like to hear it."

We got there with some tapes, and he listened. He turned around and said, "Do you have any commitments?" I didn't know what he meant. He said, "I want to know if you're free for the next few months." We were free, all right. And he sent us to Johnny Green, the head of his music department. So Green took us into a screening room and said, "I want you to look at this movie." It was a rough editing of the work print—dialogue, but no music and virtually no sound effects—but there was something about it that felt electric. When we came out I was so excited that I didn't know whether it was from being in the executive screening room of MGM, or from something about the movie itself—but it felt good.

Then, for the next three or four months, it was hassles with lawyers and department heads. Questions of union jurisdiction. Would there be patent claims against us? We had to draw circuits and give them to MGM's patent attorney in Washington to check against the files. And labor relations.

They wanted us to do it all on the lot, because they have little bungalows with a piano and a couch and you're supposed to spend eight hours a day there making music. We had a studio full of heavy, difficult to interconnect equipment; we said we couldn't transport it; they said, "That's never been done!" But Dore Schary wasn't as concerned with being traditional as with making a good movie. He said, "Let them do it in New York. Let them come out here halfway through and show us what they're doing."

That was hectic. That was night and day. We turned down all party invitations. We would grab a quick bite in the kitchen and go on working, fourteen, sixteen hours a day, because we had a deadline. We would try to go out into Washington Square for half an hour each afternoon for a stroll—that was Bebe's invention, and it saved us from going crazy.

Anyway, we brought back the assignment, and they set it up in the screening room. Dore Schary was there; Johnny Green was there; the head of the sound department was there; the producer was there, Nicky Nayfack; Fred Wilcox, the director, was there, but none of the stars. We played those scenes, and I asked permission to work the board, because I knew how loud things should be. During the landing I felt it so much that I kept making it louder and louder—and Dore Schary had very sensitive ears. But he decided then and there that that was going to be the score.

—Louis Barron (16)

Two of the most successful science-fiction films of the 1950s were not called science fiction. They were based on best-selling novels, and they were both political in the extreme: they were classic examples of the use writers make of sf to preach their sermons in metaphor. George Orwell's dismal view of the year *1984* appeared in the same year as *Forbidden Planet,* 1956.

FILMOGRAPHY
1984 (Associated British Pictures, 1956, British) 91 mins.

Producer, N. Peter Rathvon; director, Michael Anderson; script, William P. Templeton and Ralph G. Bettinson from the novel by George Orwell; art director, Terence Verity; editor, Bill Lewthwaite; special effects, G. Blackwell, B. Langley, and N. Warwick; music, Malcolm Arnold; camera, C. Pennington Richards.

Cast: Edmond O'Brien (Winston Smith); Michael Redgrave (General O'Connor); Jan Sterling (Julia); David Kossoff (Charrington); Donald Pleasence (Parsons); Mervyn Johns (Jones); Ernest Clark; Carol Wolveridge; Kenneth Griffith; Ronan O'Casey.

Orwell was a political writer from his first breath to his last, although his politics changed sides. In the 1930s he was a correspondent for lefty magazines in England, his writing marked by a searing hatred of the capitalist exploiters. His book of essays, *The Road to Wigan Pier,* and his semi-autobiographical book on poverty at home and abroad, *Down and Out in Paris and London,* cry out with rage at the privileged exploiters. Then he went to Spain. Everything Orwell did in his life is documented in his books. In *Homage to Catalonia* he tells of the bitter disillusion with the socialists and communists that came of his involvement in the Spanish Civil War. It left him with nothing. Not even life, for during World War II he learned that he was doomed to die young. So he wrote the novel, *1984*. The book served a double purpose for him. It was conceived as a buck-hustle, a probable best seller that might provide for his family when he was gone; and it was also an indictment of the inhuman treachery of governments—particularly "people's" governments. It was a great success on both counts. It is easy to read *1984* as a tract against Stalinism, which it surely was, but it is also the authentic voice of a human being whose faiths have been so shattered that he is past tears and has only sullen anger left.

The film is a somewhat simplified version of the novel, but undistorted as far as it goes. Perhaps that is what is wrong with it. Orwell was not writing for the screen. What he made most cruelly real was the drab, hopeless tedium of life under Big Brother's dictatorship, and drab and tedious is how much of the movie appears. Edmond O'Brien's performance consists principally of looking glum. It is exactly the performance dictated by the theme and story, but 91 minutes of watching people being drab and glum is excessive.

The novel remains alive, after more than thirty years, and Orwell is sometimes hailed as a literally precise prophet, not only for his political comments but even for the technology he depicted. A close examination gives him a rather poor batting average in prophecy, but maybe that is to his credit: It is possible that having *1984* as a warning helped us avoid having 1984 in fact.

Equally bad as prophecy (so far, at least) is Nevil Shute's

On the Beach,—and, perhaps, equally entitled to credit for helping to forestall the thing it warned against. The novel was another big best-seller, and the film version (1959) was again quite faithful to the original.

In the story, a nuclear war has broken out, and is all over—except that the last of the casualties have not yet died. The northern hemisphere is devoid of life. The slow atmospheric exchange of radioactivity across the Equator has given Australia a few months' extension, but their end is inevitable. Meanwhile, Australian life goes on as always, though plans are made for distribution of poison pellets to avoid the unnecessary pain of death by radiation poisoning, and a nuclear submarine makes a last, foredoomed attempt to find survivors in the United States. Strange radio signals have been received from San Francisco; but when the sub arrives they learn that it is only a broken electrical connection, blown in the wind, that had seemed to be transmitting unreadable code. At the end of the film we see the streets of Melbourne. They are empty. Nothing moves except a revivalists' banner, stirring in the wind, that says, "There Is Still Time, Brother!"

Nobody missed the political message in *On the Beach.* How they reacted to it depended a lot on what their politics were. Dr. Linus Pauling said, "It may be that some day we can look back and say *On the Beach* is the picture that saved the world." Civil Defense officials were scandalized—the Connecticut state director called it "mythological"; the one in New York agreed that it was a "fantasy" because saving the lives of a population from nuclear war "is not only possible but relatively simple."

How effective the film was as propaganda is arguable. Twenty years later, no nuclear weapon has been used in war since the film appeared. On the other hand, they still exist, bigger and better than ever, with aggregate throw-weights a couple of orders of magnitude greater than in 1959. So the jury is still out.

> (*On the Beach* is a) defeatist movie . . . (a) would-be shocker which plays right up the alley of (a) the Kremlin and (b) the western defeatists and/or traitors who yelp for the scrapping of the H-bomb. . . . (It points) the way toward eventual Communist enslavement of the entire human race.
> —Editorial, New York *Daily News*

> No punches are pulled. Its message is vigorous and meaningful for all of us. . . . to portray in human terms just what will happen if, in our childish and irresponsible way, we allow one of us to pull the trigger.
> —Editorial, New York *Times*

> It's figured that comments . . . both pro and con, represent money in the bank for UA and Kramer.
> —*Variety*

If Arch Oboler's *Five* had been a better movie, it is likely that *On the Beach* might never have been filmed. Although the circumstances and the story line are different, the message is identical. But *On the Beach* succeeded vastly where *Five* failed. It grossed more than $5,000,000 in the United States alone, and doubled that worldwide. Its star-studded cast—Gregory Peck, Ava Gardner, Fred Astaire and Anthony Perkins played leads—nicely acted Nevil Shute's well-drawn characters and read John Paxton's moving lines, and its score made *Waltzing Matilda* climb the charts as a popular song.

On the Beach and *1984* are as much a part of the fearful climate of the Fifties as *Godzilla* or *The Blob.* Considered as therapy, perhaps they are healthier. The things they tell us to fear do not come from the bottom of the sea or outer space. They arise within us. The message of these films is the same as Pogo's: "We have met the enemy, and he is us."

FILMOGRAPHY
ON THE BEACH (United Artists, 1959, U.S.A.) 134 mins.

Producer/director, Stanley Kramer; script, John Paxter from the novel by Nevil Shute; art director, Fernando Carrere; editor, Frederic Knudtson; special effects, Lee Zavitz; music, Ernest Gold; camera, Giuseppe Rotunno.

Cast: Gregory Peck (Commander Dwight Towers); Ava Gardner (Moira Davidson); Fred Astaire (Julian Osborn); Anthony Perkins (Lieutenant Peter Holmes); Donna Anderson (Mary Holmes); John Tate (Admiral Birdie); Lola Brooks (Lieutenant Hosgood); Guy Doleman (Farrel); John Neillon (Swain); Ken Wayne (Benson); Joe McCormick; Harp McGuire; Richard Meikle.

Richard Matheson's *The Incredible Shrinking Man* (1957) is not exactly *science* fiction. There is no known science that suggests any way any of its events could happen. Nor is it "fearful" in the sense of much of the rest of the 1950s product, since it is only the hero who is at risk, not the world. (But psychoanalytically oriented critics suggest that it is a metaphor for one of the most fundamental fears of all: of growing old, and thus of diminishing.)

In the film, Scott Carey (played by Grant Williams) is exposed to a strange radioactive cloud, and begins to shrink. He shrinks all through the film (to the size of a midget, then a baby, then a mouse, an insect, a grain of sand and ultimately to an atomic particle), and at each stage he has adventures. There is no more to the film than that, but each stage gives director Jack Arnold and special-effects man Clifford Stine marvelous opportunities for camera tricks and excitement.

FILMOGRAPHY
THE INCREDIBLE SHRINKING MAN (Universal, 1957, U.S.A.)
   Producer, Albert Zugsmith; director, Jack Arnold; script, Richard Matheson from his novel; art directors, Alexander Golitzen and Robert Clatworthy; editor, Al Joseph; special effects, Clifford Stine; music, Fred Carling and E. Lawrence; camera, Ellis Carter.
   Cast: Grant Williams (Scott Carey); Randy Stuart (Louise Carey); April Kent (Clarice); Raymond Bailey (Dr. Thomas Silver); Billy Curtis (Midget); William Schallert; Diana Darrin; Frank Scannell.

So did *The Lost World* when Irwin Allen decided to remake it in 1960. Like most of Allen's ventures into science fiction, the script is cynically banal and, although the special effects are adventurous, especially in a battle between a dinosaur and a helicopter, they are achieved by magnifying shots of live lizards rather than by the sort of animation Willis O'Brien achieved in the 1925 silent version. They show it. O'Brien's silent dinosaurs had been so convincing that the New York *Times* had suspected they were real, and that author A. Conan Doyle had somehow

stumbled on an actual place where they survived. At re-make time Allen realized O'Brien should be hired, and he was. But he wasn't allowed to work; they used the tarted-up lizards instead.

Also in 1960 John Wyndham's *The Midwich Cuckoos* was brought to the screen as Wolf Rilla's *The Village of the Damned.* The cuckoo is famous for laying its eggs in other birds' nests. It was Wyndham's notion that a nearly humanoid race of aliens, intent on colonizing Earth, would find a cheap and easy way to do it by impregnating as many human women as they could catch with their seed. That is what happens in *The Midwich Cuckoos,* and essen-tially the same in the MGM film. The children that result grow into terrifying young creatures, quite human in ap-pearance but capable of hypnotic domination of all pure Earthlings. Their eyes glow frighteningly, and the effect

An executive at Berkley Books told someone that my book, *The Incredible Shrinking Man*, was the novelization of the screenplay. He had no concept that it was a novel first and then a movie. In fact, he said that very few people knew this fact. He was right. He was the only one.

I'd always wanted to be involved in film. I knew it was very difficult to get in; and then, when I had a project that they wanted to buy, the stipulation was that I do the screenplay. They usually go along with that. They assume the novelist will do a lousy job and then they'll just get it rewritten. Actually, it's not that hard if you're a visual writer. If you're not a visual writer, you can't learn. But, if you can see in your mind's eye what's supposed to be up on the screen, the style is a hell of a lot easier than writing prose.
—Richard Matheson (17)

THE INCREDIBLE SHRINKING MAN (Universal, 1957)
The Wardrobe mistress holds Grant Williams's robe as he sits on the oversize hospital bed.

was scary enough to encourage MGM to make *The Children of the Damned* in 1963. This is a sort of a sequel, but almost as much of a remake: the children become sympathetic in this version, but otherwise it is essentially the same story repeated.

When I was making *Village of the Damned* I was having considerable arguments with the producers, who did not feel that my approach was right. They said I was in danger of falling between two stools— that is, "You want a horror film? You've got to have horror." And I said, "But not at all! I think it can be much more horrifying to use strangeness in an *implicit* way, rather than in a direct way." As a matter of fact, in the film there is a special trick. When the children use their telepathic powers, the eyes change and begin to glow. In the original novel, by John Wyndham, the children had very strange, very light, almost white eyes. Since those eyes don't exist, we decided to go the opposite way and just find children with very, very remarkable eyes; and on the screen dark eyes tend to be more remarkable than pale ones. Then the idea came across, from the special effects department at MGM, that they had this marvelous trick of being able to change the eyes, so that they started to glow. (It was simply a matter of making a matte, which is a little piece of film the exact size of the pupil, and to reverse it from positive to negative so that black becomes white.) The trick was effective, but I fought against it for some time, because it seemed to me that if, in order to get across the effect that the children have this influence, you have to resort to trickery, you have slightly lost the battle. . . . (I tried to) take a very ordinary village, very ordinary people, almost cliche situations between people—a quite deliberate cliche about relationships of people—and inject into this the strange children. Again, take very beautiful ordinary children. Not monster-looking children, which was one of the suggestions in the beginning: that all the children should be harelipped or hunchbacked or something. I said, "That's ridiculous!" So I took ordinary children, except that I made them behave not like children. There is something sinister, I think, about a child who does not move like a child, or laugh like a child, who has none of the physical vitality of a child. When people asked me how I got the children to act so marvelously I said, "Well, I didn't." All I told them was to do absolutely nothing whatsoever, and to walk very deliberately and sit very deliberately, and never to smile, or if they smiled, only rarely.

—Wolf Rilla (18)

FILMOGRAPHY
THE VILLAGE OF THE DAMNED (MGM, 1960, British) 78 mins.

Producer, Ronald Kinnoch; director, Wolf Rilla; script, Sterling Silliphant, Wolf Rilla, and George Barclay from the novel *The Midwich Cuckoos* by John Wyndham; art director, Ivan King; editor, Gordon Hales; special effects, Tom Howard; music, Ron Goodwin; camera, Geoffrey Faithfull.

Cast: George Sanders (Dr. Gordon Zellaby); Barbara Shelley (Anthea Zellaby); Martin Stephens (David); Michael Gwynne (Major Bernard); Laurence Naismith (Dr. Willera); Richard Vernon (Sir Edgar Hargraves); John Phillips (General Leighton); Richard Warner; Thomas Heathcote; Jenny Laird.

As a quietly civilized exercise on the fear and power of the unknown (*The Village of the Damned*) is one of the trimmest, most original and serenely unnerving little chillers in a long time. With George Sanders and Barbara Shelley heading a small, unfamiliar cast, this Metro-Goldwyn-Mayer surprise was made in England, and it must have cost the company all of a dime.

—Howard Thompson (19)

"Tired and sick film which starts off very promisingly but soon nosedives."

—*Variety*

After the Cuckoos, it was apparent that Wyndham's novels were mineable for potential films, and so *The Day of the Triffids* was made in 1963. The novel was one of Wyndham's best, and by all odds his most successful—it ran as a serial in the big slick magazine *Collier's*, and then went through many editions and saw many translations as a book. The film was a disappointment.

FILMOGRAPHY
THE DAY OF THE TRIFFIDS (Rank, 1963, British) 94 mins.

Producer, George Pitcher; director, Steve Sekely; script, Philip Yordan from the novel by John Wyndham; art director, Cedric Dawe; editor, Spencer Reeve; special effects, Wally Veevers; music, Ron Goodwin; camera, Ted Moore.

Cast: Howard Keel (Bill Masen); Nicole Maurey (Christine Durrant); Janette Scott (Karen Goodwin); Kieron Moore (Tom Goodwin); Janina Faye (Susan); Mervyn Johns; Ewan Roberts; Colette Wilde; Alison Leggatt.

The "Triffids" were three-legged ambulatory plants that came to the Earth in a shower of meteorites, which also had the property of causing much of the Earth's population to go blind. Where they come from is not easy to say. In various versions of the novel Wyndham had them coming from Venus, or alternatively from the Soviet Union; the film just lets it be from space. It is difficult to make a horde of creatures resembling coat racks with leaves look anything but funny, and Wally Veevers's special effects did not quite meet the challenge.

> John Wyndham . . . was a very gentle and a very retiring person. He was so retiring that he would never give interviews or see anybody and hardly ever came up to town. . . . I think it is one of the saddest things in the history of science-fiction films that one of his best novels, *The Day of the Triffids,* became one of the worst films. The reason it became one of the worst films . . . it was absolutely diabolical . . . was, I think, that there was a total mess and mix-up, and the producers kept on changing their minds and new bits kept on being written by about 93 writers and I think about 8 directors.
>
> —Wolf Rilla (20)

> John Wyndham was a cultivated and urbane English gentleman. Under his real name, John Beynon Harris, he had written some of the most God-awful space operas of the 1930s, but after World War II he began writing science fiction of quite a different kind. I was his literary agent from 1948 to 1953, when I closed the agency. His unobtrusive and literate prose style gave plausibility to everything he wrote about, and allowed him to reach far larger audiences than the science-fiction magazines of the time. He lived long enough to see his stories made into successful films and to enjoy the perquisites of success, but only just. The last time I saw him was in London in 1965, and he died four years later.
>
> —FP

One final bit of fallout from the fearful fifties was Val Guest's *The Quatermass Experiment* (1955—sometimes called *The Creeping Unknown*) and the other Hammer films based on the Nigel Kneale BBC television series. Professor Quatermass was England's principal television defense against creeping menaces from space in the 1950s. In *The Quatermass Experiment* a returning astronaut has been infected by a space disease which turns him into a menacing blob until Professor Quatermass electrocutes him in Westminster Abbey. In *Quatermass II* (a.k.a. *Enemy from Space*; 1957) alien intelligences have already set up a base in England, but Quatermass invades their headquarters and wipes them out. In *Quatermass and the Pit* (1968; widely distributed as *Five Million Years to Earth*) it is ancient Martians who turn up in the digging of a new Underground line in London. The Martians are interesting, and so is the story; but the special effects are not up to the demands on them. Val Guest directed and collaborated on the screenplay for the first two, but the third was turned over to Roy Ward Baker as director, and the screenplay was by the original author, Nigel Kneale, himself.

Guest himself left Hammer to make *The Day the Earth Caught Fire* (1961) for British Lion. It is an implausible story, but not quite an impossible one—according to the script uncontrolled H-bomb tests have driven the Earth out of its orbit and it is falling toward the Sun. Everything burns up, and the Thames boils away. Guest's direction moves it right along, and almost takes your mind off the fact that most of what happens on the screen takes place in an office, with the dramatic events being told to the audience as much as shown.

The earliest science-fiction film that I remember was Fritz Lang's *Metropolis*, and I was absolutely bowled over by this. I used to do odd jobs to earn a shilling so that I could go and see it again. I only got into making science-fiction films by accident. After the Quatermass films I wrote *The Day the Earth Caught Fire*, and it was seven years before anybody would let me make it. But seven years later we did. We put a picture of our own up as collateral to make it, and we were lucky enough to win an Academy Award with it.

At the end of *The Day the Earth Caught Fire* we left it that you didn't know whether the Earth had been saved or destroyed. The distributors said, "You can't leave it like that. Everybody's got to be saved." On our last shot, which was the cross of St. Paul's, they wanted angel's voices singing and the bells pealing. I had the most terrible fight with everybody, but we finally got rid of the angel voices.

Our budget was limited, and in the Thames sequence we had a cardboard river bank, but at one point only. In fact, we had fifteen fog machines in Battersea Park to shoot that sequence, and we completely ruined the Chelsea flower show, which was on at the same time.

—Val Guest (21)

As far as pure science fiction film is concerned, perhaps *Forbidden Planet* was the culmination of the Fifties. What came after that was bridge science fiction, like *1984* and *On the Beach,* or reworkings of familiar themes. It was time for a new voice to be heard, and it came. It belonged to that chronic individualist, unimpressed by the failures of others and seeking new kinds of success of his own, Stanley Kubrick.

FILMOGRAPHY

INVADERS FROM MARS (Fox, 1953, U.S.A.) 78 mins.

Producer, Edward L. Alperson; director, William Cameron Menzies; script, Richard Blake; art director, Boris Levin; production designer, William Cameron Menzies; editor, Arthur Roberts; special effects, Jack Cosgrove; camera, John Seitz.

Cast: Arthur Franz (Dr. Kelston); Helena Carter (Dr. Blake); Jimmy Hunt (David MacLean); Leif Erickson (George MacLean); Hillary Brooke (Mary MacLean); Max Wagner; Milburn Stone; Morris Ankrum; Janine Perreau.

THE CREATURE FROM THE BLACK LAGOON (Universal, 1954, U.S.A.) 79 mins.

Producer, William Allard; director, Jack Arnold; script, Harry Essex and Arthur Ross from a story by Maurice Zimm; art directors, Bernard Herzbrun and Hilyard Brown; editor, Ted J. Kent; special effects camera, Charles S. Welbourne; underwater camera, James C. Havens; camera, William E. Snyder.

Cast: Richard Carlson (David Reed); Julia Adams (Kay Lawrence); Richard Denning (Mark Williams); Antonio Moreno (Carl Maia); Ben Chapman (Gill-Man); Nestor Paiva; Whit Bissell; Harry Escalente; Sidney Mason; Bernie Gozier.

THE BLOB (Paramount, 1958, U.S.A.) 85 mins.

Producer, Jack H. Harris; director, Irvin S. Yeaworth, Jr.; script, Theodore Simonson and Kate Phillips from an idea by Irving H. Millgate; editor, Alfred Hillman; special effects, Barton Sloan; title song, Bert Bacharach and Mack David; music, Jean Yeaworth; camera, Thomas Spalding.

Cast: Steve McQueen (Steve Andrews); Aneta Corseaut (Judy Martin); Earl Rowe (Police Lieutenant); Olin Howlin (Old Man); Steve Chase (Dr. Hallen); Audrey Metcalf; Keith Almoney; Vince Barbi; John Benson; Julie Cousins.

(*The Blob* is) not so much horror as horrid.
—Arthur Knight (22)

FILMOGRAPHY
FIVE MILLION YEARS TO EARTH (Hammer/
Seven Arts, 1968, British) 97 mins.

Producer, Anthony Nelson Keys; director, Roy
Ward Baker; script, Nigel Kneale; production designer, Bernard Robinson; editor, Spencer Reeve;
special effects, Les Bowie; music, Tristam Cary;
camera, Arthur Grant.

Cast: Andrew Keir (Professor Quatermass); Barbara Shelley; James Donald; Julian Glover; Duncan
Lamont; Bryan Marshall.

MOTHRA (Toho, 1961)
Mothra buzzes an ocean liner.

SOURCES

1. Heinlein, Robert. From *Astounding Science Fiction,* July 1950.
2. Heinlein, Robert. From *Astounding Science Fiction,* July 1950.
3. Pal, George. From an unreleased, filmed interview by James Gunn, University of Kansas.
4. Monaco, James. *How to Read a Film.*
5. Lofficier, Jean-Marc. From *International MENSA Journal* January-February 1979.
6. Crichton, Michael. From *Focus on the Science Fiction Film* edited by William Johnson, Prentice-Hall, Inc., 1972.
7. Campbell, John W. From *Focus on the Science Fiction Film* edited by William Johnson, Prentice-Hall Inc., 1972.
8. Wise, Robert. From taped interview with the authors, December, 1978.
9. Wise, Robert. From *Focus on the Science Fiction Film* edited by William Johnson, Prentice-Hall, Inc., 1972.
10. Harryhausen, Ray. From *Focus on the Science Fiction Film* edited by William Johnson, Prentice-Hall Inc., 1972.
11. Bradbury, Ray. From interview with authors, January 1979.
12. Bradbury, Ray. From interview with authors, January 1979.
13. Crowther, Bosley. From *The New York Times,* April 28, 1956.
14. Fleischer, Richard. From taped interview with authors, May 1979.
15. Folsey, George. From *American Cinematographer,* August 1955.
16. Barron, Louis. From taped interview with the authors, June 1979.
17. Matheson, Richard. From taped interview with the authors. January 1979.
18. Rilla, Wolf. From *SF Symposium* edited by Jose Sanz, Instituto Nacional do Cinema, Brazil, 1969.
19. Thompson, Howard. From *The New York Times.*
20. Rilla, Wolf. From *SF Symposium* edited by Jose Sanz, Instituto Nacional do Cinema, Brazil, 1969.
21. Guest, Val. From panel discussion at *Seacon,* Brighton, England, September 1979.
22. Knight, Arthur. From *The Liveliest Art.*

Chapter 4

Dr. Kubrick's Clockwork Odyssey

In his semi-science fiction novel, *No Highway* (made into the semi-science fiction film *No Highway in the Sky*), Nevil Shute says that an aircraft designer must be a megalomaniac. He can't function if he is not. He must be so absolutely certain of his own intuitions (even when they are arguable) that he can compel a whole army corps of draftsmen and engineers to design each little air vent and shim the exact way *he* wants it and no other.

It is a lot the same with film producers. Whoever is in charge must *be* in charge if the film is to fly.

> On a large special-effects picture you may have as
> many as eight hundred people working on the film.
> That's a strong dilution of a single man's vision.
> —Gary Kurtz (2)

Much of what was wrong with Hollywood's product when the big studios were riding high was that the dominant personalities were studio heads. The directors and producers on individual films were squashed into conformity with the will of the tyrant of the moment. Scripts were manufactured by teams of writers in their sties on the back lot. Producers organized studio time and technical crews. Casting turned up actors and handed them their parts. A director came in and put them through their paces. The cutting room pieced together a final print. All the individuals concerned were experts, but none was an *auteur*. Now and then there was a rogue bull so powerful that he could not be denied, and so the likes of a Cecil B. de Mille could impress his own personality on what he made. But, after Fritz Lang, not many of them made science fiction films . . . until Stanley Kubrick came along.

In 1958 Kubrick wrote and directed the film of Humphrey Cobb's World War I novel, *Paths of Glory*. Directing plums began to fall his way, *Spartacus* in 1960 and *Lolita* in 1962. He was a man with muscle, and he used it to produce science fiction.

Kubrick was not truly megalomaniacal. He sought advice and paid attention to it. He was open to suggestions and arguments, and he even surrounded himself with experts as independent-minded and inventive as himself. But what finally appeared on the screen was Kubrick's own vision and not anyone else's. Sometimes his vision was remarkably like the original author's, as in *A Clockwork Orange*. Sometimes it was arrived at in equal-partnership collaboration, as with Arthur C. Clarke on *2001*. And sometimes it was not either of those at all. It took remarkable insight for Kubrick to find his *Dr. Strangelove* in the novel that was its genesis, Peter George's *Red Alert*.

The novel *Red Alert* is a deadpan thriller about inadvertent nuclear war. George meant you to shiver rather than laugh. Kubrick stood it on its head. *Dr. Strangelove, or, How I Learned to Stop Worrying and Love the Bomb* is not only black comedy, it almost defines the term.

The film *Dr. Strangelove* is as direct a response to the Fearful Fifties, in its way, as *Godzilla* or *The Thing*. But time had elapsed. By 1964 it was possible to see the fears more objectively. *Dr. Strangelove* looks at the catastrophic inadequacy of human institutions in the face of nuclear war, and laughs. It is as bitter as *1984* and as apocalyptic as

On the Beach. It is also uproariously funny. Kubrick himself wrote the script, with the help of Terry Southern, late of *Candy* in the Paris porn mills. The script is a masterpiece of wit and point.

One of the cardinal rules of good writing, and also of good directing, is "Don't say anything you don't have to," sometimes translated as, "Leave out the dull parts." Kubrick accomplishes this by a series of cameo scenes. There are only three real sets in the film—the interior of a B-52, the Pentagon's War Room and the office of a bomb group commander—and Kubrick cuts deftly back and forth among them. We see a SAC B-52 bomber refueling in a stately and graceful scene of airborne sexual intercourse (the background music is *Try a Little Tenderness*). The pilot, Major T. J. "King" Kong, played by Slim Pickens with maximal Air Force cowboy drawl, receives orders to proceed past the fail-safe line and drop his H-bombs on targets in the U.S.S.R. Switch to the headquarters of Burpelson Air Force Base, and we find out why. The Base Commander, General Jack D. Ripper (Sterling Hayden) has taken it upon himself to start World War III. Under established procedures the bombers cannot be recalled unless a secret signal is transmitted. Only the general knows what it is, and he won't tell.

Switch to the bedroom of the Commanding General of the Air Force, "Buck" Turgidson (George C. Scott). He is relaxing with his bikini-clad secretary when he hears that the bomb group has been ordered to attack Russia. He goes to the War Room, where a council presided over by President Muffley (Peter Sellers) is debating what to do. General Ripper has phoned the Pentagon to say that he has launched the attack and the only possible move left open for the Combined Chiefs of Staff is to follow up his group with every bomber, missile and other weapon they own; if they do, Russia will be wiped out and the Cold War will have been won; if they don't, Russia will retaliate with their own nuclear weapons and both sides will be destroyed. There is still time to recall the group, but Ripper has sealed off his Air Base and severed communications. The President orders a nearby Army unit to take the base and capture the general to make him talk. Switch to the base, where Ripper's second in command, an RAF loan officer named Mandrake (also Peter Sellers), has found out what Ripper is doing and is trying to get him to issue the recall. The Army unit attacks and sweeps aside the Air Force defenses, but Ripper foils them by committing suicide as the commander of the attackers (Keenan Wynn) breaks in. But Mandrake figures out the code, and the recall order is sent out to the bombers.

Meanwhile the President of the United States has summoned the Russian Ambassador (Peter Bull) and his own military-political advisor, Dr. Strangelove (Peter Sellers once more). They are on the hot line to Russia's Premier Kissoff, trying to untangle the problem. But they fail. Major Kong's B'52 failed to receive the recall order. Radio dead, crippled, leaking fuel, Kong pilots it to a target and himself rides the bomb down as it drops, slapping its side with his Stetson and ky-yiing. As soon as that one bomb hits a Russian "Doomsday Weapon" is triggered, and the whole world is destroyed. The end of the film shows an endless sequence of H-bomb explosions, while the background music plays *We'll Meet Again—Don't Know Where, Don't Know When. . . .*

Every actor in the film plays his role as though he were born to it—except Sellers, who plays three of them that way. Or almost. His Dr. Strangelove is a Charlie Chaplin

DR. STRANGELOVE (Columbia, 1963)
Slim Pickens (Maj. 'King' Kong) triumphs over every obstacle to launch the bomb that destroys the human race.

pastiche, a little too much larger than life. The artificial right arm that attempts to strangle him when it is not giving the Nazi salute (pace Fritz Lang's Dr. Rotwang); the frozen Mme. Tussaud smile; the wheelchair; the slip-of-the-tongue *Mein Fuehrer!* that punctuates his speech are at odds with the rest of the film. Dr. Strangelove is a villain and is played as a villain, while every other character in the film is at least in his own lights behaving supremely well. That is the very core of the comedy: that each of these persons is doing exactly what he is convinced is exactly right, and the consequence is the destruction of the human race.

But perhaps that is a matter of taste. The other performances are flawless. Keenan Wynn has only a handful of
lines, but some of them, as when he tells the RAF officer
that he thinks he was ordered to attack the base because it
had been taken over by "deviated preverts", have found
their way into the common speech. Sterling Hayden is
both terrifying and absurd as the general whose faith in
God has led him to decide to wipe out the Russians; what
has forced his hand is his revelation that water-fluoridation
is a Communist plot. (This has already led him to drink
only grain alcohol and distilled water and to give up sex: "I
do not abstain from the company of women, Mandrake.
But I do deny them my bodily fluids.") And George C.
Scott gives the finest comedy performance of his life as he
plays the commanding general of the Air Force in true
cover-your-butt military style.

FILMOGRAPHY
DR. STRANGELOVE OR: HOW I LEARNED TO
STOP WORRYING AND LOVE THE BOMB (Co-
lumbia, 1963, British/U.S.) 94 mins.

Producer/director, Stanley Kubrick; script, Stanley Kubrick, Terry Southern, and Peter George from
the novel *Red Alert* by Peter George; production
designer, Ken Adams; art director, Peter Murton;
special effects, Wally Veevers; editor, Anthony Harvey; music, Laurie Johnson; camera, Gilbert Taylor.

Cast: Peter Sellers (Group Captain Lionel
Mandrake/President   Muffley/Dr.   Strangelove);
George C. Scott (Gen. Buck Turgidson); Sterling
Hayden (Gen. Jack D. Ripper); Keenan Wynn (Col.
Bat Guano); Slim Pickens (Maj. T.J. King Kong);
Peter Bull (Ambassador de Sadesky); James Earl
Jones (Lieut. Lothar Zogg); Tracy Reed (Miss Scott);
Frank Creley; Shane Rimmer; Glenn Beck; Frank
Berry; Paul Tamarin.

If the film has a flaw, it is in the special effects. The interiors are all splendid, but the process shots are undistinguished and sometimes, e.g., the exterior shots of the B-52 as it invades Russia, distinctly wobbly. And the end is idiosyncratically Kubrick—quite like the cafe singer who terminates *Paths of Glory* or the Starchild surrealism in *2001*; none of the films are exactly "ended", except by turning up the lights and telling the audience to go home. No matter. The rest is superb. Judith Crist gave it first place on her ten-best list of the year: "one of the most cogent, comic and cruel movies to come along." Steven H. Scheuer in *Movies on TV*, his encyclopedic guide for tube-watchers, gives it more space than any other film in the book, and every word is praise. There was—of course—a storm of argument about the film, not least because of its political statements, but that had to be what Kubrick was aiming for. It might even be that Linus Pauling was wrong, and that if we are to escape nuclear disaster it is *Dr. Strangelove,* not *On the Beach,* that can claim most responsibility. *On the Beach* made a terrifyingly sober and realistic statement, but its validity rested on certain scientific facts and theories, about the lethality of fallout and the patterns of atmospheric circulation, and they could be challenged; once challenged, the thrust of the message was blunted. *Dr. Strangelove* is comic fantasy. Every character is a caricature, and there is no such thing as a "Doomsday Machine". (One hopes!) But under the extravagant metaphor there is a truth. Whatever the technological safeguards, the final decisions about nuclear attack are made by human beings, and human beings, for whatever reason, can do things that are terribly wrong. That truth was not arguable in 1964 . . . and is not now.

This masterpiece (*Dr. Strangelove*) is quite simply one of the greatest, funniest and most shattering motion pictures ever made. . . . A cinema classic that makes a personal, pertinent and devastating statement about our troubled society.

—Steven H. Scheuer (3)

Stanley Kubrick's new film . . . is beyond any question the most shattering sick joke I've ever come across. . . . My reaction to it is quite divided, because there is so much about it that is grand, so much that is brilliant and amusing, and much that is grave and dangerous. . . . Somehow, to me, (the ending) isn't funny. It is malefic and sick.

—Bosley Crowther (4)

(*Dr. Strangelove*) is the incomparable—the year's best film, a masterpiece of movie-making of a very American kind. With superb script, performances and cinematic techniques, Kubrick has triumphed in an area where few others have even ventured and none succeeded, the area of Swiftian satire.

—Judith Crist (5)

Dr. Strangelove would have been nothing without brilliant performances by first-rate actors or without sharp lines for them to say; the visual aspects were relatively unimportant. When it was over Kubrick showed the other side of his talents, with a film in which the visual was all and every part could have been played by the first actor to walk through the door of Central Casting. Or even by a chimpanzee, perhaps—and some of them were. *2001: A Space Odyssey* was his most ambitious project yet, and it took him six years.

2001 began with Arthur C. Clarke's science-fiction story, *The Sentinel*. Kubrick acquired it as part of a package of Clarke shorts, with the intention of somehow whipping them together into a coherent narrative for a film. It didn't work. The deal was renegotiated. Kubrick returned all the other stories to Clarke, keeping only *The Sentinel* for what fragments of it might be salvaged, and secured Clarke's services as collaborator on the script for a new film.

Arthur Clarke was in his forties when the contracts were signed. He was an honored prophet in a hundred countries, hobnobber with astronauts and heads of state, as famous and as successful as any science-fiction writer ever gets. He was also a person who had always known his own worth; as a youth, his fellow science fiction fans and rocket enthusiasts had called him "Ego" Clarke. Decades of applause and achievement had not humbled him a bit.

For Kubrick, Clarke was an outstanding example of the feisty, creative and independent people with whom he worked best. For Clarke, Stanley Kubrick was a Hollywood wonderkid whose wonderful qualities were not hype but real. They worked together closely—and inter-

minably. "Day after day, year after year, decade after
decade. It seemed to take so long that at one time I thought
we'd have to call it 2002!" Clarke told David Garnett after
it was all over. (1)

Nevertheless it was Kubrick's film. Clarke and Kubrick
struck that bargain. The film of the book was Kubrick's,
and his name would come first in the collaboration. The
book of the film was Clarke's, and his name would have
pride of place. As in all of Kubrick's films, perhaps more so
than in any other, Kubrick fiddled with detail, changed
plans as he went along, tinkered endlessly to get it right.
The British sand was the wrong color for his sets, so he had
ninety tons of it dyed to suit. Even Clarke was not au-
thoritative enough, so Kubrick retained space scientist
Frederick W. Ordway III as an advisor. No scientist or
writer was visual minded enough to complete the vision of
space, so Kubrick had his New York office call the editor of
Galaxy and hire their best cover artist away—and so
Richard McKenna, working engineer as well as painter,
spent the next year of his life in London to design
backdrops and hardware for Kubrick's sets. Roger Carras,
now everybody's favorite broadcast animal lover, was sent
around the world to show stills and scripts to the planet's
most famous scientists, to film their reactions as a sort of
prologue to the film itself. (It was never used.) And then,
after six years of hard work and anticipation, *2001* had its
world premiere.

Was it all worth it?

2001: A SPACE ODYSSEY (MGM, 1968)
*Bowman and Poole in Discovery's exercise wheel, en route to Jupiter. The
set was built on a steel framework and could be turned.*

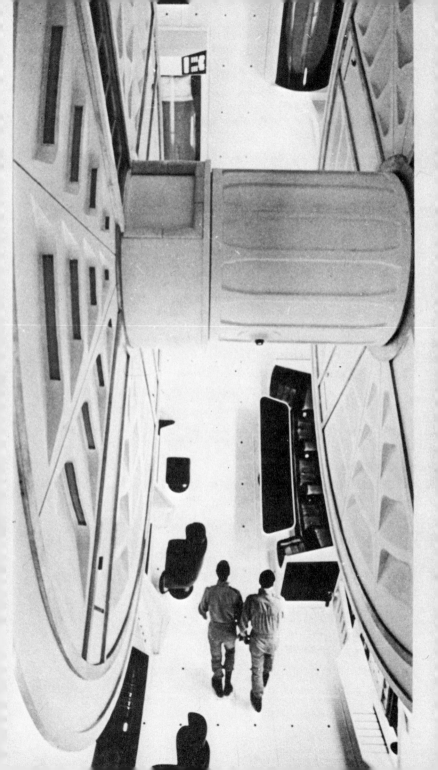

> (*2001* is) a trite setting for a series of exhibits from
> Expo '01. . . . Some have said that this picture
> cannot be truly appreciated unless one is high on pot.
> I assume that pot might make it more enjoyable, but
> then pot would also improve *Dr. Dolittle*.
> —Stanley Kauffmann (6)

For Clarke, it left him with the firm determination never
to get himself involved in the writing of another film. Six
years was too much. It had even been a financial burden,
because the money was not to come in in any quantity
until the film was released and earning its way. Even the
book, which Clarke completed two years before the film
was ready, had to sit unread and unprofitable until the
release date. Contracts had been signed. A fortune was
due on publication. But Kubrick would not allow it to come
out before the film. (Years later, Clarke remembered that
as his only serious grievance against his collaborator.) By
the time all the fiddling and painful reshaping was done,
2001 was way over budget. It cost more than ten million
dollars to make, the vastest expenditure for any science
fiction film in history to that point. And when it was released and Clarke was leaving the premiere, he heard
someone say, "Well, that's the end of Stanley Kubrick!"

But all the world knows it was not. *2001* was a success.

By the measure of the bottom line, it was not an *immense* success, at least not at first. That huge budget
overrun devoured grosses. *2001* earned a profit of 100%
on investment in the first few years, but other films have
done much more. But it is a stayer. It may be that there has
never been a day since 1968 when some audience somewhere in the world was not watching it on the screen.

I can well remember the night of the first preview of *2001*. As I stood in the foyer, I heard someone saying, "Well, that's the end of Stanley Kubrick." Another comment—this one at the world premiere, which took place in Washington on the day President Johnson announced he would not be running again. I heard an MGM executive say, "Well, today we lost two presidents."

The European premiere took place in Vienna, at the U.N. Conference on the Peaceful Uses of Space. Unfortunately, the invasion of Czechoslovakia was scheduled for the same week, which rather distracted us, but we had a cosmonaut—Leonoff, the first man ever to leave a spaceship and walk in space—as one of the delegates. After he'd seen the film he told me that now he feels he has been in space twice—which I think is the best testimonial we've had.

It is nice, when you do something that you know is good, to have it financially successful as well. You may not know this, but *2001* is the fourth most successful film in MGM history. And it looks as though it will ultimately gross 100 million dollars.

This will be my last science-fiction film. It has been a marvelous experience, four years of my life—and I have no intention of ever repeating it.

—Arthur C. Clarke (7)

Some viewers saw it repeatedly. Alexei Eisenstein saw it more than 80 times, and one or two legendary individuals may have seen it more than one hundred. It is an ambient ikon for thousands of science-fiction fans, many of whom still hold it the best film ever made. It became a major trip for the counter culture. For years after its opening it was showing in the nabes with the projector beams limned in a haze of pot smoke.

If it is hard to stop talking about *Dr. Strangelove,* for *2001* it seems impossible. Probably more has been written about it than about any other film in history—certainly more than any other science fiction film. The writing has not stopped. At least one book on it is still forthcoming, and it is the measure against which *Star Wars* and *Close Encounters* are usually gauged. What intrigues most critics is its meaning, and that is not easy to unravel.

2001 is a Rorschach blot of a film. It is built up out of image and metaphor, and if you try to argue what it says you find yourself frustrated by the fact that it does not "say" anything very clearly. Least of all in the dialogue, for usually there isn't any. (The only lines given to any of *2001*'s characters that are in any way memorable are HAL's—and he is not only not human, he is not sane.) Kubrick provides no gloss—"I don't want to spell out a verbal road map," he said. Clarke offered an interpretation in the novel version of the story, but it is far from clear that it is the same interpretation Kubrick intended; and the guessing game is part of the fun. For James Monaco, *2001* is "a masterful blending of cinematography with scientific and religious theory." Michel Clement calls it Kubrick's "visual symphony, his mysterious poem."

> *2001* . . . is a prodigious work of art. If it falls short of being a complete and perfect masterpiece, it is still a breathtaking achievement, and a near-definitive treatment of its basic themes. In terms of authority, inner conviction and total *ambience* it can be excelled by few other films of any type. And it is not a cold, intellectual construct, but a grand and eloquent message of the spirit.
>
> —Alex Eisenstein (8)

The theological elements in *2001* are indeed "mysterious", and they are not there by accident. Clarke has always made good use of the metaphysical and the surnatural *(Childhood's End, The Star, The Nine Billion Names of God)*, and Kubrick confirmed at least that much. Aliens might easily seem God-like, he said—might in fact be a "scientific" analogue of God.

> Even the M-G-M lion is stylized and abstracted in Stanley Kubrick's *2001: A Space Odyssey*, a film in which infinite care, intelligence, patience, imagination and Cinerama have been devoted to what looks like the apotheosis of the fantasy of a precocious, early nineteen-fifties city boy. . . . And yet the uncompromising slowness of the movie makes it hard to sit through without talking—and people on all sides when I saw it were talking almost throughout the film. Very annoying.
>
> —Renata Adler (9)

2001 is three films in one, a fact which is in itself no mean theological grace-note. It begins where the human race itself began: on the African savannahs some hundreds of thousands of years ago (Clarke puts it at three million years), with something like the Australopithecines. The fossil record is scanty, and open to much argument. We do not know for sure who our ancestors were just then. But we know that at some point they looked like apes and behaved like beasts, and so do the primitive folk in the beginning of *2001*. We do not know for sure how the change from apes to tool-users occurred, or when. But we know that it did happen, and it is as good a point as any to call the beginning of humanity. *2001*'s first section shows it happening.

Man had emerged from the anthropoid background for one reason only: because he was a killer. Long ago, perhaps many millions of years ago, a line of killer apes branched off from the non-aggressive primate background. . . . And lacking fighting teeth or claws, we took recourse by necessity to weapons.

A rock, a stick, a heavy bone—to our ancestral killer ape it meant the margin of survival. But the use of the weapon meant new and multiplying demands on the nervous system for the coordination of muscle and touch and sight. And so at last came the enlarged brain; so at last came man.

Far from the truth lay the antique assumption that man had fathered the weapon. The weapon, instead, had fathered man.

—Robert Ardrey (10)

In using clubs and flints, their hands had developed a dexterity found nowhere else in the animal kingdom, permitting them to make still better tools, which in turn had developed their limbs and brains yet further. It was an accelerating, cumulative process; and at its end was Man.

—Arthur C. Clarke (11)

Where *2001* departs from science is in the introduction of the Monolith. This is a gift from aliens, which has the power of stimulating the development of the Australopithecines. It inspires them to extend their reach and striking power with cudgels taken from the bones of dead prey: the first tools. Of course, they use them as weapons, and first of all against the nearest other tribe of protohumans. At the end of this section one of the primates (Clarke calls him "Moon-Watcher") throws his weapon exultantly into the sky. We see it spin on the screen, and it becomes a spaceship.

Now we enter the spaceship, and find ourselves going to the Moon. Why? Because a Monolith has been discovered there. It too exerts its unarguable will on human beings, and so they are driven to explore the moons of Jupiter.

En route, we see the inside of what spaceships have become in the year 2001, immense and automated. What the ship is automated by is the film's favorite character, the computer HAL. But HAL is going mad. The astronauts strive against HAL and manage to overcome him, but only one survives to reach the vicinity of Jupiter and find himself hurled, faster than light, to the final Monolith and rebirth as the Starchild.

ᔕᔕᔕᔕᔕᔕᔕᔕᔕᔕᔕᔕᔕᔕᔕᔕᔕᔕᔕᔕᔕᔕᔕ

Some of these worlds must be on a level that is incalculable to the human mind. These beings would probably have incomprehensible powers. . . . Once you start dealing with subject matter like that, the religious implications are inevitable, because these are really the attributes that you give to God. So you've almost got, if you like, a completely scientific definition of God.

—Stanley Kubrick (12)

ᔕᔕᔕᔕᔕᔕᔕᔕᔕᔕᔕᔕᔕᔕᔕᔕᔕᔕᔕᔕᔕᔕᔕ

Three different films. The long, wordless documentary of the Australopithecines. The super-*Destination Moon* of the lunar landing and the fight against HAL. The psychedelic light show and the surreal Starchild. They might have been made by three different *auteurs,* they have so little in common in theme or technique.

It is possible to argue against all three of the sequences, collectively or one at a time. The theme of the first segment is a perversion of an anthropological theory originally advanced by Raymond Dart, and popularized by Robert Ardrey, in his best-seller *African Genesis,* shortly before the inception of *2001.* According to the theory, it was the tools in the hand of primitive men that caused them to develop the brain, rather than the brain inventing the tools. As a theory, it is elegant, and may even be true. The addition of the Monolith only vulgarizes it. And that segment runs three-quarters of an hour long! Surely there is nothing in it that a movie-maker as skilled as Kubrick could not have said in ten minutes . . . unless what he is saying is the story of prehistory itself: endless eons, in which every minute contains danger and the risk of sudden death, but which are tediously, boringly, eternally the same.

The second section—the "2001" period of the film—is

a gadgeteer's heaven. Hugo Gernsback would have been thrilled. The Pan-Am space shuttle, the control and instrument panels, the Clavius base, the exercise treadmill, HAL's central nervous system—every frame has been carefully thought out and brilliantly invented. It all looks exactly real, from the stewardess's Velcro slippers to Poole's prefabricated food. When HAL's lunatic logic leads him to attempt to murder all his human passengers the action becomes exciting and the suspense great, and his gradual decay into imbecility as parts of his "mind" are carved away is brightly conceived and done. But why does he go mad? Is it because the planners of the mission entrusted him with the secret they withheld from the human adventurers—that they are going to investigate a Monolith—as Clarke suggests? If so, how dumb can mission planners get? One can write an alternate script in one's mind, in which HAL triumphs and carries out the mission alone. Perhaps his quicker and less fallible machine mind could have surveyed the Jovian monolith and reported back to Earth; or one in which everybody concerned had behaved a little more sensibly and HAL had not been burdened with the secret that drove him mad.

Finally, the light-show and the Cocteau-ish scenes at the astronaut's final destination are wholly sense-free, however ingeniously Clarke managed to account for them in the novel. It is not merely that they are not logical and explicable. Worse, it is impossible to construct a hypothesis under which they *would* become logical. Both Clarke and Kubrick have defended their vision—Kubrick by saying that the future will be so puzzling you and I cannot understand it at all, Clarke by his often-quoted remark that any truly advanced technology will be indistinguishable from magic. But those are not elucidations, they are apologies.

Moreover, the one thread that links these three disparate stories together is the Monolith, and as a concept that is just untenable. If it required outside help from a more advanced race to account for Man's progress, then how do you account for the outside race? Who helped them? This is the same logical flaw that destroyed Arrhenius's theory of the origin of life on Earth through spores drifting out of space, by the law of Occam's Razor. If you assume that life (or intelligence) on Earth came from somewhere outside, you only beg the question. You must then make the further assumption that *somewhere* it originated without outside intervention at all, so why not just assume that it happened here?

But, of course, none of this really matters.

The triumph of *2001* is not that it answers questions of pre-history and teleology, but that it spurs the viewer to ask them. (No one is led to question ultimate meanings in *Godzilla*.) *2001* excites the imagination and stimulates the intellect, and what more is there to ask from a science-fiction film?

Meaning aside, a great virtue of *2001* is that Kubrick has invested it with so much loving detail.

Sometime he uses the detail to pay a debt, as a sort of in-joke. When he wanted to know how computers would talk he went to Bell Labs, where a program for synthesizing both speech and music by computer had been on-going since 1961—had had beginnings even before that. The song HAL sings as he is dying is *A Bicycle Built for Two,* and he sounds exactly like that same song as synthesized by a Bell computer programmed by Dr. M. V. Mathews.

(Which was released by Decca as part of an album entitled *Music from Mathematics.*)

Some of the in-jokes are inadvertent. Science-fiction fans quickly noticed that HAL's name could be read as an encrypted message. If you replace each letter of HAL's name by the next one in the alphabet, H becomes I, A becomes B and L becomes M, thus giving the name of the ancestral home of the big number-crunchers, IBM. (But Clarke says that was only chance.)

And some are unresolved. That great Hitchcockian transition in which Moon-Watcher's tossed club turns into the space shuttle may have been on the spur of the moment. Clarke says he saw Kubrick walking back from a day's shooting, tossing a bone from hand to hand, then tossing it higher and filming it with a hand-held camera; whether that was when the idea was born he does not know. Alexei Eisenstein finds a meaning in the fact that there is no sub-title to separate the Australopithecine section of the film from the episode en route to the Moon: is this because, he speculates, Kubrick is saying that we are not that much different from the Australopithecines? And the trinitarian construction of *2001* is echoed in its opening theme music, from Richard Strauss's *Also Sprach Zarathustra.* The first three notes are C, G and again C an octave higher. Can this be read as a metaphor? Moon-Watcher the first tonic note, the Starchild the final one, and ourselves the unresolved and fleeting G in between?

Probably not. There is a limit to the subtlety even of Stanley Kubrick. Perhaps he wearied of the subtle and the mystic, because in his next science-fiction film he turned to an almost verbatim treatment of the forthright and explicit pages of Anthony Burgess's comic hell, *A Clockwork Orange.*

ᔕᓄᔕᓄᔕᓄᔕᓄᔕᓄᔕᓄᔕᓄᔕᓄᔕᓄᔕᓄᔕᓄᔕᓄᔕᓄ

> After the satiric alienation of *Dr. Strangelove*, Kubrick spent five years and ten million dollars on a science-fiction project so devoid of life and feeling as to render a computer called Hal the most sympathetic character in a jumbled scenario. . . . Kubrick's tragedy may have been that he was hailed as a great artist before he had become a competent craftsman.
> —Andrew Sarris (13)

ᔕᓄᔕᓄᔕᓄᔕᓄᔕᓄᔕᓄᔕᓄᔕᓄᔕᓄᔕᓄᔕᓄᔕᓄᔕᓄ

If *2001* represents a major turnaround in Kubrick's philosophy—from the cynical hopelessness of *Dr. Strangelove* to *2001*'s sublime metaphysic—then in *A Clockwork Orange* he turned right back. *A Clockwork Orange* is a mean-hearted work. Its only (but overwhelming) virtue is that it is brilliantly done, by Burgess as a book, and by Kubrick as a film.

The scene in *A Clockwork Orange* is England, not very many years from now. The central character, Alex, is the leader of a youth gang whose specialties are beatings, break-ins and rape. When they go too far and someone dies, the leader is caught and subjected to a kind of aversion therapy called "the Ludovico technique". The conditioning is so painful and so destructive to his personality (he can no longer even listen to "the immortal strains of the glorious Ludwig Van's magnificent Ninth") that he becomes pitiable—except to the widower of one of his rape victims, who accidentally becomes his host and surrogate parent. In a complicated and corrupt political maneuver, Alex becomes a symbol of frail humanity crushed by despotism; he is deconditioned and set free to rape and maim once more.

Alex is a sadist and a coward. Apart from music appreciation he has no visible redeeming virtue, not even loyalty to his "droogs" of the youth gang. His leisurely torture and rape of a housewife, while her elderly husband, bound and gagged, lies apoplectically helpless and watches, is an S-M freak's most delicious fantasy. Burgess says the exaltation of violence was no part of his intention, but, as in *Rollerball* a few years later, it is surely what much of the audience got. And those audiences made it a big box office winner, with grosses approaching *2001*'s at a fraction of the production cost. For a well person, there is no one to root for in *A Clockwork Orange*. The victims themselves become violators when they get the chance. Not even *1984* shows as much contempt for the human race as *A Clockwork Orange*.

But how intelligently and richly it is all brought to the screen! If a work of art can be seen apart from morality, then *A Clockwork Orange,* in film as in novel, is an artistic victory.

When *A Clockwork Orange* was about to come out in America the publisher sent me a set of galley proofs, asking for a favorable quote to put on the dust jacket. I tried to oblige. At first attempt I simply could not read the book. The Russian-Cockney future slang of the kid gangsters was utterly opaque. A few weeks later I tried again, and again failed to get past the first few pages. Then at last I broke through and read it at one sitting. It was too late for the publishers' jacket copy, and anyway I was not sure what I would have wanted to say, because I hated most of what the book said—but envied every impeccably expressed line. It seemed to me that Burgess had responded to the same social phenomenon (i.e., the rise of kid gangs) that had influenced Cyril Kornbluth and myself in writing *Gladiator-at-Law*. The worst part was that he had seen aspects to explore and scenes to invent that had not occurred to us. Burgess is a writer who is difficult to like, but impossible not to respect.

—FP

~~~~~~

> A Clockwork Orange was an attempt to make a very Christian point about the importance of free will. If we are going to love mankind, we will have to love Alex as a not unrepresentative member of it. If anyone sees the movie as a bible of violence, he's got the wrong point.
>
> —Anthony Burgess (14)

> (2001) gave us dullness and confusion. The real message, of course, is one Kubrick has used before: Intelligence is perhaps evil and certainly useless. The humanoid reaction and pointless madness of the computer shows this. Men can only be saved by some vague and unshown mystic experience by aliens. This isn't a normal science-fiction movie at all, you see. It's the first of the New Wave-Thing movies, with the usual empty symbolism. The New Thing advocates were exulting over it as a mind-blowing experience. It takes very little to blow some minds. But for the rest of us, it's a disaster. It will probably be a box-office disaster, too, and thus set major science-fiction movie-making back another ten years.
>
> —Lester del Rey (15)

~~~~~~

Considered as an episode in Kubrick's career, after the opulent splurging of 2001 the film of A Clockwork Orange seems actually restrained. Especially in a financial sense; it appears to be the equivalent of a housewife's soup-and-sandwich meal to make up for last night's prime-rib. There are no wide African landscapes recreated in the suburbs of London or forty-foot revolving stages. What is the same is the evident, perpetual, painstaking care. If Kubrick shows us nose masks on the marauders instead of lunar landing pits and penis-shaped Popsicles instead of the Jovian sys-

---

A CLOCKWORK ORANGE (Warner Bros., 1971)
Alex and his droogs enjoying a little relaxation at the Korova Milk Bar.

tem of planets and moons, he makes us believe that every detail, however inexpensive, is once again exactly *right*.

After *A Clockwork Orange* Kubrick turned to the past with *Barry Lyndon* and to fantasy with *The Shining*, taking a sabbatical from science fiction. But, as of this writing, he intends to return. He has not said what the next sf film will be, and perhaps does not yet know.

Almost any other moviemaker would have listened to the siren song of the front office and capitalized on success by repeating it. Kubrick has never done that. He could at any time have banked a quick million dollars with a *Clockwork Orange Meets the Wolfman* or *Dr. Strangelove in the Mine Shafts*. Whatever he does next it is likely that it will be something unlike everything before . . . and brilliant.

FILMOGRAPHY
2001: A SPACE ODYSSEY (MGM, 1968, U.S./British) 160 mins.

Producer/director Stanley Kubrick; script, Stanley Kubrick and Arthur C. Clarke; production designers, Tony Masters, Harry Lange, and Ernest Archer; art director, John Hoelsi; editor, Ray Lovejoy; special effects, Stanley Kubrick, Wally Veevers, Douglas Trumbull, Con Pederson, and Tom Howard; music, Richard Strauss, Gyorgy Ligeti, Johann Strauss, and Aram Khachaturian; camera, Geoffrey Unsworth.

Cast: Keir Dullea (Bowman); Gary Lockwood (Poole); William Sylvester (Dr. Heywood Floyd); Douglas Rain (HAL 9000); Dan Richter (Moonwatcher); Leonard Rossiter (Smyslov); Margaret Tyzack (Elena); Robert Beatty (Halvorsen); Frank Miller; Sean Sullivan; Edwina Carroll; Glenn Beck; Bill Weston.

A CLOCKWORK ORANGE (Warner Bros., 1971, British) 137 mins.

Producer/director, Stanley Kubrick; script, Stanley Kubrick from the novel by Anthony Burgess; production designer, John Barry; art directors, Russell Hagg and Peter Shields; editor, Bill Butler; music, Beethoven, Rossini, Purcell, Elgar, Rimsky-Korsakoff, and Walter Carlos; camera, John Alcott.

Cast: Malcolm McDowell (Alex); Patrick Magee (Mr. Alexander); Adrienne Corri (Mrs. Alexander); Aubrey Morris (P.R. Deltoid); James Marcus (Georgie); Warren Clarke (Dim); Michael Tarn (Pete); Sheila Raynor (Mum); Philip Stone (Dad); Miriam Karlin (Cat Lady); Godfrey Quigley (Chaplain); Anthony Sharp; Margaret Tyzack.

I have never learned anything about my work by
reading film critics.

—Stanley Kubrick (16)

SOURCES

1. Clarke, Arthur C. From an interview with David Garnett.

2. Kurtz, Gary. From panel discussion at *Seacon,* Brighton, England, September 1979.

3. Scheuer, Steven H. From *Movies on TV,* Bantam Books, Inc, 1977.

4. Crowther, Bosley. From *The New York Times.*

5. Crist, Judith.

6. Kauffmann, Stanley. *Figures of Light,* Harper & Row, New York, 1877.

7. Clarke, Arthur C. From *SF Symposium* edited by Jose Sanz, Instituto Nacional do Cinema, Brazil, 1969.

8. Eisenstein, Alex. From an unpublished manuscript.

9. Adler, Renata. From *The New York Times,* April 4, 1868.

10. Ardrey, Robert. From *African Genesis.*

11. Clarke, Arthur. From *2001: A Space Odyssey* (the novel).

12. Kubrick, Stanley. From an interview with Joseph Gelmis in *Newsday,* June 4, 1968.

13. Sarris, Andrew. *The American Cinema: Directors and Directions 1929-1968,* E.P. Dutton, New York, 1968.

14. Burgess, Anthony.

15. del Rey, Lester. From *Galaxy Magazine,* 1968. Author's Note: I was editor of *Galaxy* when this review appeared. Nothing in the magazine's history ever produced as much hate mail from readers, the majority of whom loved the film and two or three of whom canceled their subscriptions. FP

16. Kubrick, Stanley. From an interview with John Hofses in *Soho News,* May 28, 1980.

I worked on the novel, *Fahrenheit 451*, twice—the short version and then the long—and then I did the play with Charles Laughton. Which didn't work.

When Truffaut came along, we were originally going to do *The Illustrated Man*, but it never came about. So about a year later Truffaut came back and said, "Look, what about *Fahrenheit*? I think I can get financing for that. Do you want to do the screenplay?" I said, "No, I've worked on it too long. I'll trust you; I've seen your films."

They then proceeded to do a script. I heard all kinds of rumors about casting and financing—it's *Rashomon* time, isn't it? But I gather what happened was that Truffaut went to Oscar Werner and offered him the script, and he said, "No, you haven't stuck close enough to the novel." So, rather than change the script, Truffaut approached one or two other actors, but they were busy; and he came back to Werner and said, "If you'll take the role we'll revise it closer to the novel." I don't know if that's true or not. I think it might be. And I'm thankful to Werner if it's true.

—Ray Bradbury (1)

Chapter 5

Reeling Around the World, 1964-1972

While Stanley Kubrick was completing his triptych, from the destruction of the world to a world that richly deserved destruction, a dozen other film-makers were trying their hand at science fiction. Rather few of them were in Hollywood. Petri and Vadim, Truffaut and Godard were each turning his idiosyncratic talents to the genre. Behind each one of them was the backing of a major Hollywood studio. But it was only backing. On-the-spot control had passed across the Atlantic.

For more than a third of a century Hollywood's iron fist had dictated the world's entertainment. Now the grip was loosening. Television stole audiences from their theater chains, and anti-trust decrees made them give up their automatic bookings. Television even elbowed the majors out of studio space. The urbanization of Los Angeles taught them that their back lots were worth more as real estate than as places to shoot films—thus much of Twentieth Century-Fox became office buildings, a shopping center and the Century Plaza Hotel. The stars of the industry were forming their own production companies and taking them where shooting was cheap. *2001*, in 1968, was still made by MGM, though it was shot in England. By the time of *Westworld*, in 1973, MGM had decided that film making would thenceforth take second place to the building and operating of gambling casinos in Nevada.

By the mid-1960s Europe, the place where science fiction films began, was gearing up for a second shot. The

trendiest of the New Wave directors and the most commercial of the orthodox alike saw that sf had unexploited
opportunities. For instance, there was sex.

So in Rome, Elio Petri read Robert Sheckley's *Galaxy*
novelette, *The Seventh Victim,* bought it, added three
more corpses and released it as *The Tenth Victim* in 1965.

The Tenth Victim is a comic-inferno about a world in
which the prevailing sport is murder. It is ritualized, gamed
and legal. Petri employed three separate writers to muddy
each other's tracks in the script and took a turn at it himself;
not much is left of the straightforward lines of Sheckley's
story. In the film, beautiful blonde beast Ursula Andress
was the world's champion assassin, killing off contenders
with shots fired from her stainless-steel bra. Her chief
competition for the title was Italy's greatest super-star,
Marcello Mastroianni, in a part which gave him little to do
except let Andress defeat him. Italian films had already
acquired a tradition of candid sex; in that respect, *The
Tenth Victim* has by now come to seem fairly tame, but
Andress and Elsa Martinelli showed a lot of lovely skin.

What Italy could do, France could do better, and in
1967 Roger Vadim released *Barbarella.* The film opened
with as titillating a strip tease in free fall as has ever been
filmed. The stripper was young, gorgeous, sexy Jane
Fonda. *Barbarella*'s story was based on the French comic
strip of the same name, about a future female astronaut
whose life is an endless series of sexual and violent adventures. Even in France, Jean-Claude Forest's comic strip
ran into censorship problems, but it also contained a good
deal of imagination and wit.

It has been demonstrated over and over that one really
needs to add only one writer to destroy an original idea.
Vadim went to the trouble of hiring eight. Even though

some of them were very good—Jean-Claude Forest himself, and Terry Southern, fresh from *Dr. Strangelove,* for instance—the result was a committee effort, and shows it. It is not merely confusing. It is gibberish.

Barbarella is a futuristic sex variety show. We know at the beginning that Barbarella is some kind of interstellar spy, since the reason she strips herself naked is to present herself to the World President for orders. We don't know why she has to take her clothes off for the purpose, but we are not supposed to ask that question. We are supposed to be so pleased to see Jane Fonda in the buff that questions do not occur to us. *Barbarella* is a string of episodes in the woman's search for some missing scientist. She encounters some charming but murderous children, whose savage dolls nearly bite her to death. She visits a sort of ladies' salon where the women pass around the mouthpiece to a giant hookah; a naked man is in the bowl, and the women are smoking essence of rutty male. Barbarella is condemned to death in the Excessive Machine, source of intolerable sexual pleasure; but she burns out its tubes instead. A mysterious blind angel, symbolizing "love", is crucified in a light-hearted way. Marcel Marceau appears in the film—in a speaking part, which shows why he is so successful as a mime. It is all beautifully photographed (by Claude Renoir) in brilliant color that shows off the bright sets and costumes; but what it does not do, ever, is make any sense at all.

Barbarella almost did not get released. When Paramount Pictures' president, Charles Bluhdorn, saw what Roger Vadim had done with the studio's money he hit the ceiling. The kindest word he used was "trash". And it almost is.

FILMOGRAPHY

LA DECIMA VITTIMA (The Tenth Victim) (Embassy, 1965, Italian) 92 mins.

Executive producer, Joseph E. Levine; producer, Carlo Ponti; director, Elio Petri; script, Tonino Guerra, Giorgio Salvioni, Ennio Flaiano, and Elio Petri from the story *The Seventh Victim* by Robert Sheckley; art director, Giulio Coltellacci; editor, Ruggero Mastroianni; music, Piero Piccioni; camera, Gianni Di Venanzo.

Cast: Marcello Mastroianni (Marcello Polletti); Ursula Andress (Caroline Meredith); Elsa Martinelli (Olga); Massimo Serato; Luce Bonifassy; Mickey Knox; Salvo Randone.

BARBARELLA (Paramount, 1968, U.S.A.) 98 mins.

Producer, Dino De Laurentiis; director, Roger Vadim; script, Terry Southern in collaboration with Roger Vadim, Claude Brule, Jean-Claude Forest, Brian Degas, Tudor Gates, Clement Biddle Woods, and Vittorio Bonicelli from the book and comic strip by Jean-Claude Forest; production designer, Mario Garbuglia; art director Enrico Fea; editor, Victoria Mercanton; special effects, Augie Lohman; music, Maurice Jarre; camera, Claude Renoir.

Cast: Jane Fonda (Barbarella); John Phillip Law (Pygar); Anita Pallenberg (The Black Queen); Milo O'Shea (Durand-Durand); David Hemmings (Dilando); Marcel Marceau (Ping); Ugo Tognazzi (Mark Hand); Claude Dauphin; Antonio Sabato.

ALPHAVILLE: UNE ETRANGE AVENTURE DE LEMMY CAUTION (Alphaville) (Athos-Film, 1965, French) 100 mins.

Producer, Andre Michelin; director/script, Jean-Luc Godard; editor, Agnes Guillemot; music, Paul Msraki; camera, Raoul Coutard.

Cast: Eddie Constantine (Lemmy Caution); Anna Karina (Natacha von Braun); Akim Tamiroff (Henry Dickson); Howard Vernon; Lazlo Szabo; Michel Delahaye.

Jane Fonda comes close to saving it, with a big assist from the pure spectacle of the thing. If Vadim had banished six of the writers, leaving only Terry Southern to give the actors some funny lines to speak—or, better still, if someone other than Vadim had made it in the first place, *Barbarella* might have been superb soft-core sci-fi comic porn. But it isn't really comic. It is only after the film is over that, looking back, you realize that all the ingredients for comedy were there, so why weren't you laughing?

Even before *Barbarella,* Jean-Luc Godard made *Alphaville* (1965), about a planet where the tyrant runs a robot-policed state. *Alphaville* is a polymorphous spoof, with overtones from everything that Godard could think of. The French version was released with the subtitle *A Strange Adventure of Lemmy Caution:* Lemmy Caution is the lead of a series of detective novels by Peter Cheyney, but if the novels and the film have anything in common it is not apparent. Two scientists are named Dr. Heckle and Dr. Jeckle. When Caution decides to visit the planet Alphaville he drives there in his Ford. *Alphaville* is as cloudy as to meaning as *Barbarella*'s worst, but without the fun, and it proves that you do not really need eight writers to make a film script incoherent. Godard wrote this one all by himself.

And, also in France, Francois Truffaut bought another old *Galaxy* novelette, Ray Bradbury's *The Fireman.* Under the title of *Fahrenheit 451* it had become a great success as a book, and it was under that title that Truffaut released it as a film in 1966.

Both Truffaut and Godard were among the leaders of French film's *Nouvelle vague,* which translates to sf's New Wave and shares with it a compulsion for experiment in form, and an abiding contempt for any sort of objective meaning. Truffaut and Godard were *auteurs*—in fact, Truffaut was the man who first set forth the "*auteur* theory" of film, in the January 1954, issue of *Cahiers du cinema*.

What is an "*auteur*"? He is the genius who makes his films his personal expression. Perhaps he may be what the translation of the word suggests, an author. More often he is a director. (Truffaut's favorite *auteur* was Alfred Hitchcock.) In the *auteur* view of film-making, the personal statement of El Supremo is the only thing that matters. All the conventional components of a film—scripts, original novels, actors, production experts, cameramen—they are only the flakes of paint that the brush of the *auteur* disposes on the canvas that is his finished movie.

This is not a hopelessly wrong notion of how great films are made. Kubrick, for instance, is an *auteur* as ever was. But it tends to lead to excesses on the part of the *auteur*, as soon as he realizes he is one. If all that matters is himself, then all those other components need not be very interesting. It may even be better if they're not, as Andre Bazin says, since then "the banality of the scenario leaves more room for the personal contribution of the *auteur*."

Truffaut's version of *Fahrenheit 451* is a curious blend of sci-fi and camp, and it was cruelly received. Nevertheless it cannot be discounted. What it has to say is not heard by most people, its dismal grosses show that. But some of those who love it love it a lot.

It surely had everything going for it. Julie Christie and Oskar Werner were the brightest new stars of the 1960s, and Truffaut the most revered director. And Ray Bradbury is—Ray Bradbury.

The stars of Fahrenheit 451.

What's really great about *Fahrenheit* is that we had
lines around the block for twelve weeks. This was in
Westwood Village, near the UCLA campus; I went to
the studio and said, "Hey, look at these crowds,
these young people. This is the cinema audience of
the future. Now, be very careful where you release
this film. Don't put it in the big cities indiscriminately.
Put it in college towns and you'll get your money
back." The studios didn't listen to me. They just
released it anywhere, and it died.

—Ray Bradbury (1)

ᵔᵔᵔᵔᵔᵔᵔᵔᵔᵔᵔᵔᵔᵔᵔᵔᵔᵔᵔᵔᵔᵔᵔᵔᵔᵔᵔᵔᵔᵔ

Two months ago *Fahrenheit 451*, in script form, was a hard and violent film, inspired by worthy sentiments and altogether on the serious side. In shooting it, I realize that I have been trying to give it a lighter tone. . . . If I had to start the film over, this is what I'd say to the art director, costume designer and cinematographer by way of instructions: "Let's make a film about life as children see it, with the firemen as toy soldiers, the firehouse as a model and so on." I don't want *Fahrenheit 451* to look like a Yugoslav film.

—Francois Truffaut (2)

ᵔᵔᵔᵔᵔᵔᵔᵔᵔᵔᵔᵔᵔᵔᵔᵔᵔᵔᵔᵔᵔᵔᵔᵔᵔᵔᵔᵔᵔᵔ

Bradbury is a pure child of science fiction. First he was a teen-aged fan, then contributor to *Thrilling Wonder* and all the other sf pulps of the early 1940s—and then, early, a senior statesman of the field. He was the first to break ground for science fiction in some of the most prestigious general magazines; the one science fiction writer whose works are the obligatory sf school children are given to read; the one writer who is called on without fail when a World's Fair pavilion needs a science fiction theme or an interdisciplinary conference on the future needs a science fiction spokesman. He has never lost touch with his roots in science fiction; and they go almost as deeply in film. They go deeper, if you count genetics. His mother was so enamored of the movies that she gave him the middle name "Douglas" after Douglas Fairbanks. Bradbury is a film addict who has seen every important movie ever made ("some of them twenty times," he says), and has worked in and around the film colony since he was old enough to vote. His own verdict on *Fahrenheit*, more than a decade later, is "flawed but beautiful".

(Fahrenheit 451) is flawed but beautiful, and the last scenes are some of the most beautiful scenes ever put on the screen. It's not my ending; it's not in the book that way.

By a wonderful accident, the last week of shooting it began to snow. People said, "Well, let's wrap it up and go back to the studio." Truffaut said, "No, we'll use the snow." He was smart enough to go with this beautiful gentleness of the falling white, in that scene of the little boy being taught these wonderful words by his dying grandfather. The snow has that fragility and beauty to it, so every time I see the Book People wandering through the forest, reciting in the snow, I weep. It's so beautiful! But that's not me. That's Truffaut. He was smart enough to go with an accident of nature and turn it into a brilliant ending.

—Ray Bradbury (1)

Fahrenheit 451 (the novel) is a lucid and poetic cry of rage against the know-nothings. The central character, The Fireman, is not in the business of putting fires out. He starts them. His business is burning books. The government has determined that all books are dangerous to the social order, and when a secret cache of them is found the fire trucks roll to burn them up. In the story, the Fireman becomes a convert to literacy. He goes off to a secret colony where the people themselves have become books, by committing the work to memory, line by line. Try to crush us as you will, Bradbury says to would-be tyrants, we will always find a way to survive and serve beauty and truth! He wrote the story in the early 1950s, when truth and freedom were at some risk in America. As in much of Bradbury's best work, the story is almost a poem, and the "living books" a poetic metaphor.

In Bradbury's novel, the metaphor worked.

In Truffaut's film, it did not. Good science fiction sometimes entails considerable risk, as the author takes the great chance of pushing his imagination so far, and testing the receptivity of his audience so greatly, that if it went one step further it would crumble and become ludicrous. Truffaut's *Fahrenheit* went that one step too far. Under his direction, Christie and Werner performed as though well dosed with Valium, and there was much too much vagueness in the *Nouvelle vague.*

~~~~~~

Truffaut made the jump into the English-language cinema despite his lacking command of the English language. *Fahrenheit 451* is consequently as verbally clumsy as it is visually graceful and emotionally expressive. Truffaut ran for cover back to the womb of the French language.

—Andrew Sarris (3)

Fahrenheit 451 isn't a very good movie but the idea—which is rather dumb but in a way brilliant—has an almost irresistible appeal: people want to see it and then want to talk about how it should have been worked out. *Fahrenheit 451* is more interesting in the talking-over afterward than in the seeing.

—Pauline Kael (4)

~~~~~~

For an *auteur*, Truffaut seemed strangely reluctant to commit himself. He left much of the detail to subordinates, and bothered to make only hurried last minute changes when he felt they were wrong. ("In making a film, it's sometimes better not to be too trusting," he complained in his journal, after finding one of the most important sets was "not very well done.") When he discussed the score with composer Bernard Herrmann, he concurred that "his score should not have any meaning"—and surely got what he asked for.

Stanley Kubrick's finicking and inventive attention to detail might have given *Fahrenheit* enough solidity to engage an audience's emotions. Bradbury's own poet's disdain for plausibility might have made it an allegorical delight. Truffaut achieved neither.

Perhaps the difficulty is that two poets were collaborating on a single theme, as though T. S. Eliot had been assigned to rewrite *Leaves of Grass*. But whatever it is that Truffaut was reaching for, he missed it.

FILMOGRAPHY
FAHRENHEIT 451 (Anglo-Enterprise, & Vineyard, 1966, British) 111 mins.

Producer, Lewis M. Allen; director, Francois Truffaut; script, Francois Truffaut and Jean-Louis Richard from the novel by Ray Bradbury; production designer, Tony Walton; art director, Syd Cain; editor, Thom Noble; special effects, Charles Staffel; music, Bernard Herrmann; camera, Nicholas Roeg.

Cast: Oskar Werner (Montag); Julie Christie (Linda/Clarisse); Cyril Cusack (The Captain); Anton Diffring (Fabian); Bee Duffell (The Book-Woman); Jeremy Spenser; Gilliam Lewis; Caroline Hunt.

In 1966 the pendulum of science-fiction movies began to swing back to the United States with Richard Fleischer's *Fantastic Voyage*, a totally preposterous but pictorially vivid film in which Raquel Welch and a couple of buddies go submarining down the alimentary canal with gun and camera. (That was a Robert Benchley joke from the 1920s, but he never expected anybody to make it into a film.)

Fantastic Voyage was budgeted at four and a half million dollars and ran two million dollars over. Almost every dime was spent on special effects. The stars were serviceable— newcomer Raquel Welch ornamenting a cast that included Stephen Boyd, Edmond O'Brien and Arthur Kennedy— but wasted in parts which gave them no lines worth saying, and did not even let Welch take her clothes off. O'Brien, older and fatter than in *1984*, played his part with the same torpid resignation. Boyd was called on to be heroic but not intelligent—like a naval mine, he was not required to think or feel, only to explode on command.

Many of the best science fiction films start with real science fiction writers to provide a story. *Fantastic Voyage* started that way. The original story was by a collaborative team that included Jerome Bixby, once editor of *Planet Stories* among other certifiable sf credits. David Duncan wrote the script. Richard Matheson was called in for a touch-up. But it was Harry Kleiner who did the final draft, and maybe that's most of what's wrong with *Fantastic Voyage.*

The film concerns a turncoat Czechoslovakian scientist, who has worked on a process for making things little— *really* little, so that a live and fully equipped Army corps can be put into a bottle cap. The Americans have the same process, but both sides have been defeated by the fact that anything reduced automatically comes back up to size after sixty minutes. (Why does it do this? How does the process operate? Don't ask.) Enemy agents have wounded the scientist in an assassination attempt, leaving an inoperable bloodclot in his brain which will shortly kill him. O'Brien dispatches Welch, Boyd and a couple of others in a new submarine which they just happen to have in the next room. They shrink the submarine and crew, and the adventurers are off to navigate the fluid systems of the scientist to the brain, where they will destroy the clot with a laser.

If you will believe any of that, you will believe anything. Of course, science fiction need not limit itself to what is presently known. Great leaps of theoretical imagination are part of some of the best sf. But any science fiction writer worth taking seriously owes his audience certain obligations. One obligation, if he is up to it, is at least to know what scientific laws he is breaking. Even more important, he is bound by the consequences of his own lies; that is the whole nature of what Hal Clement calls "the science fiction game".

Fantastic Voyage accepts no such responsibilities. It does get the internal workings of the human body pretty near right. The rest is all foolishness. Any event which the director or script writer thought would look good on the screen is allowed to happen.

At the very beginning, Stephen Boyd is put onto a secret elevator which lowers him and his car several stories into a great underground laboratory. Having got off at the bottom floor, what is the next thing he does? He gets into an electric golf cart and drives back *up* several flights. That is merely silly. Other errors in logic are fatal. At the end of the trip, the submarine becomes disabled. The crew is trapped; if they stay with the sub inside the brain they will come back to normal size in just a few minutes, killing their patient and no doubt themselves in the crush. So they

abandon the sub and swim out the tear ducts of the
patient's eye—just in time to return to normal size safely.
But they've left the submarine itself in the brain! What is
going to happen when it comes back to size? The producers assumed their audiences would not be smart enough to
ask questions like that, and, as the film was a great box-
office success, perhaps they were right.

> When the movie ended, (my daughter) Robyn
> turned to me at once and said, "Won't the ship
> expand now and kill the man, Daddy?"
>
> "Yes, Robyn," I explained, "but you see that be-
> cause you're smarter than the average Hollywood
> producer. After all, you're eleven."
>
> —Isaac Asimov (8)

FANTASTIC VOYAGE (Fox, 1966)
The Proteus and its crew in a blood vessel.

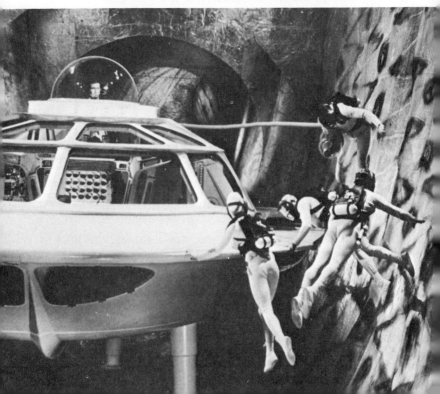

I was called in to do a rewrite on *Fantastic Voyage*. After reading David Duncan's script, I told them they were crazy to want a big rewrite. It only needed a little polishing here and there. They chose to differ. I didn't get a job, and they rewrote it into a comic strip.

—Richard Matheson (5)

Fantastic Voyage started as a long treatment by Otto Klement, with whom I'd collaborated before, and myself. It was about a 170-page story, not a script. This we sold to 20th Century-Fox. From that David Duncan attempted to get a script. Apparently it wasn't satisfactory, so Twentieth put Harry Kleiner on and he came up with the script that was finally used.

The film was essentially a special-effects picture. Our treatment was totally different. Otto and I did it as a turn-of-the-century, Jules Verne kind of thing. Do you remember *Journey to the Center of the Earth*? Atmospherically it was very much like that. The bronze laboratories, bronze instrumentation, crystal technology and so forth. We had very much more of a human story, because we had an external frame at both ends, with a scientist named Sam Breton who discovered the process of miniaturization, and the excitement this generated—whereas in the final picture they threw it away with one line. Edmond O'Brien says, "Oh, we've found a way to make people submicroscopic."

Then—for one thing—they updated it. This took away all the sense of wonder that we had attempted to suffuse the original with. For another, they threw in a dirty, communist, atheist spy, Donald Pleasance. I guess they couldn't think of any other way of contriving conflict between characters, so they came up with that original bombshell. The special effects I thought were great—I guess it won the Academy Award that year for special effects. But what I was sad about when I attended the premiere was the complete loss of the sense of wonder, the sense of awe, the sense of mystery. They referred to it briefly when they first entered the body. They were looking around and saying, "Holy cats, a brand-new world! Isn't it miraculous that God in His infinite wisdom keeps all of this going?"

That was the essence of our story, that wonder never stopped. Whereas very quickly, in *Fantastic Voyage*, they got into a simple action film. Somebody was trying to sabotage the laser. Somebody was trying to sabotage the ship. Who was it? It was cops and robbers inside the human body.

—Jerome Bixby (6)

One of the things people don't realize when they think of *Fantastic Voyage* is that the word "miniatures" really doesn't apply. Almost everything that was built was giant, not miniature. We had just one miniature—of the submarine—but all the sets that were built were vastly and grossly magnified. It took up almost a whole sound stage just for the valves of the heart.

The sets don't exist any more. All of the stuff was very fragile—plastic filaments—and one of our big problems was to keep the sets all in one piece while we were shooting. If there was too much heat the things would just blow apart. A lot of Mylar was used, a lot of experimental filters.

Some of the technical effects were accidentally found. I always wondered how they were going to resolve the situation of dissolving the blood clot in the brain once the laser hits it. And then I knocked over a bottle of acetone onto some of this material, entirely by accident, and it dissolved the material beautifully. Nobody knew that it would until it happened, and there it was.

Most of the scenes were supposed to be underwater, but nothing was shot that way. Mostly it was down with slow-motion photography, and putting a little smoke in the atmosphere so that it looked like there was something there, and the proper use of filters. The feeling of moving in water was by suspending the people on wires and by shooting at about two and a half times normal. Of course, all the body motion of the actors was swimming motion. They were hanging by wires. It's amazing, the work the cameraman did. The wire never shows, and it's almost impossible to have it not show.

It's a very strange thing—in movies you always set your own traps, and then you step into them. To get rid of reflections on the wires we wiped them with acid, which pitted them and made a rough surface, and then painted them black and shot them against dark backgrounds. However, when you do that you weaken the wires. We were constantly having trouble with wires breaking. Each actor had about five wires on him—but with the actors twenty or thirty feet off the floor it got a little hairy.

—Richard Fleischer (7)

FILMOGRAPHY

FANTASTIC VOYAGE (Fox, 1966, U.S.A.) 100 mins.

Producer, Saul David; director, Richard Fleischer; script, Harry Kleiner, adapted by David Duncan from a story by Otto Klement and J. Kewis Bixby; art directors, Jack Martin Smith and Dale Hennesy; editor, William B. Murphy; special effects, L.B. Abbott, Art Cruickshank, and Emil Kosa, Jr.; music, Leonard Rsenman; camera, Ernest Laszlo.

Cast: Stephen Boyd (Grant); Raquel Welch (Cora Peterson); Edmond O'Brien (General Carter); Donald Pleasence (Dr. Michaels); Arthur O'Connell (Colonel Reid); Arthur Kennedy; William Redfield; Jean Del Val.

Fantastic Voyage's six million-plus was as fabulous a production budget for 1966 as any *Star Wars* or *Superman* today. If the script is a disaster, the special effects are superb. Fleischer spent six months experimenting before the cameras turned, and built with a lavish hand: a set representing the interior of a human heart a hundred and thirty feet wide; a seventy-foot replica of the inner ear; a forty-two-foot submarine; a military headquarters that cost a million and a quarter by itself, complete with computers, radar and closed-circuit TV. The camera director, Ernest Laszlo, ordered the sets made in white or colorless plastic. The riot of color on the screen was all lighting.

That was what made *Fantastic Voyage* a success, but what a marvel it might have been if, added to the bubbly white cells on the attack and the cavernous arteries the sub glides through, there had been a *story.*

In 1968 the pace begins to pick up again. There were two major science fiction films, both American, both in their individual ways great successes . . . and both made from actual science fiction stories.

Charly was filmed by Ralph Nelson from *Flowers for Algernon,* a novelette from *The Magazine of Fantasy and Science Fiction* by Daniel Keyes.

In the film, Charly is the retarded handyman in a medical laboratory which is experimenting on a chemical that stimulates intelligence. The drug is tried first on a laboratory mouse, Algernon. It works. He becomes supermouse. It is tried on Charly himself, who then becomes the greatest all-round genius in the world . . . for a time. Tragically, the effects of the drug turn out to be transitory, and not repeatable. The super-genius will become a halfwit again. Worse. With all his intelligence and insight he knows exactly what he will become, and can do nothing to avert it.

The story is simple enough, but it is sensitively written, and sensitively acted by Cliff Robertson, who earned an Oscar for it.

But what to make of Daniel Keyes? His career is a puzzle. His first ambition was to be a writer. To support his career, he took a job as reading fee critic for a literary agent; to support his own career, the agent got him a job as editor of a string of pulp magazines. Then Keyes wrote *Flowers for Algernon.* As a magazine story, it won the Hugo award for best story in its length for the year. When he expanded it to novel length, the book version made it on to the select list of science fiction novels that have sold more than 1,000,000 copies in a single edition. Keyes is now a college professor; he published a second novel a few years ago and a few other short pieces—but nothing with the impact of *Flowers for Algernon/Charly.*

Flowers for Algernon strikes directly to the core of what is wrong with most science fiction. There are no people in the stories. We are very strong on gadget, we are very strong on theory and concept, but we have yet to create our Gatsby, our Ahab, Emma Bovary, Huckleberry Finn. But *Charly* did that, both in the story and in the movie. That scene in which Cliff Robertson, after having had his intelligence upped, is standing before the conclave of the world's greatest scientists, and he's holding this dead mouse in his hand and he looks down at it and says, "Charly Gordon is a man who will very soon be what he was"—it wrenches your heart. I mean, I cry every time I see that scene. It's heartbreaking, and it's pure science fiction.

—Harlan Ellison (9)

Almost as successful as *Charly* critically, and even more so in the grosses, was Franklin Schaffer's *Planet of the Apes,* made from Pierre Boulle's novel, *Monkey Planet.* Boulle is not usually known as a science fiction writer, but *Monkey Planet* is pure sf, and so is the film. According to the story, future astronauts crash on a planet in which evolution has taken a different turn. Primates rule it, just as on Earth. But on the new planet the humans like you and me somehow have fallen behind, and it is the ape branch of the primate family that run things . . . or so it seems. But appearances are deceptive and, after harrowing adventures in which three of the four astronauts are either rendered dead or brainless, the one survivor discovers that the planet is not after all a new one. It is our own familiar Earth, in the far future, to which they have inexplicably traveled.

As a novelist, Boulle has an unusual distinction: his novels are usually better as films than as books. (The other principal exhibit is his *The Bridge on the River Kwai.*) *Planet of the Apes* turned out well indeed, partly for adventure, partly for social satire, perhaps most of all for the marvelous makeup by John Chambers (over a million dollars' worth of ape masks and accessories alone). Finding your favorite movie star under the fur is part of the fun. Perhaps part of the credit goes to the fact that one member at least of the production staff was in a position to know what good dramatic science fiction could be. Mort Abrahams, the associate producer, had himself produced American television's first all-science fiction series, *Tales of Tomorrow,* back in the innovative if poverty stricken dawn of the industry.

Planet of the Apes did so well that it spawned four sequels: *Beneath*—, *Escape from*—, *Conquest of*— and

Battle for the Planet of the Apes. As always, the blood
rapidly ran thin. It was even tried, briefly, as a television
series, but nothing new was ever added in any of the
exploitations, and the basic gimmick soon wore out.

Not only the "big" films of the Sixties deserve mention;
some minor ones had interesting traits. Among them are
three in particular—*The Creeping Terror,* because it
shows how bad a film can get even when at least one
person working on it, John Lackey, knows what he is
about and works hard to realize it; *Robinson Crusoe of
Mars,* because it turned out so much better than anyone
had reason to expect; and Martin Caidin's *Marooned,*
because it illustrates a point.

Mike Hodel calls *The Creeping Terror* "the worst
science-fiction film ever made." That is an awesome responsibility to load on any one single picture, but the film
comes close to justifying it. Direction, acting, script, sets—
everything that you can imagine is wrong with it. It was
made on a zero-based budget, but goes out of its way to be
even worse than it had to. (Hodel points out that although
it is supposed to be set in Colorado, key scenes clearly
show the California state flag.)

The way I came to make the monster for *The
Creeping Terror* was unpremeditated. One day my
car didn't work. I went to a car-parts store, covered
with grease, and I happened to realize that I was next
door to a place where a friend of mine had been
working on a film. I went in and asked about him and,
of course, nobody knew where he was—because
that was all of two weeks ago and, you know, worlds
change in the motion picture industry in two weeks.
There were people hustling around, looking as pro-

fessional as they could, which wasn't very, and I could see that a film production was in the beginning stages. I found myself talking with the producer, and he said he was doing a science-fiction movie. I said, "Oh, I design science-fiction things." He said, "Creatures? Monsters?" I said, "Yes, yes!" Well, he grabbed me by the collar and plunked me down at his own desk and said, "Draw me a monster. I want one that will swallow people—preferably several people at once—and enjoy it."

So, I figured he wanted something like a double-barreled job, or even a four-barrel, so I scribbled him one off. It seemed to be a moment of inspiration. I don't know quite what was on my mind at the time, but I produced on a large sheet of pink paper a drawing of something that I would later come to know and love as "The Creeping Terror".

I built it out of polyurethane foam, in the raw form—from the resin. It weighed five or six hundred pounds. It had eight people inside of it—eight groaning, cursing stuntmen, because every time we went over rough terrain they got the full dust-in-the-face treatment. I was in charge of directing the creature, yelling, "Up in front, down in back! Pull to the left! Pull to the right!" It was like a large, undulating omelette. As it developed, I realized that I was getting into something very sculptural in its character. The swallowing action could be really spectacular. But the script pretensions of the producer were in many ways coming to naught. He kept wanting to go to fancy locations, and he couldn't possibly raise the money for it.

—John Lackey (10)

THE CREEPING TERROR (Teledyn, 1964)
Half a dozen grips getting ready to make The Creeping Terror *creep.*

Robinson Crusoe of Mars, on the other hand, is very nearly very good indeed. Ib Melchior had the notion of converting Daniel Defoe's *Robinson Crusoe* into a space adventure film and collaborated on the script with John C. Higgins. The director was Byron Haskin (who also directed *Destination Moon* and *War of the Worlds* for George Pal). The part of Robinson Crusoe's sidekick was played by Adam West, first step to his career as TV's Batman. The story is full of nice little touches and inventive special effects. It isn't a big film, but it pleases; *Time* called it "a pleasant surprise . . . modest yet provocative", and for once *Time* had it just right.

Much of *Robinson Crusoe of Mars* was shot in Death Valley, and so was much of the John Sturges production of *Marooned.* Martin Caidin's novel is only marginally sci-

FILMOGRAPHY

ROBINSON CRUSOE ON MARS (Paramount, 1964, U.S.A.) 110 mins.

Producer, Aubrey Schenck; director, Byron Haskin; script, Ib Melchior and John C. Higgins from the novel *Robinson Crusoe* by Daniel De Foe; art directors, Hal Pereira and Arthur Lonergan; editor, Terry Morse; special effects, Lawrence Butler; music, Val Cleve; camera, Winton C. Hoch.

Cast: Paul Mantee (Commander Christopher Draper); Vic Lundin (Friday); Adam West (Colonel Dan McReady).

CHARLY (Selmur and Robertson Associates, 1968, U.S.A.) 106 mins.

Producer/director, Ralph Nelson; script, Stirling Silliphant from the novel *Flowers for Algernon* by Daniel Keyes; art director, Charles Rosen; editor, Frederic Steinkamp; music, Ravi Shankar; camera, Arthur J. Ornitz.

Cast: Cliff Robertson (Charly Gordon); Claire Bloom (Alice Kinlan); Lilia Skala (Dr. Anna Straus); Leon Janney (Dr. Richard Nemur); Dick Van Patten; Ruth White.

PLANET OF THE APES (Fox, 1968, U.S.A.) 112 mins.

Producer, Arthur P. Jacobs; director, Franklin J. Schaffner; script, Rod Serling and Michael Wilson from the novel *Monkey Planet* by Pierre Boulle; art directors, Jack Martin Smith and William Creber; editor, Hugh S. Fowler; special effects, L.B. Abbott, Art Cruickshank, and Emil Kosa, Jr.; music, Jerry Goldsmith; camera, Leon Shamroy.

Cast: Charlton Heston (George Taylor); Roddy McDowall (Cornelius); Kim Hunter (Dr. Zira); Maurice Evans (Dr. Zaius); James Whitmore (Assembly President); Robert Gunner; Linda Harrison; James Daly.

ence fiction. It is about the perils of astronauts in orbit, and the hardware is very like what we have all been seeing on our television sets from Merritt Island and elsewhere—in fact, an actual Saturn-5 launching film clip is worked into the movie. All Caidin made up is an incident: that a group of astronauts become stranded, and that they are rescued by another space ship. The surprise in the film is that the stranded astronauts are American, the rescuers Russian.

One of the claims made for science fiction is that it not only sometimes predicts future events, but (at least now and then) actually causes them to happen. It may have happened with *Marooned.* An item of persistent gossip in the space community says that the film was shown to an audience of space scientists in Moscow, who were impressed by its message of Soviet-U.S. cooperation in space. Next time an American team came visiting (it is said) they mentioned the film and intimated that some such venture might actually be tried—and thus the Apollo-Soyuz rendezvous of 1974 came to be. Apart from that, the film is distinctly minor, although it had good performances by Gregory Peck and Gene Hackman and the New York *Times* called it "a handsome, professional and future-minded space drama in fine color."

Also minor, and also having to do with Soviet-American cooperation, was the 1969 *Colossus: The Forbin Project,* based on the science-fiction novel, *Colossus,* by D. F. Jones. The cooperation this time is not encouraging to human morale. It is between two great computers, the American Colossus and the Soviet Guardian, each of which has been charged with control of its nation's nuclear forces. The computers jointly decide to take over the world. *Colossus: The Forbin Project* is not a very memorable film, but it shows a kind of maturity that print science fiction had been used to for some time, but was rare in films. Its makers allowed it to reach its natural conclusion without forcing it to a happy ending. . . except, of course, for computers.

In the late 1960s a new giant was born.

Even giants are born small, and George Lucas's first production was nothing like *Star Wars*. Lucas was then a college student in southern California, and as part of his requirements for a degree he made a twenty-minute short called *THX 2238 4EB*. Out of school a year or two later, he was taken on by Francis Ford Coppola, who saw the short and made it the first production of his new company, American Zoetrope. It was released in 1971 as *THX 1138*.

THX 1138 is a diatribe against the police state, like *1984*. The police are robots, and they are soothingly gentle as they direct the lives of humans—like Jack Williamson's *The Humanoids*. *THX* has a simple story line. Lucas imagines a future world underground, teeming with people. They are kept placid and unresentful by regular drugging; but a woman among them, LUH 3417, tampers with her drugs and those of her lover, THX 1138 himself. No longer tranquilized, they are roused to have sexual intercourse—a punishable offense, which results in the death of LUH and the imprisonment of THX in an immense open white space. He and another prisoner escape from it—simply by walking away. They steal a car, flee the pursuing robots on their motorcycles through endless miles of tunnels, board a nearly empty train and are carried to the far marches of the underground city. The companion is killed, but THX continues his flight. He has no real hope, for the tireless robots must sooner or later catch up with him. But the central authority with pure computer logic calculates on a cost/effectiveness basis that it is simply not worth while to pursue him further, and so he then escapes to the arid surface of the Earth.

The story of *THX 1138* is in fact like a good many others in almost all respects; what is not like anything else is the look and sound of the film. *THX* is now seen, if anywhere at all, only on television reruns, which is a pity. The blinding white-on-white photography is only an annoyance in the living room. In a motion-picture theater it saturates the senses.

Television, on the other hand, may be an improvement when it comes to the sound, because at least you can turn the volume down. In the film there is a constant overlapping noise of spoken messages, mostly the voices of computers. Some are in clear. Some are cloyingly sweet. Some are tricked up with every distortion electronics can impose on a voice: they buzz, or sing, or echo. Both Lucas and Coppola are from the rock generation, and there is something of that in their treatment of dialogue: the words are important, but they are almost impossible to understand—sometimes wholly impossible, as in most of the battle sequences in Coppola's *Apocalypse Now.*

FILMOGRAPHY

THX 1138 (Warner Bros., 1971, U.S.A.) 88 mins.

Executive producer, Francis Ford Coppola; producer, Lawrence Sturhahn; director, George Lucas; script, George Lucas and Walter Murch from a story by Lucas; art director, Michael Haller; editor, George Lucas; music, Lalo Schifrin; camera, Dave Meyers and Albert Kihn.

Cast: Robert Duvall (THX 1138); Donald Pleasence (SEN 5241); Don Pedro Colley (SRT); Maggie McOmie (LUH 3417); Ian Wolfe; Marshall Effron; John Pearce.

When they came to make Lucas's original short into a full length feature, Lucas and Coppola brought formidable talents to bear. "Anyone fascinated with the potentials of film must watch *THX 1138*," the Los Angeles *Times* said, quite rightly. The filming is brilliant, and it was accomplished without immense quantities of money for special effects. The huge empty white plain was shot in a fairly small TV studio. For the tunnel chase sequences, they simply borrowed the unfinished diggings of San Francisco's BART subway.

But all that ingenuity gets between the audience and the characters. It is difficult to care about THX. He does not seem to care much about himself. About the only thing he does in the entire of his own volition is to run away, and what he runs to does not seem a great deal better than what he has left behind.

THX 1138 is a film pregnant with meaning and astonishing in its look, but it was a financial failure. Lucas learned from it. When he got around to his chef d'oeuvre, *Star Wars,* he insisted that it was guaranteed free of any meaning at all.

1971 gave us *THX 1138* and Stanley Kubrick's last science-fiction film to date, *A Clockwork Orange.* It also was the year that brought Michael Crichton and Kurt Vonnegut, Jr., to the screen.

Crichton's *The Andromeda Strain* was never labeled as science fiction. Perhaps that was part of the reason for its immense success as a book, for it reached some of those large sections of the reading public, then overwhelming and still formidable, who will only read science fiction when it is called something else. When it came to be made into a film the director, Robert Wise, insisted that it was not

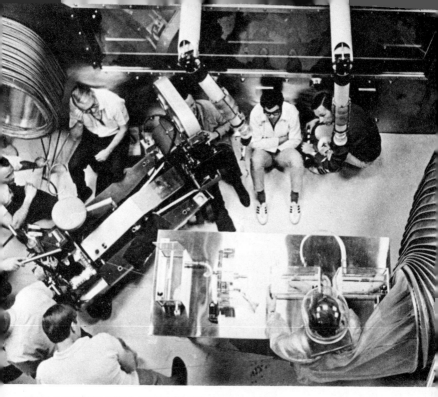

THE ANDROMEDA STRAIN (Universal, 1971)
On the set of The Andromeda Strain, Robert Wise (upper left) directing.

science fiction but science fact. But Wise himself had directed *The Day the Earth Stood Still* twenty years earlier; some of the special effects were by Douglas Trumbull, one of the brains behind *2001*; and the story speaks for itself. A satellite has crashed in New Mexico. It carries germs of a plague from outer space, which infects the residents of a nearby town, killing all except a baby and a drunk. The survivors are quarantined in a huge, glittering, sterile installation, while Earth's top doctors and biologists strive to prevent the organism's escape and the consequent annihilation of humanity.

∿∿∿∿∿∿∿∿∿∿∿∿∿∿∿∿∿∿∿∿∿∿∿∿

FILMOGRAPHY
THE ANDROMEDA STRAIN (Universal, 1971, U.S.A.) 130 mins.

Producer/director, Robert Wise; script, Nelson Gidding from the novel by Michael Crichton; production designer, Boris Levin; art director, William Tuntke; editor, Stuart Gilmore and John W. Holmes; special effects, Douglas Trumbull and James Shourt; music, Gil Mellé; camera, Richard H.Kline.

Cast: Arthur Hill (Dr. Jeremy Stone); David Wayne (Dr. Charles Dutton); James Olson (Dr. Mark Hall); Paula Kelly (Karen Anson); George Mitchell (Jackson); Kate Reid (Dr. Ruth Leavitt); Ramon Biere (Major Manchek); Peter Hobbs (General Sparks); Mark Jenkins; Kermit Murdock; Richard O'Brien.

∿∿∿∿∿∿∿∿∿∿∿∿∿∿∿∿∿∿∿∿∿∿∿∿

The story came out of a very real concern of just a few years before that, when many scientists warned of just such a potential danger in returning crews from the imminent Apollo moon landings. At great expense, the first returning astronauts were quarantined and studied before being allowed to rejoin the human race, and at even greater expense, as a corollary to prevent the export of terrestrial diseases to possible Selenites or Martians, all landing craft were sterilized within an inch of their lives during assembly. We now know that the risks are not very large, because life of any kind seems scarce off the surface of our own planet. But no one knew that for sure in 1971, and Wise deliberately gave *The Andromeda Strain* an almost documentary look, choosing actors who were not especially well known so that audiences would perceive them as real people rather than movie stars. It all worked very well. *The Andromeda Strain* was a great success.

Robert Wise calls *The Andromeda Strain* science *fact.* Kurt Vonnegut, Jr., is equally emphatic in the opposite direction. His novels, he says, are not science fiction. They are *fiction.*

What writers say about themselves is seldom to be trusted, because they see their work from the inside out instead of the view given to us as readers. Vonnegut's close connection with science fiction is not to be doubted. Some of his first stories appeared in *Galaxy,* and early on he visited the Milford Science Fiction Writers' Conference.

Like most novelists, Vonnegut puts pages of his autobiography into his books. Bits and pieces of Milford pervade them: his "Kilgore Trout", for instance, does sound a lot like Milford regular Theodore Sturgeon, author of (among other things) *Killdozer.* Milford is a combination trade school and encounter group. It is cliquish, inner-directed and intensive, and it did not appeal to Vonnegut. From then on, he distanced himself from science fiction in every way he could—except in what he wrote.

FILMOGRAPHY

SLAUGHTERHOUSE FIVE (Universal, 1971, U.S.A.) 105 mins.

Producer, Paul Monash; director, George Roy Hill; script, Stephen Geller from the novel by Kurt Vonnegut, Jr.; production designer, Henry Bumstead; art directors, Alexander Golitzen and George Webb; editor, Dede Allen; music, J.S. Bach arranged by Glenn Gould; camera, Miroslav Ondricek.

Cast: Michael Sachs (Billy Pilgrim); Ron Leibman (Paul Lazzaro); Eugene Roche (Edgar Derby); Valerie Perrine (Montana Wildhack); Sharon Gans (Valencia); Robert Blossom (Wild Bob Cody); Kevin Conway; Gary Waynesmith; Sorrell Brooke.

Again, the story of *Slaughterhouse Five* speaks for itself. It is the story of Billy Pilgrim, ex-GI and veteran of the firestorm that annihilated Dresden while he was a prisoner of war in the pens located at #5 Slaughterhouse Street. Pilgrim has become "unstuck" in time (Or else he fantasies that he has—the second reading allows the interpretation that the film is not science fiction but a sort of dream.). Sometimes Pilgrim is in the PW camp, watching his buddies and the city die. Sometimes he is the star attraction in a sort of sideshow on the distant planet Tralfamadore, along with the most beautiful and sexy of women, the movie starlet Montana Wildhack. As an exhibit, he is the captive of a race of aliens who have accidentally destroyed the entire universe (but the destruction hasn't quite finished happening yet). For their entertainment, he and Montana eat, sleep, make love and do all the other pitifully mortal things that their captors have long since outgrown, while the aliens watch and applaud. Pilgrim's vision is not limited to Tralfamadore; he also sees his own future on Earth, in scenes of violence and bloodshed.

Slaughterhouse Five was directed by George Roy Hill. Hill was fifty when the film was released, veteran of the New York stage (*Thoroughly Modern Millie*), of a well-remembered and gently comic Peter Sellers film, *The World of Henry Orient,* and of the wondrously successful *Butch Cassidy and the Sundance Kid.* He approached the convoluted story of *Slaughterhouse Five* with respect, and filmed it with care and more than three million dollars. But it does not quite work. Vonnegut is a discursive, introspective, stylized writer. He does not translate easily into film, where the brilliant little interpolations and exactly appropriate turns of phrase fall between the frames and are lost. Even Hill did not succeed in making *Slaughterhouse Five* intelligible to audiences who had not read the book, and the film died at the b.o.

A serious fault in *Slaughterhouse Five* is the tackiness of the ''sci-fi'' scenes on Tralfamadore. If they were to be done at all, they should have been done better, say by a Douglas Trumbull. The following year Trumbull got a film of his own to do; he approached his subject with as much intelligence and care as Hill with *Slaughterhouse Five,* but from the opposite direction.

Silent Running (1972) started out with a strike against it, since most casual theater-goers expected it to be about submarines. It wasn't. It took place entirely in space. In the story, the Earth is completely built over and sterile. There is no room for growing green things, and they survive in the universe only in spaceborne hothouses. These hothouses are immense, expensive, and essentially useless to the busy manufacturers and consumers of Earth, who decide to discontinue them as an unwarranted frill.

Bruce Dern plays the part of one of the draftees running these ecological museums. He comes to love them, and when the order comes down to terminate them he rebels. He fakes mechanical trouble, gets rid of the rest of the crew and settles down to a hermit's life. His only company is three robots, Louie, Huey and Dewey.

What *Silent Running* lacks most is believability. Is there any *imaginable* combination of events which could make preserving forests in space cheaper than setting aside a few acres somewhere on the Earth? There is not. But the film also lacks pace and plot. The script of *Silent Running* must be one of the shortest ever to produce ninety minutes of film, even though four writers combined to create it. There are long sections with no dialogue at all, or with Bruce

Dern speaking reflectively and haltingly, and above all draggingly slowly, to the robots, who cannot answer. For audiences in a hurry, it is an interminable bore.

But for audiences willing to enter Trumbull's spaced-out world, it is soothing and delightful. Certainly it is made with immense skill. Dern avoids the space ships coming to "rescue" him by slipping in among the rings of Saturn, in a handsome sequence originally created for, but not used in, *2001*. The robots themselves are marvelous. They are obviously too tiny to contain human beings, and yet their movements are far too coordinated and natural to have been done by animation or split-screen. In fact, they do contain human beings: the actors are child amputees, sometimes walking on their hands to animate a robot shell in ways that a less ingenious *auteur* could never have created. And the robots are childlike—trusting, voiceless, sometimes mischievous—and when one of them is destroyed Dern's sorrow is shared by the audience.

Considering *Silent Running* and *Slaughterhouse Five* together, one so beautifully fills the gaps in the other that it almost seems worth wishing for the return of the terrible old studio tyrants. What if a Goldwyn or a Zanuck had put Vonnegut and Trumbull together in a room, with orders to assemble the best parts of both and fit them together into a film? Both Trumbull and Vonnegut are wise and forthcoming human beings, far less given to mean ego clashes than others in their professions. They should work well together. . . . But that is a dream. The reality is that *Silent Running* lacked story. It may also have lacked money. It was Trumbull's misfortune to have to make it for a million three when that was no longer really enough to pay for a dazzle of special effects.

But $1,300,000 is still two hundred times as much as the students at U.S.C. had when they came to make their first version of *Dark Star*.

The first version (1971) ran only forty-five minutes, but its cost was not much over $5,000 and change. No professional company could possibly have done it. As amateurs, the southern Californian students were exempt from the demands of the unions, which saved a fortune. But they were also exempt from the technical skills the unions offered, to say nothing of the resources of a professional studio. For money and experience and technical backup, they substituted wit and ingenuity.

Dark Star sends up *Star Trek,* and it is *funny.* The crew of *Dark Star* have the same mission as Captain Kirk and his *Enterprise.* They dart about the universe, seeking potential trouble spots and disarming them. They don't waste time arguing with worrisome planets, though. They simply blow them up. Their "thermostellar" bombs are so sophisticated that they guide themselves to a target, talk back to the crewmen and even beg for the chance to go off. The ship's captain happens to be dead, but he still talks to the crew—not very coherently—through taps wired into his preserved brain. Everyone on the ship has gone out of his mind long since, as detached from reality as Bruce Dern in *Silent Running*, as hallucinatory as Billy Pilgrim in *Slaughterhouse Five.* As ship's mascot they have a bulging, blubbery alien who is as much of a nuisance to them as *Star Trek*'s Tribbles or Robert A. Heinlein's flat cats. Everything that can go wrong has. *Dark Star* is black comedy, satire and a lot of fun.

The 45-minute student version was shot on 16mm film, but a professional producer, Jack Harris, put up the money to transfer it to theater-sized 35mm, and to shoot enough additional scenes to bring it up to feature length. In the theater version (1974) it achieved spotty release in a few out-of-the-way theaters, but even so made money—even the beefed-up version cost only $60,000 all told. It costs more than that to do the opening titles on a film like *Star Wars*.

In 1972 another country was heard from, as Mosfilm released the Soviet production of Stanislaw Lem's *Solaris*.

As with both Crichton and Vonnegut, Stanislaw Lem likes to keep a space between himself and "science-fiction writers"—especially American science fiction writers. Those who can read his many works in the original Polish sometimes call him the greatest science fiction writer alive. Those who read only the English translations sometimes wonder why. An Italian proverb says, *Tradutore tradittore,* meaning, "To translate is to betray." Lem is usually twice betrayed before he gets into English. Most of the existing translations are double, Polish into French or German and then the French or German into English, and it is hard to see what is left of this allusive, witty, often subtle writer after that. Even so, he has a devoted clique in America, made up only partly of literary persons with no other experience of science fiction to compare him to. Lem's contacts with American science fiction writers have been as shaking for him as Vonnegut's visit to Milford, and have left him just as reluctant to associate with them again. And yet among them are some of his greatest admirers.

Solaris—the book—is an untypically heavy handed Lem novel, and it is perhaps appropriate that it was made as a joint Russian-Polish film by Andrei Tarkovsky, still in his 30s and best known for such movies as *Ivan's Child-*

hood. The name "Solaris" belongs to a planet. This world has been studied for a long time by terrestrial astronauts, orbiting around it, but its puzzling qualities have not been solved. Among other things, something in or on Solaris has the power of giving the astronauts "companions" who not only seem to them their exact hearts'-desires (as in Stanley G. Weinbaum's *The Dream Beasts*), but also double as spy instruments for whoever, or whatever, is reciprocally studying the astronauts. The filming is imaginative and sometimes, as in the opening scenes on Earth, warm and human. But in terms of audience and box office, it has not made much of a mark in the West.

Solaris was first seen in America in its original Russian-language print, at a few conventions and special screenings. The print did not even have English subtitles, and the reactions of the audiences were quite as mystified as those of Leningraders watching the undubbed *The Thing*. A later release print in English was spottily distributed, and disappeared soon. But the film's partisans are adoring. Philip Strick, in fact, calls it "the most intelligent and questioning science-fiction movie ever made." And it is unquestionably at least the most famous Russian science-fiction film since *Aelita.*

FILMOGRAPHY
SOLARIS (Mosfilm, 1972, Soviet) 165 mins.
    Director, Andrei Tarkovsky; script, Friedrich Gorenstein and Andrei Tarkovsky from the novel by Stanislaw Lem; art director, Mikhail Romadid; music, Eduard Artemiev; camera, Vadim Youssov.
    Cast: Donatis Banionis (Christ Kelvin); Natalya Bandarchuk (Hari); Yuri Jarvet (Snouth); Nicolai Grinko; Vladislav Dvorzhetski; Anatoli Solintsin.

FILMOGRAPHY

SILENT RUNNING (Universal, 1972, U.S.A.) 90 mins.

Producer, Michael Gurskoff; director, Douglas Trumbull; script, Michael Cimino, Deric Washburn, and Steve Bochco from a story by Douglas Trumbull; editor, Aaron Stell; special effects, Douglas Trumbull, John Dykstra, and Richard Yuricich; music, Peter Schickele; camera, Charles F. Wheeler.

Cast: Bruce Dern (Freeman Lowell); Cliff Potts (Wolf); Ron Rifkin (Barker); Jesse Vint (Keenan); Mark Persons, Cheryl Sparks, Steven Brown, and Larry Whisenhunt (Drones).

SOURCES

1. Bradbury, Ray. From a taped interview with the authors, January 1979.

2. Truffaut, Francois. From "The Journal of Fahrenheit 451" in *Focus on the Science Fiction Film* edited by William Johnson, Prentice-Hall, Inc., 1972.

3. Sarris, Andrew. *The American Cinema: Directors and Directions, 1929-1968,* E.P. Dutton, New York, 1968.

4. Kael, Pauline. *Kiss Kiss Bang Bang,* Little, Brown & Co., Boston, 1968.

5. Matheson, Richard. From a taped interview with the authors, January 1979.

6. Bixby, Jerome. From a taped interview with the authors, August 1979.

7. Fleischer, Richard. From a taped interview with the authors, May 1979.

8. Asimov, Isaac. From *In Joy Still Felt,* Doubleday, New York.

9. Ellison, Harlan. From a taped interview with the authors, January 1979.

10. Lackey, John. From a radio discussion with the authors, KPFK, Los Angeles, January 1979.

Chapter 6

Tooling Up for the Big Bang, 1973-1976

By the early 1970s the term "science fiction" had lost most of its pejorative sting.

Partly the change was a function of numbers. From its first self-aware beginning in the 1920s to the mid-1970s the science fiction audience had been increasing regularly, like compound interest, at a rate of six or seven per cent per year, from perhaps a hundred thousand when the first issue of *Amazing Stories* appeared to something approaching two million by 1973. Two million is not even one one-hundredth of the U.S. population. But it is a lot of individual human beings. Especially it is a lot of individual *readers,* and readers themselves are an increasingly rare breed.

Even more the change was a function of respectability. By 1973 the academic world had discovered science fiction books and magazines. More than a thousand colleges had some sort of courses in science fiction by then, as well as an uncounted number of high schools. Doctoral dissertations were written on science-fiction books and authors. Scholarly journals appeared, and science fiction writers were more and more often invited to lecture at colleges— as well as at management conventions, scientific gatherings and the odd Kiwanis meeting. Science fiction had not quite come all the way *in*. But it was no longer disgracefully *out*.

Science fiction in film and TV follows the curve of science fiction in print—usually at a respectful distance of a couple of decades—and the networks and the studios had come to see science fiction as respectable too. *Star Trek* helped a great deal. During its three-year prime-time life, it was never better than marginal in the ratings—would have been canceled at the end of the second year, if it had not been for the whipped-up blizzard of letters that fell on NBC. But in syndicated reruns it was astonishing. There was hardly a city in America, hardly even any in all the western world, where *Star Trek* was not being shown in reruns every day. Sometimes more often than that; there is a city in Texas where, if you had a big enough antenna, you could watch *five Star Trek* reruns every Monday through Friday, with an extra bonus on the weekend. Even more astonishing was *Star Trek*'s commercial fallout of books and games and maps and Spock ears and put-it-together models. By 1973 *Star Trek* had become the second most profitable merchandising show in the history of television.

In the film studios, this acceptance of science fiction did not quite extend to tolerance of the term itself. Producers still denied that their films were "science fiction" even when they were. Reviewers like Pauline Kael still went on record to say that all science fiction films struck her as "faintly dumb"—and when she came to review sf films she liked, as with *Sleeper* and *Young Frankenstein,* managed to do so without once employing the terms "science fiction", "sf" or even "sci-fi".

And indeed, the sf films of the mid-1970s weren't "sci-fi". Only a handful exploited space or monsters. The bulk of them explored social problems here on Earth, even as comedy.

Michael Crichton's *Westworld* gave not only comedy but chills, in a marvelous robot-after-man chase. This was not an adaptation of a Crichton novel, like *The An-*

dromeda Strain. This one he wrote directly as a screenplay, refusing even to allow it to be novelized by someone else, and went on to direct the film to boot. Crichton shows a great talent for visualizing the pictorial parts of science fiction in *Westworld.* It was an inspiration, for instance, to show some of the scenes through the robot's infra-red eyes, so that we see a mosaic of colored pixels in computer grids. It is the same false-color enhancement one finds at Jet Propulsion Laboratories when a spacecraft is returning pictures from space, and why no one thought to use it earlier is hard to understand.

The locale of *Westworld* is an X-rated future Disneyland called "Delos" (=de Los Angeles?). It is manned exclusively by robots. Two tourists, Richard Benjamin and James Brolin, visit it for a weekend of fantasy fulfillment. As in the Anaheim original, Delos is divided into different "lands", but here they are called "worlds". Westworld is a reconstructed cowtown of the 1880s. Medievalworld and Romanworld are also made available, for those whose golden-age dreams go farther back. In all three of them, every "living" thing is a robot, except the tourists; there are even robot horses and robot rattlesnakes. The robots are at the disposal of the paying customers, to be used for any purpose they like. The girls are copulatable. (Consciousness had not yet been raised enough in 1973 to say whether the same was true of the men.) Everyone is killable. It does not greatly harm the robots to be killed. They are carted away by night to the repair shops, to return the next day as good as new . . . until something goes wrong (according to the high-powered advertising for the film, it goes "worng"), and the robots begin to fight back for real.

∽↶∽↶∽↶∽↶∽↶∽↶∽↶∽↶∽↶∽↶∽↶∽↶∽↶∽↶∽↶∽↶∽↶∽

FILMOGRAPHY

WESTWORLD (MGM, 1973, U.S.A.) 89 mins.

Producer, Paul N. Lazarus III; director/script, Michael Crichton; art director, Herman Blumenthal; editor, David Bretherton; special effects, Charles Schulthies; automated image processing, John Whitney, Jr.; music, Fred Karlin; camera, Gene Polito.

Cast: Yul Brynner (Gunslinger); Richard Benjamin (Peter Martin); James Brolin (John Blane); Norman Bartold (Medieval Knight); Dick Van Patten (Banker); Victoria Shaw (Medieval Queen); Alan Oppenheimer (Chief Supervisor); Michael Milker; Steve Franklin; Linda Scott.

∽↶∽↶∽↶∽↶∽↶∽↶∽↶∽↶∽↶∽↶∽↶∽↶∽↶∽↶∽↶∽↶∽↶∽↶∽

It is a pity that there is a certain amount of fat-headed nonsense in the film. "Fat-headed" nonsense may be defined as ordinary nonsense which has been gratuitously interjected, serving no important plot or dramatic purpose—e.g., the silly quirk in *Westworld* that stipulates that the robots can be distinguished from the human customers only by their hands, because "they haven't got the hands right yet." (This is roughly equivalent to saying that Texas Instruments got its TI-55 calculator all finished, but couldn't quite manage to design a snap for the carrying case.) There are other failures of internal logic in the robot's weaponry and visual systems; but these are only annoyances. The chase at the end is brilliant, as the flayed and charred body of gunman Yul Brynner remorselessly pursues his most recent murderer, Richard Benjamin. The film was inexpensively made, too. The special effects were relatively modest, and the sets obviously whatever was ready to hand. "Romanworld" is Harold Lloyd's old estate. "Medievalworld" came right out of the set warehouses. "Westworld" is any studio's standing back-lot cowtown (and Brynner even wore his old costume from *The Magnificent Seven* as a gunslinger). It grossed $3.5 million in its first American release, paying back its investment with a profit, and has been earning ever since.

Even funnier—perhaps the funniest science-fiction comedy ever made—was *Sleeper* (1973), written, directed, inspired and acted by that master comedian of the 1970s, Woody Allen. Pauline Kael says that Allen has "the city-wise effrontery of a shrimp", and *Sleeper* is that bodacious shrimp's victory over the forces of future evil.

In *Sleeper,* Woody Allen has been frozen for two hundred years by R.C.W. Ettinger's "corpsicle" scheme. He is brought back to life in the year 2173, and meets Diane Keaton, a 22nd century poet. The two of them become involved in the struggle against a *1984*-style dictator, of whom nothing remains but his nose.

Sleeper is not significant for its plot. It is all glorious schtick, like all of Woody Allen. He extracts comedy from the angst and anomie of the 1960s and 1970s. Wherever he is in films, in a banana republic or two centuries in the future, he has obviously just left a Greenwich Village pot party, where he came prepared with all the right conversational gambits and no one liked him anyway. *Sleeper*'s schtick deals with clones and synthetic foods and robots, as well as the sexual and political muddles of late 20th century man. Allen is a gloriously literate person. He reads everything and is interested in everything; perhaps the central message of all his films is that the world is so confusing that it cannot be handled even when you know everything anybody can be expected to know.

There is a certain amount of nonsense in *Sleeper,* but Allen saved himself the embarrassment of its being fat-

headed nonsense by hiring Ben Bova (then editor of
Analog) as a consultant on the film. It shows. There are
plenty of departures from logic in *Sleeper,* but there aren't
any *unnecessary* ones.

FILMOGRAPHY
SLEEPER (United Artists, 1973, U.S.A.) 88 mins.
　　Producer, Jack Grossberg; director, Woody Allen;
script, Woody Allen and Marshall Brickman; produc-
tion designer, Dale Hennesy; art director, Dianne
Wager; editors, O. Nicholas Brown and Trudy Ship;
special effects, A.D. Flowers; music, Woody Allen;
camera, David M. Walsh.
　　Cast: Woody Allen (Miles Monroe); Diane Keaton
(Luna Schlosser); John Beck (Erno Windt); Mary
Gregory (Dr. Milik); Don Keefer (Dr. Tryon); Don
McLiam (Dr. Agon); Bartlett Robinson (Dr. Orva);
Marya Small; Chris Forbes.

The third major 1973 science-fiction film, *Soylent
Green*, had no comedy in it at all. It was made from Harry
Harrison's novel, *Make Room, Make Room,* and it detailed a world of the not very far future in which uncontrolled child-bearing had brought about such overpopulation
that starvation is near for everyone. A police state sees that
nothing can be wasted. Nothing is, not even the meat on
the bodies of the dead. They are processed to make the
government food handouts known as "Soylent Green".

　　There is a ghoulishness to *Soylent Green* even beyond
its cannibalistic theme. Edward G. Robinson, dying while
he made it, portrays a dying old man in the film. When his
actual death occurred, it gave an ugly little tweak to the
publicity. The film does not have a great deal beyond
ghoulishness to offer, and almost all of that was injected by

the film people. Harrison's novel was a purely cautionary tale about overpopulation; his word "soylent" was a coinage from "soy beans" and "lentils". The cannibalism was an inspiration from Hollywood.

FILMOGRAPHY
SOYLENT GREEN (MGM, 1973, U.S.A.) 97 mins.
Producers, Walter Seltzer and Russell Thacher; director, Richard Fleischer; script, Stanley R. Greenberg from the novel *Make Room! Make Room!* by Harry Harrison; art director, Edward C. Carfagno; editor, Samuel E. Beetley; special effects, Robert R. Hoag and Matthew Yuricich; music, Fred Mylow; camera, Richard H. Kline.

Cast: Charlton Heston (Detective Thorn); Edward G. Robinson (Sol Roth); Leigh Taylor-Young (Shirl); Chuck Connors (Tab Fielding); Joseph Cotten (William Simonson); Brock Peters (Hatcher); Mike Henry; Stephen Young; Celia Lovsky.

Soylent Green is a realistic film, at least in the first part. It's a look into the near future, and the idea was to make the people as recognizable to the people of today as possible, because it's a very short extrapolation from what we have presently in our society. I shot it in a rather documentary-like style. But then, once they take off into this other world, there's a poetic quality I tried to get. Although the people are behaving in a normal way, the whole thing is slightly elevated, away from super-realism. You really don't have to identify too much with the people who are in that section of the film. You just see this other, bizarre world through their eyes.

—Richard Fleischer (1)

Edward G. Robinson said to the director of *Soylent Green*, "Dick, I don't understand my part. I don't know what I'm supposed to do. I have no idea who the character is."

So I took him aside and said, "I wrote the book, and who you are in this picture is me. That's how old I will be. You have my Army background. You have my physical background. You're the only person in this whole book/film who has lived in a world that is fairly good, that has sunshine, birds, happiness, warmth. Everyone else here thinks that this rotten, grim, drab world is the only game in town. You connect the two."

He said, "Thank you very much," went away, thought about it, came on. They had shot his scene a couple of times earlier. He had terminal cancer, which no one knew at the time; he preferred to go on acting rather than lying at home and looking at the ceiling. Tremendous man. He had muffed his lines twice. It was a key scene, but at sixty-nine years of age you're allowed to muff your lines twice. A key scene is a very large scene. He insisted on a closed set, which means the only people there were the gaffers and best boys and electricians who have seen a million pictures and are bored to tears. You should have seen these guys. After they had done the scene—it's the eating scene, close to the beginning, very important to the film—Dick Fleischer said, "Cut!" and all these horrible old electricians and rotten old carpenters clapped. He had created something. They had seen a dull scene—and what a real artist created out of it.

—Harry Harrison (2)

Soylent Green won the SFWA's best-film Nebula, and so, a little later, did the Mel Brooks *Young Frankenstein.* This is rather odd. By most standards, *Young Frankenstein* (1974) is hardly science fiction at all.

Like *Sleeper, Young Frankenstein* is made up of nearly pure schtick, but this time performed as broadly as any Billy Minsky burlesque skit of the 1930s. It is full of sight gags and sex gags. The hump on the current Igor's back keeps wandering around. When Madeline Kahn is raped by the monster, her scream turns into a full-throated Jeanette MacDonald rendering of "Oh, sweet mystery of life" as she finds she likes it.

Mel Brooks's comedic style is more Abbott and Costello than Woody Allen; it is the obsessive dedication of a borscht-circuit *tummeler,* a Milton Berle, an Ed Wynn. The gags come so fast that the cumulative effect forces you to laugh even when you don't want to, even if it is only irritation that brings it about. But there is a higher kind of wit in *Young Frankenstein*, too, in throwaways like the changing railway sets and scenes as the young doctor journeys to Transylvania.

It is easy for *Young Frankenstein*'s reliance on jokes about rape and physical deformities to give offense. It is *meant* to work on the narrow edge of being inexcusable, because that is how Mel Brooks gets his laughs. His ultimate excuse is that he gets them.

But what was the ultimate excuse for *Zardoz,* in the same year? It is full of intrinsically comic ideas which do not turn out to be funny. Perhaps they are not meant to. It is hard to tell what John Boorman, who both wrote and directed it, does intend.

There are big production values in *Zardoz*, but perhaps

The trade union of science-fiction writers is the Science Fiction Writers of America. Each year it gives "Nebulas" for the best novel, short story and so on of the year, and in the early 1970s it decided to add an award for Best Dramatic Production. The first feature film honored was *Soylent Green*; the second, *Young Frankenstein*.

The Nebulas have made as much trouble for SFWA as all the tyrannical editors and rapacious publishers in the world put together, but the dramatic awards set a new high in aggravation. To honor the writers of *Soylent Green* properly, three awards had to be given, not one, and the hand-crafted trophies cost several hundred dollars some members were reluctant to spend. Two years later, *Young Frankenstein* caused even more trouble. When someone from Mel Brooks's staff was invited to come and receive the trophy a secretary said, "Listen, just mail it to us." The *Young Frankenstein* award is what caused the SFWA membership to vote to abolish it again . . . just in time to be unable to give one to *Star Wars*.

—FP

they are not big enough—Pauline Kael thought that one of its troubles was that it was a five million dollar movie that had to be brought in for a million four. (She calls it "discothèque H. Rider Haggard.") But it has worse troubles than that.

The story: In the year 2293, women run the world. The price they have paid for their mastery (or mistressy) is that they have given up their sexuality and their capacity for love. Out in the marches, beyond the great force screen that protects these Eternals, lives a slave population of Brutals who include real, studsy males. A great flying stone god-head urges the Brutals to revolutions, and spits weapons through its stone teeth to help the fight along. One of the characters is a sort of policeman, Zed, played by Sean Connery—or rather, the character is Sean Connery, playing the same character he always plays, but the people in the film address him as "Zed". He disrupts the placid matriarchy. The guns help, but his ultimate weapon is simply his own jock body, displayed in a loincloth. The swooning female Eternals rediscover sex. They join with Zed to exterminate the surviving Eternal males (and all of the females that won't go along with the new regime, too). A new hybrid race, fathered by Brutals and mothered by Eternals, shows the way to a happy future.

Or so John Boorman wants us to believe. It is hard to believe anything about *Zardoz*. Even the title. ("Zardoz" is the name of the mysterious flying head. Remember, one of the projections the Wizard of Oz visited on Dorothy and her sidekicks? Wizard of Oz = Zard Oz, get it?) But the film has its worshippers. One of them is Philip Strick, who knows too much about both science fiction and film to be discounted; he calls it an "extraordinary achievement. . . although the science-fiction fans in general disliked it intensely."

If you believe that the function of science fiction film, or one of its functions, is simply to display pretty images on the screen, then perhaps *Zardoz* really is an extraordinary achievement. Parts of it are dazzling. It has an optic computer that glitters like the brightest gems the world has ever seen. It jumbles brilliant color and stark misery together to stir the senses; *2001*'s light show is no more colorful.

On the other hand, if you believe that the function of science fiction, or one of its functions, is to make the audience think, then you can understand why the fans detested it. *Zardoz* is simply not to be taken seriously, not for one picosecond. Not in its details. (How come the Eternal women never happened to be turned on by studsy Brutals before? What exactly is the flying head?) Not in its overall thrust, which, if it has one, seems to be that it is better to be a jock than a genius.

It would not have taken much to convert all the visual magic of *Zardoz* into a story that satisfied the audience's intelligence and stirred it to think. If Boorman had had the wisdom of Woody Allen, he could have hired any of a hundred science-fiction writers to supply the internal logic the story does not have. He might not have had to go that far. Perhaps it might have required no more than a decision by him that internal logic and plausibility *mattered*.

Yet Strick goes on to call it "a luminous and compassionate exploration of what, without our realizing it, has for too long been regarded as unexplorable." (3) How can views differ so?

There is one possible explanation. It rests on that difference between print and film science fiction which has been at the root of so many disagreements. Sense or senses, which should take pride of place?

—But wouldn't it be loverly if we could have both?

FILMOGRAPHY
ZARDOZ (Fox, 1974, U.S.A.) 105 mins.

Producer/director/script, John Boorman; production designer, Anthony Pratt; editor, John Merritt; special effects, Gerry Johnston; music, David Munrow; camera, Geoffrey Unsworth.

Cast: Sean Connery (Zed); Charlotte Rampling (Consuella); Sara Kestelman (May); John Alderton (Friend); Niall Buggy (Arthur Frayn); Sally Anne Newton; Bosco Hogan.

1975 brought three new science-fiction films, all of them distinguished by being highly controversial: *Rollerball, The Stepford Wives* and *A Boy and His Dog*.

Norman Jewison's *Rollerball* could easily have earned an XXX rating, if the Code measured the pornography of violence rather than sex. Its cast suffers every insult to which flesh is susceptible. If they are not run over by motorbikers, they are smashed by a cestus. If they are not deliberately dehelmeted and skulled, they are burned alive. And all this violence, we are told, is good for us.

The story takes place in the year 2018. Wars between nations are over. They were replaced years before by wars among great corporations; but those, too, are now history. The Game has taken over. The shadowy rulers of the world are The Game's executives, and their purpose in creating and running The Game is to provide an outlet for the common man's need for violence.

The Game combines the most violent features of football, motorcycle racing and Roller Derby, and the world's champion gamester is James Caan. He is not only at the top of the charts, he is well content to be there—he is doing the Lord's work, after all, even though for unclear reasons it has meant that he must divorce his beloved wife and take all subsequent sexual pleasure with a series of rent-a-chicks supplied by the executives. There is no blemish anywhere in his world, until the chief executive tells him that, for the good of The Game, he is going to have to retire.

Things go downhill for Caan after that. The rules of The Game are constantly changed on him, so that there are no more penalties for anything, including cold-blooded murder. His buddies are decimated. One becomes a living vegetable, kept breathing as a brainless hulk on a machine until Caan himself elects to pull the plug. The climax of the film is one great superbowl of a Game in which every player on both teams is destroyed, except Caan himself. Sole survivor on the track, bearing the chrome-plated cannon ball that is their puck, he hesitates before the boxes where the cowed executives tremblingly await his next move. It is like that moment in *Spartacus* when the black gladiator, having spared Kirk Douglas, hesitates before the nobles and then swarms futilely and heroically up the wall to attack them. Caan doesn't. He tosses the puck into the goal and skates away. It is a highly symbolic act.

But what, exactly, does it symbolize?

In fact, what is *Rollerball* itself? Is it a cold-blooded commercial exploitation of the sado-masochist violence-freak market? Or is it a tract for humanism, on the side of the angels? William Harrison, who wrote both the original short story and the screenplay for the film, is a creative writing professor at the University of Arkansas. He tells his students that he is unhappy with the film. After he turned in the script, he took the money and ran; what happened after that is not his doing. What happened after that, he says, changed a story that deplored violence into a film that celebrates it. Dr. Betty Hull, who also teaches creative writing (as well as science fiction and film) thinks the film is high-principled and commendable, although she is displeased with that fraction of the audiences who seem to draw the opposite message.

Rollerball is unmistakably a tract for peace, but what troubles me is the way some people in its audiences react. They yell with delight every time an opponent is creamed, and toward the end they begin yelling with just as much delight when it's a member of their own team that gets it. I wouldn't like to meet any of those people in a dark alley.

—Elizabeth Anne Hull (5)

It is not really clear that violence (or sex, for that matter) on the screen is much of a social evil. The intuitive assumption is that seeing it done will lead people to do it, but the only controlled studies seem to show that that does not happen. Nevertheless, *Rollerball*'s mingy-mouthed "message" is an affront. Whatever effect it may have on an audience's behavior, it certainly numbs their sense of shock in the film itself, so that one of the most repugnant acts shown does not deal with the repetitious mutilation of people. It is a scene in which some drunken party-goers stagger into a grove and deliberately burn down the trees with flame pistols.

Rollerball's brief sermons between acts of mayhem are not what the film is about. The mayhem is what the film is about. It is exactly parallel to the average Times Square porno flick. *Deep Throat* pauses between its complicated copulations to give the audience a chance to recharge for the next bout. *Rollerball*'s intermissions are on the same design. *Rollerball* cannot be seen as a cautionary tale about some possible future world in which many viewers delight in watching butchery. That world is here, and *Rollerball* exploits it. . . . And yet—

And yet, if one of the purposes of science fiction is to make people think, then *Rollerball* does achieve that purpose for at least some of its audiences. It demands discussion, and it gets it.

FILMOGRAPHY
ROLLERBALL (United Artists, 1975, U.S.A.) 129 mins.

Producer/director, Norman Jewison; script, William Harrison from his story; production designer, John Box; art director, Robert Laing; editor, Antony Gibbs; special effects, Sass Bedig, John Richardson and Joe Fitt; music, Andre Previn; camera, Douglas Slocombe.

Cast: James Caan (Jonathan E.); John Houseman (Bartholomew); Maud Adams (Ella); John Beck (Moonpie); Moses Gunn (Cletu); Pamela Hensley (Mackie); Ralph Richardson; Shane Rimmer; Barbara Trentham.

Released at almost the same time, the 1975 *The Stepford Wives* seems also to offer two contradictory messages. At one level, it suggests that suburban husbands view their wives as no more than convenient sources of housekeeping, child-rearing and sex. At another, it seems to say that that's all they're really good for, anyway.

In well-to-do Stepford, the husbands are unhappy because their wives are turning to women's lib and generally disturbing the placid comfort of their homes. They form a club, the Men's Society, and hatch out a plan. One of their members, Dale Coba (Patrick O'Neal) used to work in Disneyland. His idea is to build Animatronic duplicates of the wives, get rid of the originals and live happily with the replacements. It all works out very well for the husbands until a new neighbor, Joanna (Katharine Ross) discovers what is going on. She fights back; the men win and she too is made tractable.

The novel is by Ira Levin, better known for *Rosemary's Baby*. William Goldman wrote a faithful enough adaptation, but the film is tepid.

It did, however, succeed in giving offense to a lot of people concerned in the womens' rights movement. In Levin's novel, the difference between live Joanna and the machine others came across clearly, by internalizing Joanna's reactions. In Ryan Forbes's film, you see only what they do, not what they think. Pauline Kael said, "There isn't a hell of a lot of difference between Joanna and the robot housewives right from the start," and called the film "degrading".

I dislike *The Stepford Wives* for reasons that go beyond its being a cruddy movie; I dislike it for the condescension implicit in its view that educated American women are not responsible for what they become.

—Pauline Kael (4)

〜〜〜〜〜〜〜〜〜〜〜〜〜〜〜〜〜〜〜〜〜〜〜〜〜〜

FILMOGRAPHY
THE STEPFORD WIVES (Columbia, 1975, U.S.A.)
115 mins.
  Producer, Edgar J. Sherick; director, Bryan
Forbes; script, William Goldman from the novel by
Ira Levin; editor, Gene Callahan; music, Michael
Small; camera, Owen Roisman.
  Cast: Katharine Ross (Joanna); Paula Prentiss
(Bobby); Peter Masterson (Walter); Nanette New-
man (Carol); Tina Louise (Charmaine); Patrick
O'Neal; Carol Rosson; William Prince.

〜〜〜〜〜〜〜〜〜〜〜〜〜〜〜〜〜〜〜〜〜〜〜〜〜〜

There were similar reactions to another 1975 film, *A Boy and His Dog,* brought to the screen by L. Q. Jones from Harlan Ellison's award-winning science-fiction story.

A Boy and His Dog is a post-holocaust film, laid in the year 2024. The surface of the Earth has been burned nearly sterile, and the only inhabitants are starving, looting barbarians. A few well-to-do survivors have high-technology underground retreats, but their existence is equally precarious and the shelters are run in a regimented style. The Boy is a wanderer. His companion is the Dog, and the two have the curious capacity to communicate with each other by telepathy. In the team's adventuring about the world they encounter a girl from the underground, who invites them below. But the pair are not happy there. They take the girl back to the surface. Then, running short on food, the Boy kills the girl and serves her to the Dog.

A Boy and His Dog is controversial, at least partly because Harlan Ellison is. Ellison has been a highly visible part of the science-fiction community since he was a teenaged fan, and the film arises from that community. It was financed, to a small degree, by money raised from science fiction fans at a convention, and its first showing, in a rough cut that the available projectors could not well handle, was at the World Science Fiction Convention in Washington, D.C., in 1974. When it was released the following year its runs were short in commercial theaters, perhaps as much because it was not accompanied by the sort of saturation advertising that has converted many low-budget films into box-office triumphs as for any flaw in the film itself. What is more surprising is that it created so little interest in the science fiction community itself.

But the reception given to all three films suggests the attainment of a sort of maturation plateau in science fiction. Each was controversial, *Rollerball* for its violence, the other two for their sexist aspects. What was noteworthy was that they were disparaged or praised on their merits, and not simply dismissed because they were representatives of that unimportant genre called ''sci-fi''.

~~~~~~

FILMOGRAPHY
A BOY AND HIS DOG (LQJaf Films, 1975, U.S.A.)
89 mins.

Producer, Alvy Moore; d rector, L. Q. Jones; script, L. Q. Jones from the novella by Harlan Ellison; production designer, Ray Boyle; editor, Scott Conrad; special effects, Frank Rowe; music, Tim McIntire; camera, John Arthur Morrill.

Cast: Don Johnson (Vic); Susanne Benton (Quilla June); Tim McIntire (Blood's Voice); Alvy Moore (Dr. Moore); Jason Robards (Lew); Tiger (Blood the Dog); Helen Winston; Charles McGraw.

~~~~~~~~~~~~~~~~~~~~~~~~~~~~~~~~~~~~~~~

On sum, I think *A Boy and His Dog* is quite a good film. I do not like the sexist aspects of it, which are L. Q. Jones's. I despise his last line. I think it's in very bad taste; it destroys the character of the dog; it's not the last line in the story, and I find it really repellent and offensive. He loved it, and audiences seem to love it—the kind of audience I despise.

After the girl is dead, to save the dog's life he has had to cook the girl and serve parts of her to the dog. *He* has not eaten any—it very specifically said in the story that he hadn't. And he says, "She asked me if I knew what love is. Well, I know what love is—a boy loves his dog." That's the last line of the story.

Well, in the film, after they're walking away from the smoldering fire and you know that they've cooked and eaten the girl, the kid says to the dog, "I don't know why she got all mushy over me." And the dog says, "She may not have had particularly good judgment, but she sure had good taste." Now, that's a line male-chauvinist asshole audiences roar at. I resented the hell out of that line, and tried to get L. Q. to change it. He wouldn't change it. He did change a lot of sexist lines that were in it earlier, but I had to come up with the money, because he had no money to re-loop them. I went to a convention and sold hundreds of frames of the movie—three frames for ten dollars—and I brought the money back and dumped all these dollar bills on his desk and said, "Here. Now take it back to Ryder Sound Studios and throw it back on the spools."

—Harlan Ellison (6)

Logan's Run (1976) also came straight out of the science fiction community. It was based on the novel by William F. Nolan and George Clayton Johnson, both straight out of science fiction. Unfortunately the script writer, David Zelag Goodman, and the director, Michael Anderson, had less respect for the purity of the science-fiction concept. The novel was not terribly deep. Even so, the film trivializes it.

Logan's Run shows a society in which the problem of population is solved by killing off everyone over the age of 25. (In the novel, it was 30.) The liquidation is disguised as a sort of razzle-dazzle "ascension" into a more glorious state, and most people appear to fall for the fraud. Those who don't are captured and put away by the "Sandmen", one of whom is the film's protagonist. He reaches his own termination and decides to try to escape. Unfortunately, there is nothing to escape to, except ruined and empty cities. He returns to civilization, tricks a great gaudy computer into blowing itself up and thus changes the world—to what, we are not told.

FILMOGRAPHY
LOGAN'S RUN (MGM, 1976, U.S.A.) 118 mins.

Producer, Saul David; director, Michael Anderson; script, David Zelag Goodman from the novel by William F. Nolan and George Clayton Johnson; production designer, Dale Hennesy; editor, Bob Wyman; special effects, L.B. Abbott; music, Jerry Goldsmith; camera, Ernest Laszlo.

Cast: Michael York (Logan); Jenny Agutter (Jessica); Richard Jordan (Francis); Roscoe Lee Browne (Box); Farrah Fawcett-Majors (Holly); Peter Ustinov (Old Man).

Michael Anderson is one of the best of the uncelebrated directors; his *The Dam Busters* was among the most satisfying (and most successful) of British World War II films. He does not appear to be comfortable with science fiction, and is probably at least partly to blame for the lackluster film of *1984*, which he also directed. Nevertheless, *Logan's Run* has adequate performances, and some really spectacular special- effects scenes, and it was a great success commercially, leading to a (very poor) brief television series and a number of tie-in novel sequels.

H. G. Wells got his worst film adaptation ever in 1976, with Bert Gordon's production of *Food of the Gods,* a tedious film which retained little of Wells and substituted typical quickie Hollywood silliness in its story line. Almost as bad was *The Land That Time Forgot* (1975), Kevin Connor's adaptation of one of the few non-Tarzan stories by one of science fiction's best known writers, Edgar Rice Burroughs, ever to reach the screen. (The script was partly written by Michael Moorcock, but shows none of his inventiveness and color.) Much better, but rather strange, was the film version of Walter Tevis's novel, *The Man Who Fell to Earth* (1976) directed by Nicholas Roeg from a script by Paul Mayersberg. Tevis, an English professor, has written a number of science-fiction stories (*The Ifth of Ooth,* etc.) and such box-office successes as *The Hustler.* The film of *The Man Who Fell to Earth* is not much like any of Tevis's other works; it is low-key and somewhat ambiguous. David Bowie's performance of the androgynous alien who comes to our planet to ask for help is the only one that matters in the film, and it is an acquired taste. Not all audiences responded to it. *The Man Who Fell to Earth* might have been an event in any less crowded year, but in

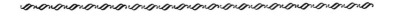

No round-up of the 1970s would be complete without a mention of Roger Corman, although to be sure he got his start in the mid-Fifties, at Samuel Z. Arkoff's American International Pictures. The 1950s were the era of Grade B sci-fi flicks, but those made by AIP were generally something less. Corman learned, and continued the tradition. AIP made money on grosses that would not have covered the advertising budget on a "real" picture, so Corman's *The Monster from the Ocean Floor* (1954) cost less than $20,000. It brought in $200,000. In 1956 he made *The Day the World Ended* for about $70,000; it earned almost half a million. While at AIP he produced and/or directed such notable sf films as *I Was a Teenage Werewolf* (1953), *The Attack of the Crab Monsters* (1957), and a successful series of films loosely based on Poe stories starring Vincent Price. Science fiction became less important in the releases of New World Pictures, the company Corman formed after leaving AIP, but one sf film, *Deathrace 2000* (1975), cost about half a million and returned rentals of almost ten million. Since *Deathrace*, Corman has increased his budgets, producing the unsuccessful *Battle Beyond the Stars*, among others.

1976 it barely had time to get out and make back its production costs before it was brushed aside.

One of the attractive commercial traits of science fiction is its longevity. Novels published twenty-five, fifty or even more years ago appear in new editions and reach substantial new audiences every year. Sometimes they reach the same audience all over again, as persons who read a book as teen-agers buy a copy to read it again in mature years. The audience for science fiction films continues in the same way. As new viewers are recruited, they hear of the existence of a *Forbidden Planet* or an *Invasion of the Body Snatchers* and seek them out. Tens or hundreds of thousands of people will go to see the same film over and over again; word of mouth and repeat viewing contribute substantially to sf film audiences. For the films of 1975 and 1976 that slow process did not have time to work. When a supernova explodes, the light of all the other stars in a galaxy is drowned out; and in 1977 the Big Bang of science fiction films arrived.

SOURCES

1. Fleischer, Richard. From an interview with the authors, May 1979.
2. Harrison, Harry. From a panel discussion at *Seacon,* Brighton, England, September 1979.
3. Strick, Philip. From *Science Fiction Movies,* Octopus Books Ltd., London, 1976.
4. Kael, Pauline. From *Kiss Kiss Bang Bang,* Little, Brown & Co., Boston, 1968.
5. Hull, Elizabeth Anne. From talk given at Tulsa, Oklahoma SF convention, July 1979.
6. Ellison, Harlan. From a taped interview with the authors, January 1979.

Chapter 7

Hyperspace, Hyper-Grosses, Hype

Never in the history of Planet Earth was there a film like *Star Wars*. Its box-office grosses passed $800,000,000. It made back its production cost in its first test release, in only 25 scattered theaters. The sales of *Star Wars*-related merchandise almost equaled the box office—even though for its first high-volume Christmas sales season the merchandise did not yet exist, so millions of kids found empty boxes, and an IOU from the manufacturers, under their Christmas trees. The album of its *score* grossed $20,000,000. It is the first film in history whose dollar income can be described as a substantial fraction of a *billion*. Then there was *Close Encounters of the Third Kind*, almost as dazzling a moneymaker and something like a theological revelation besides. *Star Wars* by itself could have been a fluke—startling, but discountable as a million-to-one miracle. Two such films in a row convinced the movie magnates. The floodgates fell open and the projects burst forth. Paramount dusted off dead *Star Trek,* hooked the electrodes to its neck and brought it back to life. Long-stalled *Superman* and *Buck Rogers* were rushed to the screen. Secret 007 was pushed into sci-fi in *Moonraker.* TV could not be left out and, though the *Battlestar Galactica* series died of its own wretched mindlessness, *Mork and Mindy* topped the charts. Even the multiply written and never produced *Martian Chronicles* of Ray Bradbury made it to filming at last, though only as a television miniseries. English and Italian film-makers got the fever and rushed multi-million-dollar exploitations before the cameras and into export. In the two years after *Star Wars* big budget science fiction productions were popping up at the rate of nearly one a month. The fans who used to grub through the movie listings for anything resembling science fiction suddenly had a bewildering cornucopia of offerings to choose among. The audiences who didn't like sf began to have trouble finding a theater showing something that was not.

Lucas and Spielberg did not create the science fiction film market. It was growing, growing, growing for decades before their films went into release. What they did was to make it clear that no studio, producer or star could afford to ignore science fiction any more. Ever. Money talked. When the chorus of dollars reached the hundreds of millions, it screamed.

Star Wars caught everybody by surprise, even the man who had made it. George Lucas thought it might gross $16,000,000 or so, maybe half again as much if they were very lucky. Making it for $9,000,000 promised a pleasant little profit. But, as all the world knows, his guess on the grosses was wrong by more than an order of magnitude.

Star Wars was not Lucas's first attempt at science fiction, but *THX 1138* hadn't made it. He then turned to the nostalgia of the 1960s, when he had been a teen-ager, and produced *American Graffiti,* and that made it big. Even before *American Graffiti* was released, in August 1974, the industry talk was hot enough so that Lucas could name his own project. He named *Star Wars.*

Star Wars takes place, Lucas says, in "a galaxy far away and long ago." Why in the past rather than the future? Because Lucas did not want it to seem like conventional science fiction. He described it, in a pre-release interview, as a sort of spaghetti Western in space.

The story line of *Star Wars* hardly needs telling, it has been told in so many forms before. The once and future Luke Skywalker pulls the Sword from the Stone (this time the sword is photonic, and gives him command of The Force) with the help of the local Merlin (played by Alec Guinness), and for the sake of his Guinevere (Princess Leia) defeats the Black Knight (Darth Vader) with the assistance of his Round Table and assorted ensorcelled aides (including a teddy-bear Wookie and a couple of charming robots). T. H. White told that story about Camelot, but even then it was already old. It is the simplest and oldest story there is, because at root it is only the story of fighting Evil for the sake of Good. *Star Wars* wastes no time in trying to explain *why* one side is Evil and the other Good. The same script could be played from the other side, as war stories always can. The Bad Guys are defined as the enemy, and the enemy is always defined as the Bad Guys. There is nothing to learn about the nature of Evil from *Star Wars,* in spite of Obi Wan Kenobi's mystic preachments (coming from the living mouth of Alec Guinness). There is nothing to learn about science, either, in spite of the wondrous technology the film displays. If one defines ''space opera'' as that which exploits the staggering vastness of future machines and space settings without consideration of plausibility or science, then *Star Wars* is purest *Thrilling Wonder Stories* corn. If one defines pornography as that which exploits the sensuality of human beings without concern for their identity as persons, then it is purest porn. It is county-fair cotton candy. It does not contain a trace of the minimum daily requirement of any vitamins or minerals at all . . . but, oh, how sweet it is! It is *fun.* It is everyone's favorite ten-year-old comic book, but bigger than life and displayed in blazing, sense-saturating actualization.

Star Wars is what literary-critics call a "pastiche", meaning that it is made up of borrowings. The skeletal sandworm is from *Dune*. "The Force" is the same sort of mystic intervention as E. E. Smith's Lens. The immense, corrupt Galactic Empire owes something to Asimov's *Foundation*. The robots are close descendants of *Forbidden Planet's* Robby (who in turn derives from Kuttner and Asimov). The great machine corridors and vertical shafts resemble those of the Krel, again in *Forbidden Planet*. The space combat not only looks like scenes from air-war films of the past but was actually made by animating spaceships, frame by frame, over such film-strips. The repeated attacks on the Death Star at the film's climax might almost have been made in the same way from the conclusion of the World War II bomber film, *The Dam Busters*. Sometimes the borrowings are specific and literal, of the sort that in music are called "quotations". Sometimes they are general, from an entire class of story. Taken together, they constitute very nearly the whole of *Star Wars*. The triumph of *Star Wars*, what makes it truly a masterpiece of its kind, is that Lucas and his close associate Gary Kurtz orchestrated all these things together magnificently. Star Wars is not Bach, but it is at least Offenbach. It delights.

What is most delightful is the superb special effects, achieved by a Kubrick-like attention to every detail and frame. Money was spent open-handedly where it was needed. Intelligence filled in when the money ran out. The famous space-bar scene is a compromise. The original designer of monstrous aliens could not deliver them all, and Kurtz had to send out for five-and-dime Hallowe'en masks to complete the costuming. Lucas said to Michael

Pye and Lynda Miles, "The fact is that we didn't have the money, and the key to special effects is time and money. I had to cut corners like crazy. I cut scenes left and right. And I cut out over 100 special effects shots. The film is about 25 percent of what I wanted it to be." (3)

But it was the right 25 percent. The economies do not show, not in a single frame.

The title *Star Wars* was an insurance policy . . . we calculated that there are something like $8 million worth of science fiction freaks in the USA, and they will go to see absolutely anything with a title like *Star Wars*.

—George Lucas (1)

Star Wars is full of throwaway bits, so that it rivals *2001* in repeat viewings. If you missed Frank Herbert's sandworm the first time you saw it, you notice and appreciate the distant skeleton in the desert the second time, or the tenth. When the Wookie cries out wordlessly, Jay Kay Klein says that on the fourth or fifth viewing he was able at last to distinguish words: it is calling, "Mama!" However bizarre its events, however eclectic its sources, *Star Wars* comes together as a pleasing whole. Perhaps it reflects the character of its makers, Lucas and Kurtz. One of the amazing things about this amazing team is that they not only paid the people who worked for them but overpaid them. They took money out of their own shares and handed it over to those actors and technical people who they thought deserved bonuses. Have any other producers in the history of the industry done that? Fifty-year Hollywood veterans scratch their heads, trying to come up with a single name.

(In creating the sound track for *Star Wars*), the approach was basically this: The characters were outlined, of course, in the script, but for the robot R2, for example, there were no lines. The script would occasionally say, "R2 makes a sound here, indicating he's happy." Or, "R2 makes an angry noise." Only some sort of vague emotional connection was made at that point. The voice of the robot wholly came out of a long process, after the film was finished, of trying out different sounds in the context of the conversations in the film. It was picking sounds that had the right emotional envelope, that gave the right emotional feeling, without having any recognizable content.

I did read some basic texts on language, but I wouldn't define myself as an expert of any kind on it. I tried to learn how language as we know it is structured. What kind of descriptions there are of the kind of elements which become human speech. I listened to a lot of foreign languages, different kinds of speech—in particular the non-word sounds, the parts of our speech which are almost sound effects. Useful inspirations were the kinds of sounds babies made, because here you have an intelligent creature which has not yet learned a developed language; yet they're able to communicate a good deal. I imagined R2 as a small child that is just learning to talk. I worked on his language almost a word at a time. I'd start with a very tiny noise, and then I'd start connecting these noises. I produced a lot of phonemes, little bits of sounds, by trial and errors, and established lists of them: "These are all angry sounds. These are cute, sympathetic sounds; and here's a list of sounds that seem like they're informational phrases." I think that if you taped your tongue down and tried to talk you might end up sounding something like what I'm talking about. The Wookie is the same thing.

—Ben Burtt, Jr. (2)

STAR WARS (Fox, 1977)
Ben Kenobi uses telepathy to get past the Imperial troops, while R2D2 and C3PO look on.

FILMOGRAPHY

STAR WARS (Fox, 1977, U.S.A.) 121 mins.

Producer, Gary Kurtz; director/script, George Lucas; production designer, John Barry; art director, Norman Reynolds; editors, Paul Hirsch, Marcis Lucas, and Richard Chew; special effects supervisor, John Dykstra; special dialogue and sound effects, Ben Burtt, Jr.; music, John Williams; camera, Gilbert Taylor.

Cast: Mark Hamill (Luke Skywalker); Harrison Ford (Han Solo); Carrie Fisher (Princess Leia); Peter Cushing (Grand Moff Tarkin); Ben Kenobi (Alec Guinness); Anthony Daniels (C3PO); Kenny Baker (R2D2); Peter Mayhew (Chewbacca); David Prowse (Lord Darth Vader); Phil Brown; Jack Purvis.

ᘓᘓᘓᘓᘓᘓᘓᘓᘓᘓᘓᘓᘓᘓᘓᘓᘓᘓᘓᘓᘓᘓᘓᘓᘓᘓ

At the time that *Star Wars* came out there hadn't been any adventure science-fiction films in quite a while. We knew that if the picture was successful there would probably be some other product in the same line—which is the way the movie business functions. If only ten or fifteen per cent of it was any good it would be worth while to me, because I've always been a great science-fiction film fan and would like to see it all. That's sort of the way it turned out.

I'm sure that at some point several of the large pictures are not going to make any money. Then the industry's going to say, "Well, no one is interested in science fiction again." But that never was true, of course. The only criterion is whether a picture is good or not, has good characters and is interesting to see.

—Gary Kurtz (4)

ᘓᘓᘓᘓᘓᘓᘓᘓᘓᘓᘓᘓᘓᘓᘓᘓᘓᘓᘓᘓᘓᘓᘓᘓᘓᘓ

Such success could not fail to be followed up, and while *Star Wars* was still in early release a sequel was begun. Lucas had written his own script for *Star Wars*. For *The Empire Strikes Back* he made the excellent choice of Leigh Brackett, who combined solid contributions to the science-fiction pulps of the 1940s and thereabouts with screenplays for such memorable films as *The Big Sleep*. Brackett had cancer. She was terminally ill when she signed the contract, in November 1977, but finished and delivered the script shortly before her death the following year.

There was no trouble with financing for *The Empire Strikes Back*. If Lucas was only able to make *Star Wars* a quarter of what he intended, *Empire* was close to a hundred per cent.

Empire starts with Darth Vader combing the Galaxy for Skywalker and his chums and finally locating them on a planet of ice. He attacks; they escape, but they split up. Skywalker goes to a jungly sort of planet to receive advanced Jedi training from a super-guru named Yoda, who looks like an Edd Cartier illustration of a Hobbit and is actually played by a sort of Muppet. Han Solo and Princess Leia flee to a cloud city run by another new character, Lando Calrissian (the first black to show up in that galaxy long ago), where Skywalker joins them, Vader pursues them, and in a protracted battle involving both conventional armaments (i.e., light-sabers) and mystic tricks of the Jedi knights Vader tells Skywalker that he is the boy's father.

This seems like a swell plot gimmick. The trouble is, it also seems to be contradicted by Obi Wan Kenobi's earlier statement that Luke's father is dead. Is somebody lying? Is there some surprise development which can make the statement true without making a liar out of the essence of honor itself, Obi Wan? Wait and see. . . .

And it is all superbly well done, with the use of every special effect known to the studio technicians. There is stop-frame animation, painted-in animation, models of all sizes and degrees of function, painted backdrops blended with foreground action and computers to patch together half a dozen separate shots to make a seamless whole—not counting Frank Oz's Yoda.

But perhaps a hundred per cent is, after all, too much.

Empire's special effects have almost become the film. The audiences are beginning to spend as much time trying to guess how an effect was done as in allowing themselves to live in the action. Perhaps the direction is at fault. Because of his health and his determination to do only the things he really wants to do Lucas did not direct *Empire*. He turned that chore over to Irvin Kersher. But Lucas was there as Executive Producer.

In any case, *Empire* was, of course, an enormous success—close to a hundred-million gross in the first two months. If it was not *as* huge as its predecessor, well, nothing else ever has been, either.

∿∿∿∿∿∿∿∿∿∿∿∿∿∿∿∿∿∿∿∿∿∿∿∿∿∿∿∿

> People say, "How can you take *Star Wars* seriously?" I don't take it seriously. It's a real gas! I enjoy it. I even saw it in French once, and it's even better, somehow.
>
> —Harry Harrison (5)

∿∿∿∿∿∿∿∿∿∿∿∿∿∿∿∿∿∿∿∿∿∿∿∿∿∿∿∿

Star Wars lives on. It follows its principals wherever they go. When John Williams moved on to replace Arthur Fiedler at the Boston Pops, his first concert featured Bach, Fritz Kreisler, Isaac Stern in the second Wieniawski violin concerto—and personal appearances by See Threepio and Artoo Deetoo. It will probably follow all of us for years to come. Lucas and Kurtz tell us they intend a total of nine "Star Wars" movies, three cycles of three films each, of which the two already released are the first and second episodes of the second series.

∿∿∿∿∿∿∿∿∿∿∿∿∿∿∿∿∿∿∿∿∿∿∿∿∿∿∿∿

> The budget on *Star Wars* was actually a fairly low budget for the time it was made. It was one of the lowest budget pictures to come out that year, science fiction or otherwise.
>
> —Gary Kurtz (6)

∿∿∿∿∿∿∿∿∿∿∿∿∿∿∿∿∿∿∿∿∿∿∿∿∿∿∿∿

Ben Kenobi and Darth Vader cross light sabers.

FILMOGRAPHY
THE EMPIRE STRIKES BACK (Fox, 1980, U.S.A.)

Producer, Gary Kurtz; director, Irvin Kershner; script, Leigh Brackett and Lawrence Kasdan from a story by George Lucas; production designer, Norman Reynolds; art directors, Leslie Dilley, Harry Lange, and Alan Tomkins; editor, Paul Hirsch; special effects, Brian Johnson and Richard Edlund; sound designer, Ben Burtt, Jr.; music, John Williams; camera, Peter Suschitzky.

Cast: Mark Hamill (Luke Skywalker); Harrison Ford (Han Solo); Carrie Fisher (Princess Leia); Billy Dee Williams (Lando Calrissian); Anthony Daniels (C3PO); Frank Oz (Yoda); Kenny Baker (R2D2); Peter Mayhew (Chewbacca); Alec Guinness (Ben Kenobi); David Prowse (Darth Vader).

It would seem that that is going to be difficult to sustain, at least without getting into *Luke Skywalker Meets Godzilla* story lines. Perhaps the plan is real. Perhaps the concept was firm at the very beginning, and all questions will be answered, and perhaps there will even turn out to be some profound hidden agenda in it all, some hint of message or meaning. But it is certain that nothing of the sort appears in the first two.

If *Star Wars* had no message, then *Close Encounters of the Third Kind* was wholly message.

Close Encounters is not exactly science fiction. It is not exactly a "fiction" film at all, in the same sense that *Destination Moon* was not. The Pal film was a pre-enactment of an actual event that simply had not happened to occur yet. So is the Spielberg—or it is, at least, if you happen to be of the same faith as the film, and therefore believe in the reality of flying saucers and the imminence of real and open contact with visiting extraterrestrials.

For Ray Bradbury, *CE3K* was "a religious experience". For J. Allen Hynek, the former Air Force saucer-buster who became a convert and was retained as technical advisor to the film, it was a sort of documentary. Very little of the story was "made up". Almost every concept and bit of business, and some of the actual lines, were transcribed faithfully from actual reports of UFO-spotters around the world. Even the title is a technical term taken from the special vocabulary of UFOlogy.

The film opens with the basic Bermuda Triangle story, as it has been told over and over, with an invented addition. The flight of planes which disappeared off the southern Atlantic coast of the United States during World War II reappears in the southwestern desert, intact and empty.

CLOSE ENCOUNTER OF THE FIRST KIND—CE I
DEFINITION: A UFO in close proximity (within 500 feet) to the witness. . . .
CLOSE ENCOUNTER OF THE SECOND KIND—CE II
DEFINITION: A Close Encounter of the First Kind that influences the environment in some fashion, usually by leaving physical evidence of its presence or creating electromagnetic interference. . . .
CLOSE ENCOUNTER OF THE THIRD KIND—CE III
DEFINITION: A Close Encounter of the First or Second Kind with "occupants" or entities associated with it. This kind of UFO sighting most fires public interest and controversy. Over 1,200 alleged incidents of this type have been catalogued from all available sources by UFO researchers.

—Allan Henry
in *The UFO Handbook* (7)

Are these only fantasies? Emphatically, no, if we can believe the many reports. . . . Many reports of allegedly real experiences of just such encounters with occupants of UFOs . . . have come to me from many parts of the world. The events portrayed in the novel *Close Encounters of the Third Kind* were based in part on such actual reports. In particular, the appearance of the "extraterrestrials" in the novel were based on the most frequently reported features of such beings.

—J. Allen Hynek (8)

Only the pilots are missing. We then see a series of UFO phenomena occurring all over the world, at a great religious meeting in India and in small towns and cities around the U.S.A. Cars are paralyzed by failure of their electrical systems, while road signs and mailboxes jiggle madly. A house is invaded by UFO forces, spilling food out of the refrigerator, while a little boy wanders out to look at the alien and then disappears. Mysterious flaming lights zap across a highway, while drivers stop to stare. Everyone sees these things. No one will report them, not even the pilots and air traffic controllers who witness a radar incident; it is an article of the UFO faith that most sighters keep quiet, for fear of ridicule.

All these early scenes are drawn from actual UFO reports, and they are presented without any attempt to unite them, except as examples of Something Strange. Then the film begins to develop a plot. We follow one particular sighter, who has become obsessed with the need to draw, build or visit a strange-looking mountain. In one of the silliest scenes ever put on a screen, he runs out of his house like a madman, seeking trash, rubble, scoops of earth, any material at all to use to reconstruct this mountain, head-high in his living room. His wife thinks he has gone mad. So would most of us in similar circumstances, no doubt; but so persuasive is Spielberg's film, or so desperate is the need of audiences to believe, that hardly anyone gets up and walks out of the theater.

Of course, the film tells us that there is a reason behind his preposterous acts. The Aliens are making contact with a chosen few human beings. Their way of doing so is to imprint in their minds the image of this mountain. It is a hypnotic compulsion, and when the subjects discover that the mountain really exists (as they do because some hush-hush government activity is going on there, and civilians are being evacuated, which attracts the interest of the television news reporters) they all try to go there, in spite of the military's attempts to keep them away. And what they find is the landing site for the UFOs.

The rest of the film is one great, extended scene. First a clutch of tiny scout ships flash by. Then bigger, slower ships; and at last the immense Mother Ship lands and begins emitting strange musical sounds. Air Force scientists duplicate them electronically. Organized communication with the aliens has begun.

This is Spielberg's make-or-break scene, and he takes considerable risks in it. "Science" can't tell us much about what first communication with aliens is really like. It has never happened. But logic can, and all that we know suggests that it would be stumbling, inconclusive, and frustrating.

From the roof of the mother ship's central core, far above Neary, hung a cluster of odd-shaped leaves or petals spread out in a circle like the leaves of an artichoke. They seemed to encase a busy, fiery core in which lights came and went. . . .

Under the roof of the mother ship, encased by the gigantic petals, hung a kind of swarm of active, pulsating entities. They seemed to Neary, even from this distance, to be the UFOs with which he was now familiar, never at rest, shifting color, position, speed, shape. They vibrated to different rhythms as they shouldered in beside each other.

—Stephen Spielberg (9)

CLOSE ENCOUNTERS OF THE THIRD KIND (Columbia/EMI, 1977)
The frail crew of the mother ship confront human civilization head-on a
last.

FILMOGRAPHY
CLOSE ENCOUNTERS OF THE THIRD KIND
(Columbia/EMI, 1977, U.S.A.) 135 mins.

Producers, Julia and Michael Phillips; director/ script, Steven Spielberg; production designer, Joe Alves; art director, Dan Lamino; special effects, Douglas Trumbull; visual effects concepts, Steven Spielberg; music, John Williams; camera, Vilmos Zsigmond with Douglas Trumbull, William A. Fraker, Douglas Slocombe, John Alonzo, Laszlo Kovacs, Richard Yuricich, Dave Stewart, Robert Hall, Don Jarel, and Dennis Muren.

Cast: Richard Dreyfuss (Roy Neary); Francois Truffaut (Claude Lacombe); Teri Garr (Ronnie Neary); Melinda Dillon (Jillian Guiler); Carey Guffey (Barry Guiler); Bob Balaban (Interpreter Laughlin); Warren Kennerling; Philip Dodds; J. Patrick McNamara.

Spielberg's act of courage is to show it just that way. The film does not give very many clues to what is going on. To get them at all, the audience has to pay close attention—not many movie-makers would trust their audience for that. To put them together into some sort of comprehension, the audience must use its intelligence, and even fewer film people will risk *that*. Spielberg dares, and wins. The scene is a triumphant climax.

Regrettably, there is an anticlimax to follow it. The great ship opens its portals, and out march the lost child, the crews of the vanished Bermuda Triangle aircraft and half the rest of history's missing persons. The aliens reveal themselves, shadowily and briefly, as spindly, pale, childlike creatures. They invite a few of their chosen volunteers to join them on their trip back into space . . . and then are gone.

However, Spielberg did not exactly chicken out on giving a more tangible ending to the film. He simply decided that it was not needed. He shot only 135 pages of his 160-page script, and after the preview he cut out some of the scenes that he had shot and included in the first print.

He may have had a more commercial reason than appears, because in the summer of 1980 he shrewdly put back the cut scenes, added in some that had been left out and re-released the film as *Close Encounters of the Third Kind, The Special Edition.* It is not a new film. It is not even very different in any respect from the first release; some of the mad behavior of the contactees in the middle of the film has been (mercifully) shortened, and the ending has been opened up to give us a good look at the interior of the alien ship.

Considered as science fiction, *Close Encounters of the Third Kind,* in either version, has nothing to say that is not either a cliche or an absurdity.

However, that is not where the action is. *CE3K* is a triumphant affirmation of afaith. It is to UFOlogy what *The Sign of the Cross* was to the Christian religion. And, like *The Sign of the Cross,* it is a magnificent spectacle. Even an unbeliever cannot see that great final ship approach without a tingle of excited delight.

It is what comes after that that separates the sheep from the goats among the viewers. For the unbeliever, the aliens are a cop-out, blurring out of focus to conceal a lack of imagination, and the film stops just when, in showing the *consequences* of this contact, it might at last become inventive. For the saucerer, it stops just where it should; and the aliens are an obvious metaphor for a transcendantal reality.

In the long run, all of UFOlogy rests on faith. There is no evidence that is not anecdotal. To accept any of this evidence as real requires faith that at least some of the authors of the anecdotes are both truthful and themselves undeceived, for in all the tends of thousands of UFO reports there is a terrible lack of confirming physical evidence. When there is any at all, it is never unambiguous. Some of the best photographs have been shown to be (or were later confessed to be) fakes. Some of the most apparently trustworthy witnesses have later destroyed their own credibility. The very size of the number of reported Close Encounters argues against their reliability. With all those thousands of reported "visits" it is hard to believe that some one saucerite somewhere would not drop a shoelace, a used Kleenex, an exhausted wristwatch battery—some artifact, *any* artifact, that would un-equivocally show its alien origin. Nothing of that sort has ever been discovered.

But—absence of proof is not proof of absence. It is nearly impossible to prove any kind of negative. If there is no incontestable proof that Close Encounters have occur-red, there is also no proof that they have not. And so we come back to faith.

If your faith tells you that tens of thousands of sighters and contactees cannot all be either lying or wrong, then you can believe that flying saucers are real. If your faith tells you that, since a great many of them have been shown to be illusions or frauds, it is safe to dismiss them all, then you can believe that they are not. Exactly the same argu-ments apply to the supernatural religions, to the existence of ESP phenomena and to many political philosophies, and the world at large has come no nearer to resolving any of those disputes, either.

So it is pointless to discuss *Close Encounters* in terms of plausibility. UFOlogists would argue quite fairly that we cannot know what is plausible about creatures of whom we know nothing at all. *Close Encounters* is a magnifi-cently realized dramatization of a research discipline as carefully studied as astrology and as widely accepted as the belief in ghosts. It is true that the basic phenomena it describes are dismissed as untrue by most scientists. But only a century ago so were meteorites and ball lightning.

And in the eyes of the titans of the movie business, none of that mattered.

Whether Spielberg was cynic or consecrated believer was not important. What was important was the long lines at box offices all over the world. Even before either *Star Wars* or *Close Encounters of the Third Kind* were in the theaters, the word was out. They were *big*. Twentieth Century-Fox's stock jumped in the New York Exchange, because the financial world knew the studio at last had a real winner. Every producer, director, script writer and star in Hollywood began looking around for a similar winner of his own. The "$8 million worth of science fiction freaks" had multiplied, and the audiences were waiting. So Donald Cammell took a Dean Koontz novel about a computer that took over an automated home and raped the lady of the house in order to create the first machine-human hybrid, and made it into *Demon Seed*. Taylor revived H. G. Wells's *The Island of Dr. Moreau*. Ralph Bakshi came out of his *Fritz the Cat* underground to make the animated version of *Wizards*—all in 1977. By 1978 there was a new major science-fiction production every few weeks. Some were good. A few were spectacular; and one even made a convert out of Pauline Kael.

⟨≈≈≈≈≈≈≈≈≈≈≈≈≈≈≈≈≈≈≈≈≈≈≈≈≈≈≈≈≈≈⟩

I think the greatest film of our time is *Close Encounters*. I've said that many times now. It's one of the few philosophical films that's ever been made. It's a transcendental experience. You feel as if you've been changed forever, and for the good. You want to come out and say, "Yes! I love the human race! I love the universe, I want to go out there! Let's believe in ourselves as God's creations. Let's treat ourselves with reverence."
—Ray Bradbury (10)

Close Encounters—oh, my God, the second coming! Down comes this galactic chandelier and out comes the Pillsbury doughboy and says, "We're going to save your ass!" Very, very silly stuff.
—Harlan Ellison (11)

⟨≈≈≈≈≈≈≈≈≈≈≈≈≈≈≈≈≈≈≈≈≈≈≈≈≈≈≈≈≈≈⟩

The Invasion of the Body Snatchers (1978 version) is a perfect example of what is best about bad science-fiction movies. Bad science fiction can be good sci-fi. *Invasion* is *great* sci-fi. It does not trouble the intellect. But it scares you when it should, makes you gasp in shock when it wants to, holds your attention to the last frame, surprises you, startles laughs out of you and even warms you to the terrors and yearnings of its characters. It gives the same immediate pleasure as a grape NeHi gives a ten-year-old.

The Invasion of the Body Snatchers takes place in San Francisco, with a sort of prologue on an unidentified alien planet somewhere in space. Pictorially, the prologue is the most beautiful part of the film. We see filmy growing things filling an alien landscape. They slip and slide, and bubble up out of that world's atmosphere, through space, settling into the skies of our own Earth. In San Francisco they bloom into delicate red flowers which people discover and enjoy, and sometimes take home. This is a mistake. Once in your house, they become evil. They spawn ugly umber blooms, which grow into milkweed pods the size of a man. In fact, they turn out to contain men. Or women. Or children—or, at least in one case, a dog-human crossbreed. The pod creatures become the exact mental and physical duplicates of the nearest slumbering human being. When they are ripe, the human conveniently crumbles into dust and the surrogate emerges from the pod to take his place in the world. They are so close to the originals that only the nearest and dearest of the replaced victims can detect the change, and sometimes not even they. But a San Francisco public health inspector perceives what is going on, and tries to do something about it. One of the first victims is a jock dentist, the lover and roommate of the inspector's lab assistant. A psychiatrist friend, played by Leonard Nimoy, is brought in on the problem. He promises help—but turns out himself to be a pod-surrogate and part of the conspiracy. (As, one by one, does nearly every other character in the film.)

As the pod people grow more numerous and daring, they speed up their conquest. They appear openly in the streets, carrying pods to replace the few holdout humans in San Francisco. They ship pods by truck and sea all over the world; they meet planes at San Francisco International to convert their passengers into instant pods. The public health inspector and the girl battle against them with valor and intelligence—and a passel of first-rate special effects, as in the grand climactic scene where he destroys a nursery of pods in a spectacle of electric short-circuits and burning sheds. But he loses. In fact, we all lose, all us replaceable human beings. The end of the film tells us that there is no hope of survival for the human race—except as pod-created duplicates.

The whole thing is beautifully done, and when it is over the audience gets up from its seats in a good humor and exits, chatting about the film. What else can one ask of a sci-fi flick? Not much.

But if it were printed science fiction, in *Analog,* say, or in *The Magazine of Fantasy and Science Fiction,* the readers would ask a little more. The letter columns would be full of cranky questions: *Why* can the pods only replace humans when the humans are asleep? The script writer probably could have made up an interesting answer if he had seen any need for it. For a film audience, he did not perceive the need. Or how come one of the creatures was a fusion between dog and human, when nothing like that ever happened again? Or, if the dentist was one of the first to succumb, how did it happen that a garbage truck manned by doppelgangers was there to receive the crumbs of his model? How did the creatures communicate? By tele-pathy? Apparently yes, because they reached out to each other quickly and easily; but also apparently no, because they could identify normal humans only by surface clues. The creatures evidently remembered their ancestral lives on the dying planet; how? By what biological miracle did the human originals dry up and crumble as soon as the pods were hatched? Et any number of ceteras.

The answer to all these questions is the same. The scenes gave instant pleasure, like a child's shockingly sweet candies. The film-maker did not expect the audiences to ask embarrassing questions.

And yet in print science fiction those questions are among the keenest pleasures of reading. They are part of that wonderful bonus at the end of a really good science-fiction story, when the reader plays over the author's inventions in his mind. Could this ever be true? Has the author failed to see the implications of his story? Has he missed a critical contradiction? And—if all these tests are passed—then the reader carries the story on in his own head. That pleasure seldom exists with sci-fi. Sci-fi pleases the senses and stimulates the glands. But it is not likely ever to stir the intellect.

The novel from which both versions of the film were made was *The Body Snatchers,* by Jack Finney. Finney was a successful commercial writer of the 1950s and thereabouts, whose nearest present equivalent may be Michael Crichton. He wrote "bridge" science fiction, aimed at an audience of people who would not have been reading sf if they had known what it was that they were reading. Much of his work appeared in the big slicks, *Collier's* and *The Saturday Evening Post,* and he is on record that he doesn't think much of science fiction, doesn't like to admit that was what he wrote and won't even agree that he ever wrote any without an argument about the definition of terms. And in a sense he is right, since what he wrote is probably better diagnosed as sci-fi.

Inn *The Invasion of the Body Snatchers,* I was working specifically on creating sounds for the pod creatures—the pod births and the pod screams. There's a sort of ground line to all the things I've been working on in the last two years—*Star Wars, Body Snatchers* and *Alien*—of trying to get an emotional effect without using a recognizable sound, or one that seems human-produced. Something that sounds like it comes from an intelligent creature, yet did not relate to anything familiar—did not sound like a person, or a refrigerator motor. It had to have complexity, and seem to carry enough information to be intelligent. . . . In the *Body Snatchers*, the idea of the birth sequence was simply to give the feeling of birth taking place. All of the sounds in that sequence were organic sounds. They were derived, in many cases, from actual birth sounds. I recorded unborn fetuses with an ultrasonic microphone—the heartbeat in the placenta, the sound of fluid swishing through the veins.

—Ben Burtt, Jr. (12)

I saw (Don Siegel's version of *Invasion of the Body Snatchers*) many times. I always liked his original version, but I wanted to take that theme—to pay homage to the first one, and take the theme through a whole other series of variations and, using different characters, essentially go back to *some* of the key points. . . . We went back to Jack Finney's book and really studied a little bit more about the genesis of the pods—where they came from, how they drifted through space, what happened to people after they disintegrated. And that kind of suggests the whole garbage truck idea: how these things could be disposed of in a big city. How, in fact, the big city could be taken.

(I see my version as) sort of a sequel. Another rendition of the theme. I think the Kevin McCarthy character suggests a sequel when he says what were supposed to be the last lines of the first movie before they tacked on that ending. Banging the doors and running for twenty-two years, from the old movie right up to this one. He passes the torch to Donald Sutherland. Who drops it.

—Philip Kaufman (13)

FILMOGRAPHY
INVASION OF THE BODY SNATCHERS (United Artists, 1978, U.S.A.) 115 mins.

Producer, Robert H. Solo; director, Philip Kaufman; script, W.D. Richter from the novel by Jack Finney; production design, Charles Rosen; editor, Douglas Stewart; special effects, Dell Rheaume and Russ Hessey; special sound effects, Ben Burtt; music, Denny Zeitlin; camera, Michael Chapman.

Cast: Donald Sutherland (Matthew Bennell); Brooke Adams (Elizabeth Driscoll); Leonard Nimoy (Dr. David Kibner); Veronica Cartwright (Nancy Bellicec); Jeff Goldblum (Jack Bellicec); Art Hindle (Geoffrey); Kevin McCarthy (Running Man).

Even purer sci-fi, in fact sci-fi right out of the comic books, is *Superman*. It is garish and wholly unbelievable; what a surprise that it should also be rather endearing!

Superman is not only big and long, it is two films for the price of one; it is a double feature all by itself. Film Number One is a wedding cake of a movie. It contains endless vistas, enormous faces sitting in judgment, dazzling super-scientific gadgets. Its star is aging Marlon Brando, supported by aging Trevor Howard and other aging stars. If Samuel Goldwyn had ever produced a sci-fi super-spectacle, this first half of *Superman* would have been it. Film Number Two (which continues without interruption from the first) is *Batman* plus four years. That is, it is aimed at an audience of sixteen-year-olds rather than twelves. Film One is sci-fi. Film Two is not even sci-fi, it is comics.

It is gratifying that both parts work. It is also gratifying, and astonishing as well, that they work together, since they have so little in common. They do not even have the same actors. Superman in Film One appears as infant (later as child and youth), none of which are played by Christopher Reeve. None of the other actors in Film One survive into Film Two at all. (Not counting the odd ancestral recording found in a cave of ice.) Not even the *names* are the same, because Superman does not become Superman until Lois Lane christens him.

In fact, the dichotomy is so complete that the young Superman and the mature one do not seem even to have the same genes. Consider the evidence. What are Super-man's special traits? Everyone knows them: He is immensely strong; he can fly through the air; he is blindingly quick; he has X-ray vision. Do any of these traits show up in his parents? They do not. Obviously something funny has happened on the way from the planet Krypton.

FILMOGRAPHY

SUPERMAN (Warner Bros., 1978, Great Britain) 143 mins.

Executive producer, Ilya Salkind; producer, Pierre Spengler; director, Richard Donner; script, Mario Puzo, David Newman, Robert Benton from a story by Puzo, based on characters screated by Jerry Siegel and Joel Shuster, production design, John Barry; editor, Stuart Baird; director of special effects, Colin Chilvers; director of optical visual effects, Roy Field; director of mattes and composites; director of process photography, Derek Meddings; music, John Williams; camera, Geoffrey Unsworth.

Cast: Marlon Brando (Jor-El); Gene Hackman (Lex Luthor); Christopher Reeve (Superman/ Clark Kent); Ned Beatty (Otis); Jackie Cooper (Perry White); Glenn Ford (Pa Kent); Trevor Howard (First Elder); Margot Kidder (Lois Lane); Valerie Perrine (Eve Teschmacher); Terence Stamp (General Zod); Maria Schell (Bond-Ah); Phyllis Thaxter (Ma Kent); Susannah York (Lara); Jeff East (Young Clark Kent); Aaron Smolinski (Baby Clark Kent).

Some pretty funny things happened in the making of the film, too—at least they would have been funny if you didn't happen to be an investor. It was produced by the father and son team of Alexander and Ilya Salkind. They allowed a writer, David Michael Petrou, to stay with the film through all of its locations and travails and if his account of it all, *The Making of Superman, The Movie,* is anywhere near accurate, it must have been a riot. Everything took forever. There were times when a day's work produced four seconds of film. There were times when it produced none. Deadlines were rarely met. Authorities were divided—not only were there two Salkinds producing the film, but for a while there seemed to be two directors, neither of whom was sure what was going on. They began pre-production in Rome, built hundreds of thousands of dollars' worth of sets there, and then abandoned it all and moved to England to start from scratch again. Shooting in England took so long that the rented studio ran out of time; they had to tear down their sets, wait till another film was shot in the space, then rebuild them for another go. Casting was last-minute. They didn't have Christopher Reeve until five weeks before the cameras began to roll. They cast Keenan Wynn for the newspaper editor, Perry White, on the day they began shooting his scenes—five thousand miles away. He got to England so late that they rushed him before the cameras without making allowance for his age and jet lag and he collapsed; the part was open again, and they sent out an S.O.S. for Jackie Cooper. They spent months trying to find the right person for the young Clark Kent's terrestrial mother, then, in a burst of inspiration, Ilya Salkind gave it to Phyllis Thaxter (Phyllis Thaxter is his mother-in-law.). Before *Superman,* the Salkinds were best known for an unusual feat. They had made a film of *The Three Musketeers* and, when it was complete, discovered they had immensely overshot. They had four or five hours of usable film. Another producer might have toiled to reduce it to playable length, but they had a better idea. They snipped it in the middle, released the first half as *The Three Musketeers* and the second half, a little later, as the "sequel," *The Four Musketeers.* But both halves did big business, and they and everyone else involved made a fortune. There is a kind of intelligence at work in the Salkinds that one cannot help but respect; all the same, if you were going to make a movie of the making of *Superman,* you might want to cast their parts with Cheech and Chong.

Mario Puzo wrote the basic script for *Superman,* fresh from three high-powered successes in a row—both *Godfathers,* and *Earthquake.* If any writer in Hollywood had clout enough to get a film down his way, Puzo was it. Did that save his script from tampering? No. After Puzo had taken his money and gone away the rewrite teams came in. The earthquake sequence, so close to Puzo's own *Earthquake,* was added this time by someone else. (And in Los Angeles, on New Year's Day of 1979, an extra one was added as a real quake shook the Studio Theater while *Superman* was being shown. Patrons stayed in their seats, evidently figuring it was some part of Lex Luthor's plan.) (16) The silly device of rotating the Earth backward to reverse time and bring Lois Lane back to life was also added by someone else, and Puzo hated it. He called it "a writer's cheat on an audience. . . . If he can do that he can do anything."

I wrote the screenplay (of *Superman*), and then they got four or five other people to rewrite it. . . . There was a lot of dialogue I didn't like. I think I wrote part of the speech up in Krypton. They made it a little more high-flown, a little more pretentious. What happens is, you write a draft, then you have conferences, then you read stuff other people have done and you tell them stuff, and by the time you're finished, you don't know what's yours and what's not. The sequence I know is mine is the ballet sequence up in the sky. I had written that much more elaborately, where they fly over the Taj Mahal and other scenic wonders of the world. But I guess they ran out of money, so they settled. I was sitting there with someone, and I kept saying, "I didn't write that. I didn't write that." I think I said that a lot through the picture.

—Mario Puzo (14)

Perhaps it is the hordes of writers who trampled over the script that make it fall into disparate pieces. More likely it is a manifestation of Hollywood distrust for the audience. Some people in film seem to think that audiences will not sit still for a single story in a feature-length film: thus *2001* and even *Things to Come,* as well as *Superman.* It takes a consistency of theme to hold the pieces together, and the film of *Superman* doesn't have one. What it has is common knowledge. Everybody *knows* the story of Superman long before they enter the theater, and the two halves of the film are joined by everyone's childhood bubblegum.

Superman has been a piece of the common heritage since the 1930s. Philip Wylie's novel, *Gladiator* (1930) was about a man with superhuman strength, and it inspired two young science fiction fans, Jerry Siegel and Joseph Shuster, to create their own story about a man with superhuman everything. They sold the rights to a comic syndicate for pitiful money, and they sold them outright, so that when The Man of Steel became very large business the money was long spent and they could only watch from outside. (Forty years later the proprietors voluntarily gave them a sort of modest pension out of the profits.) Mort Weisinger, once editor of *Thrilling Wonder Stories,* took over the *Superman* comics; science-fiction writers like Kuttner and Bester wrote episodes, and *Superman* became the most successful comic series ever put on paper. Not just on paper. It ran as a series on radio and as a serial in the Saturday afternoon movie houses; Dave Fleischer made it into cartoon shorts in the early 1940s, and it lasted five years on the early television of the 1950s, and as daytime reruns ever since. (George Reeves played Superman in the TV series, and was so firmly identified with it that he couldn't get another job when the series ended; two years later he killed himself.) For four decades *Superman* has been everywhere you looked, even on the tee-shirts of school children, even as a Broadway musical, and so the great burden of explanation and tying threads together was lifted from the film. It does not have to say who Lex Luthor is, or why Superman conceals his identity under the cloak of the mild-mannered reporter from the *Daily Planet.* Everybody knows. All the film has to do is fill out the familiar notions and illustrate them with colorful detail.

> (*Superman*) is, surprise of surprises, a "woman's picture" on a peculiarly primal level. . . . "It's not so much how good-looking he is," sighed a friend. "It's the feeling that he can pick you up and carry you away. . . . He's so simple, so direct. No intellectual B.S. I'm so *sick* of all these men who've been through *est.* It's mental masturbation. They keep coming up with excuses not to get close to a woman, to take risks in any way. Superman takes risks all the time."
>
> —Patricia Goldstone (15)

And it surely does that very well. When, in the prologue, the three traitors are sentenced, their punishment is to be recorded for all eternity into a sort of super-silicon chip, a device that Cordwainer Smith might well have invented. Luthor's hideout under Grand Central Station *looks* like Grand Central Station, just as a twisted criminal master-mind like Luthor would have desired it. The mating flight of Lois Lane and Superman is joyous. If some of the plot turns (e.g., spinning the Earth backward to save Lois Lane) are dumb enough to make a cat puke, the signals have long been given that none of the film is to be *be-*

lieved. Star Wars was a naive film, and that was part of its strength. Watching it, you were invited to pretend that all this marvelous fairy tale was real and you were a part of it. *Superman* is far more cynical. It is a nostalgia trip, and part of the appeal of nostalgia is in the wry amusement at past innocence. But it all works. Christopher Reeve is the best Superman ever. In real life, almost as much as in the film: he can actually act, he comes of a high-powered family (father a poet, mother a newspaperman, sister an M.D., one brother an archaeologist, the other a Ph.D. at Yale) . . . and he is, of course, incredibly good-looking. However the Salkinds achieved it, they have given new life to the legend of *Superman*.

On the other hand, the film of *Buck Rogers* may well kill him off once and for all.

This is not easy to do, because for more than half a century Buck Rogers has been a winner. He came out of the heartland of science fiction where, known as Tony Rogers, he was the hero of two novelettes. Written by Philip Nowlan and Lt. Dick Calkins, they appeared in *Amazing Stories,* back when the magazine was young, as *Armageddon 2419 A.D.* and *Airlords of Han.* "Han" was not some planet far off in space. It was simply Japan. At least, it was the super-scientific and enlarged Japan the authors expected in the 25th century, by which time they supposed it would have conquered the world.

In the *Amazing* story, Tony Rogers fell asleep in a coal mine in the early 20th century and slept for five hundred years; when he awakes, he finds America ravaged by the oppressor. But he also finds patriotic guerrillas hiding out in the forests, refusing to surrender. He joins them, leads them and with them conquers the Asiatics. An alert editor for a comic syndicate saw this one, too, and so Tony, rechristened "Buck", became the hero of one of the longest-lived newspaper strips in history, as well as of a very successful kiddytime radio show in the 1930s. That didn't end it. Buck Rogers was as much a household name as Superman. For most of its lifetime, science fiction was defined in the vocabularies of the uninitiated as "that Buck Rogers stuff". Buck kept showing up in Saturday-afternoon movie serials and in endless Big Little Books.

What is most wrong with *Buck Rogers* as a movie is that it wasn't made to be one. It was made to be a TV series. Stringing together bits and pieces into a theater film was a good money idea—it is supposed to have grossed over $25 million, on an investment most of which was already written off against production costs for the television series—but it is a shabby film. The special effects designed to look good on the 21-inch screen look tacky in a movie theater.

FILMOGRAPHY
BUCK ROGERS (Universal, 1979, U.S.A.) 89 mins.

Executive producer, Glen A. Larson; producer, Richard Caffey; director, Daniel Haller; script, Glen A. Larson and Leslie Stevens; art director, Paul Peters; editor, John J. Dumas; special effects, Bud Ewing; music, Stu Phillips; camera, Frank Beascoechea.

Cast: Gil Gerard (Buck Rogers); Pamela Hensley (Princess Ardala); Erin Gray (Wilma Deering); Henry Silva (Kane); Tim O'Connor (Dr. Huer); Joseph Wiseman (Draco); Felix Silla (Twiki); Mel Blanc (Twiki's voice).

The story, on the other hand, looks equally tacky in both places. In a less crowded year, it might have seemed less trite and trivial; but it followed *Star Wars,* and half-good space spectacle had to be matched against very good space spectacle.

Exactly the same was true of *Battlestar Galactica.* In fact, the case was even worse. *Buck Rogers* at least had its origins in the heartland of early science fiction. The origins of *Battlestar Galactica* lay only in a hustle for bucks. It was shot for television, and the theater version is actually a cut (from three hours), blown up (to 35 millimeter) salvage job. If there is a worse way to make a movie, it is hard to think of it. John Dykstra's special effects are wasted on a wholly mindless plot. All it was meant to do was to introduce the characters for the television series that was meant to follow, and that's all it does—and rather dull, foreseeable characters they are.

It is impossible to take either *Battlestar Galactica* or *Buck Rogers* in any way seriously. Their makers did not intend seriousness. The two films illustrate the conviction of Universal (which produced them both) that, whatever the physical age of science fiction audiences, their hearts are childlike and their minds empty.

It is not entirely fair to judge these two by the standards of real films. They are admittedly tacked together ersatz, made up of a pinch of henbane, a touch of greed and a few reels of video tape. But the most unfair blow of all is that both of them made money.

In the year or two after *Star Wars,* there were half a dozen science-fiction films that did not rip it off. They didn't come because *Star Wars* had shown the way. They came along because the time was ripe for the exploration of some new science-fiction subjects in the movie theater. One natural subject was cloning, and it got its shot at the screen in *The Boys from Brazil,* with Laurence Olivier and Gregory Peck. Nazi Peck has cloned a bunch of duplicates of Adolph Hitler. Zionist Olivier finds out about it, and spoils the scheme. One of the good things about *The Boys from Brazil* is that it touches all its scientific bases; whether or not the thing could be done is far from certain, but at least it does not fly in the face of the laws of science by having the clones, e.g., emerge fully born with little moustaches. There is a lot more Nazi-hunting than science fiction in *The Boys from Brazil,* and not much need for special effects wizardry.

There is a lot more political propaganda than science fiction in *The China Syndrome,* but its plot comes right out of a 1939 *Astounding Stories.* It is the same story as Lester del Rey's *Nerves,* and also the same story as Three Mile Island, which conveniently for the producers took place just as the film was making its rounds of the theaters. *The China Syndrome* is a cautionary story; it is warning us of something that hasn't happened yet, but may be in the cards. It is also a sort of pre-documentary, in the same sense that *Close Encounters of the Third Kind* and *Destination Moon* were. Unlike them, the event it described began to happen twelve days after the film's premiere on March 16th, 1979. The bull's-eye hits in the picture are remarkable. *China*'s reactor had a defective pump that vibrated itself to destruction; Three Mile had two defective pumps that vibrated so badly they were stopped to prevent destruction. *China*'s accident involved a bad valve and a stuck gauge. So did Three Mile's. *China*'s near-meltdown threatened "an area the size of Pennsylvania." Three Mile's was *in* Pennsylvania.

Without any current-events relevance, but with a certain amount of charm, the Warner *Time After Time* joined Jack the Ripper to H. G. Wells's *Time Machine,* causing young H.G. himself to journey to present-day San Francisco when he discovers the Ripper has used his machine to evade justice. It has good effects and good acting, in a cast headed by Malcolm McDowell and Mary Steenburgen. It also had one of the bloodiest flash scenes ever put on a motion-picture screen, as we open a door onto a room that has just been redecorated with the Ripper's trademarks.

But the worst Jack the Ripper could do was not a patch on the handiwork of Ronald Shusett's *Alien.* A space ship of human beings (well, mostly human beings—one turns out to be a robot), in the course of exploring the Galaxy, finds an ancient space ship built by creatures who were not human at all. One of them survives and, in a series of bloody and terrifying encounters, attempts to take possession of the human ship. The story of *Alien* is a lot like the early work of A. E. Van Vogt, from his *Black Destroyer* and *Discord in Scarlet* period—a fact which did not escape the notice of Van Vogt, who requested payment from the producers. The story is not very complicated, though; it is simply the war between the human (and robot) crew and the protean Alien, who can appear in any form, in any place. The special effects are superb.

Alien was a great success—cost less than $15 million to make, returned (according to its producer, Ronald Shusett) over $100 million at the box office in its first year or so. What made it a success? It wasn't just the special effects or the terrifying Alien itself; it was something else, and thereby hangs a tale. *Alien* appeared to the accom-

FILMOGRAPHY

THE CHINA SYNDROME (Columbia, 1979, U.S.A.) 122 mins.

Producer, Michael Douglas; director, James Bridges; script, Mike Gray, T.S. Cook, and James Bridges; production designer, George Jenkins; editor, David Rawlins; special effects, Henry Millar Jr.; camera, James Crabe.

Cast: Jane Fonda (Kimberly Wells); Jack Lemmon (Jack Godell); Michael Douglas (Richard Adams); Scott Brady (Herman De Young); James Hampton (Bill Gibson); Peter Donat (Don Jacovich); Wilford Brimley; Richard Herd.

THE BOYS FROM BRAZIL (Fox, 1978, U.S.A.) 123 mins.

Executive producer, Robert Freyer; producers, Martin Richards and Stanley O'Toole; director, Franklin J. Schaffner; script, Heywood Gould from the novel by Ira Levin; production designer, Gil Parrondo; editor, Robert Swink; music, Jerry Goldsmith; camera, Henri Decae.

Cast: Gregory Peck (Josef Mengele); Laurence Olivier (Ezra Lieberman); James Mason (Eduard Siebert); Lilli Palmer (Esther Lieberman); Uta Hagen (Frieda Maloney); Steve Guttenberg; Rosemary Harris; John Rubinstein.

TIME AFTER TIME (Warner Bros., 1979, U.S.A.) 112 mins.

Producer, Herb Jaffe; director, Nicholas Meyer; script, Nicholas Meyer based on a story by Kearl Alexander and Steve Hays; production designer, Edward C. Carfagno; editor, Donn Cambern; special effects, Larry Fuentes and Jim Blount; music, Miklos Rozsa; camera, Paul Lohmann.

Cast: Malcolm McDowell (H.G.Wells); David Warner (Stevenson); Mary Steenburgen (Amy); Charles Cioffi (Lt. Mitchell); Andonia Katsaros; Patti D'Arbanville.

paniment of huge advertising budgets; its television commercial—the tagline was, "In space no one can hear you SCREAM"—was on every station, all the time.

There were, it seems, two lessons to be learned from the year 1977. One was that big-budget special-effects films like *Star Wars* could make a lot of money. The other was that you could make a lot of money in a quite different way with, apparently, any old kind of product at all.

> *Alien* . . . works on your nerves and emotions with the practiced hand of a torturer extracting a confession. The movie is terrifying, but not in a way that is remotely enjoyable.
>
> —David Denby (17)

ALIEN (Fox, 1979)
The derelict spaceship where the alien eggs are found.

◇◇◇◇◇◇◇◇◇◇◇◇◇◇◇◇◇◇◇◇◇◇◇◇◇◇◇◇◇

FILMOGRAPHY

ALIEN (Fox, 1979, U.S.A.) 124 mins.

Executive producer, Ronald Shusett; producer, Walter Hill, Gordon Carol, and David Giler; director, Dan O'Bannon; production designer, Michael Seymour; editor, Terry Rawlings; special effects, Brian Johnson and Nick Allder; music, Jerry Goldsmith; camera, Derek Vanlint.

Cast: Sigourney Weaver (Ripley); Tom Skerritt (Dallas); Veronica Cartwright (Lambert); Harry Dean Stanton (Brett); John Hurt (Kane); Ian Holm (Ash); Yaphet Kotto (Parker).

◇◇◇◇◇◇◇◇◇◇◇◇◇◇◇◇◇◇◇◇◇◇◇◇◇◇◇◇◇

In the *Star Wars* year of 1977 Twentieth Century-Fox had a second science-fiction iron in the fire.

The studio had, in a transient moment of somebody's enthusiasm, acquired a *Galaxy* novella by Roger Zelazny, called *Damnation Alley*. It was out of Zelazny's usual line of territory. There was no extra-terrestrial color in it, nor any of the cloudy heroic fantasy of, say, his "Princes in Amber" series. *Damnation Alley* was a straightforward adventure yarn. The time is the not very far future. The United States has been devastated in a nuclear holocaust. All the continent between the coasts is poisoned, horrid, inhabited by vicious enemies; and one man has to drive across it. Having bought the story, Fox of course began changing everything about it—threw in some giant insects and a couple of pretty girls, gave it a new title—the usual precautions Hollywood likes to take against anything surviving of an author's original inspiration. Then they filmed it.

Then they put it on the shelf—for a year.

Somehow the mixture didn't jell. Fox pondered whether it was worth while to spend the money to release it. The prevailing opinion was that it would just mean throwing good money after bad, and so it languished.

Then *Star Wars* happened, and somebody got an idea. *Star Wars* was sci-fi, and it was a certain bonanza. This other property, what-do-you-call-it, was also sci-fi. It was not in any other way very much like *Star Wars*.

But the audiences might not know that. So they changed the title back, and the TV experts were called in. They produced a commercial, and they played it on every channel for the opening. They spent about as much money on promotion as it cost to produce this low-budget turkey in the first place and, lo and behold, when *Variety*'s list of top-fifty grossing films came out that month, *Damnation Alley* was right up there near the top. Domestic rentals reached close to $20,000,000, and a joke began going around Hollywood:

Q. What is the definition of a "feature film"?

A. It is one of several elements which combine to make up a major promotion effort.

By 1980, almost every new film was spending a million dollars or more on TV commercials alone in the first weeks of release. The timing was important. If the film was bad, word of mouth would sooner or later kill it—but if the rataplan of TV commercials dragged hordes of people into the theaters in the first week, maybe even just in the first weekend, five or ten million dollars would come into the till before the word got around.

The producer of a film is not normally the person who spends the advertising money. That's done by the distributors, a fact which is fruitful of bad blood and lawsuits. Film distribution contracts are inordinately complex but, under them, the distributor generally agrees to bear certain costs and to have the privilege of recouping them before the profits on the film are returned to the producer. These are called "prep costs". They include the cost of making prints of the film, the costs of arranging press junkets and other publicity projects—and the costs of the TV commercials. Sometimes the prep costs amount to more than the total budget for many films—for *Star Trek, The Motion Picture* they came to $11 million. Sometimes they are unclear—which is why Ronald Shusett asked for an audit to find out why *Alien,* after selling a hundred million dollars' worth of tickets by his count, was still in the red on its initial investment.

After you pay your money at the ticket window, the theater you're in keeps a piece of it for its expenses and profit. The rest goes to the exhibitor. If he has spent a million dollars in prep costs, he keeps the first million to recoup his costs. The next million (or as many millions as come in) are the "rental" grosses, and out of them he takes 40% or so for his trouble and sends the rest along to the producer.

The trouble with all that is that it exposes the distributor to great temptation. His profit comes from the 40% of the net after prep costs are deducted. But he doesn't really pay the prep costs; they are recouped off the top. So distributors may be willing to spend almost a dollar on commercials to bring a dollar's rental in. The flip side of the coin is no better; if a distributor decides not to risk promotion money on a film, there is not much a producer can do. Brian de Palma offered to put his own money into promoting *Home Movies.* The distributor said he could do that only if he agreed to take the costs out of his producer's share—which, on a flop film, is zero.

Abuses or none, simple or complex, the uses of promotion are clear. No filmmaker dares risk opening without it. It is not just TV commercials. It is everything that can call attention to a film and make people willing to go out of their homes to see it. It is hype. Every word that comes from a studio, a director or a star is hype. Every publicized act is hype. Signing Marlon Brando for *Superman* was hype—it let the public know, years before the film was released, that this was not a cotton-gym-suit and cardboard-scenery *Superman,* it was a major production that could well afford to pay nearly $4,000,000 to one of the most famous actors in the world for what was essentially a bit part. The first release of *Close Encounters of the Third Kind* itself was a kind of hype—to get the customers to come back and see the same picture over again, for the sake of a little extra footage inside the alien spaceship.

So, when it came close to time for release of the three huge blockbuster sci-fi movies that closed out the 1970s, the publicity and promotion drums began to beat.

On the first day of August, 1979, a machine appeared in Pennsylvania Station, New York City. Commuters and vacationers paused to look at the flickering pictures from the internal slide projector. They didn't get much for their trouble. What they saw was the good old spaceship *Enterprise,* photographed from a dozen different points of view but not in any way different from the one that had graced a million *Star Trek* reruns. They also got a look at its aging crew, in a series of posed stills, and an unctuous voice-over about how great *Star Trek, The Motion Picture* was going to be—nearly half a year later, when it was scheduled for release. That was it. But that was the beginning. The other two biggies, *Moonraker* and *The Black Hole,* were not far behind.

FILMOGRAPHY

DAMNATION ALLEY (Universal, 1977, U.S.A.) 95 mins.

Executive producers, Hal Landers and Bobby Roberts; producers, Jerome M. Zeitman and Paul Maslansky; director, Jack Smight; script, Alan Sharp and Lucas Heller from the novel by Roger Zelazny; production design, Preston Ames; editor, Frank J. Urioste; special effects, Milt Rice; music, Jerry Goldsmith; camera, Harry Stradling Jr.

Cast: Jan-Michael Vincent (Tanner); George Peppard (Denton); Dominique Sanda (Janice); Paul Winfield (Keegan); Jackie Earle Haley (Billy); Kip Niven (Perry).

MOONRAKER (United Artists, 1979, U.S.A.) 126 mins.

Producer, Albert R. Broccoli; director, Lewis Gilbert; script, Christopher Wood from the novel by Ian Fleming; production designer, Ken Adam; editor, John Glen; visual effects supervisor, Derek Meddings; special effects, John Evans John; music, John Barry; camera, Jean Tournier.

Cast: Roger Moore (James Bond); Lois Chiles (Holly Goodhead); Michael Lonsdale (Drax); Richard Kiel (Jaws); Corinne Clery (Corrine Dufour); Bernard Lee (M); Desmond Llewelyn (Q); Lois Maxwell (Moneypenny); Geoffrey Keen; Emily Bolton.

THE BLACK HOLE (Disney, 1979, U.S.A.) 97 mins.

Producer, Ron Miller; director, Gary Nelson; script, Jeb Rosebrook and Gerry Day from a story by Rosebrook, Bob Barbash, and Richard Landau; production designer, Peter Ellenshaw; art directors, John B. Mansbridge, Al Roelofs, and Robert T. McCall; editor, Greg McLaughlin; director of miniature photography, Art Cruickshank; miniature effects, Peter Ellenshaw; music, John Barry; camera, Frank Phillips.

Cast: Maximilian Schell (Dr. Hans Reinhardt); Anthony Perkins (Dr. Alex Durant); Robert Forster (Capt. Dan Holland); Joseph Bottoms (Lt. Charles Pizer); Yvette Mimieux (Dr. Kat McCraw); Ernest Borgnine (Harry Booth); Tommy McLoughlin (Capt. S.T.A.R.).

The Black Hole promises everything but delivers only grief—it is truly the Ayatollah Khomeini of movies.

—Anji Valenza
(Review in *Tightbeam*.) (18)

Of the three super-spectacles that ended the decade of the 1970s, one was mildly disappointing. The trouble was that that was the best of the three. The other two were astonishingly inept.

Perhaps it is not fair to consider *Moonraker* as a science-fiction film. It is a James Bond film, and its producer, Albert Broccoli, denied flatly that it was science fiction to begin with.

If he had had the wisdom to stop there, all would have been well enough and we would have been spared the necessity of discussing this mindless spoof; but what the man actually said was, "The premise of *Moonraker* is not science fiction, it's science *fact.*"

Science fact. Oh, *shame*. *Moonraker* begins by showing "Jaws" surviving a parachuteless fall from a plane, and ends with the silliest depiction of free-fall ever put on a screen. James Bond has made his way to a sort of Gerard O'Neill space colony—it really serves no purpose to explain how. It is rotating, so there is a sort of centrifugal pseudo-gravity, which is right enough, except that at the hub there is no gravity at all—which is also right. Then the film goes wrong. Bond and one of the decorative women who follow him around have to make their way across this "no-gravity" zone at the hub and you would not believe how perilous and how agonizing it is. You especially would not believe it if you knew anything about zero-G environments. That's not the worst. To confuse his enemies, Bond decides to stop the habitat rotating. He does this by pushing a button. It then instantly stops, and at once everybody begins floating around. . . . Well, no matter what the producer may have the temerity to say, no one should really take a James Bond epic seriously. But there is no such excuse for the Disney studio's *The Black Hole*.

Disney had, and still very nearly has, the best film technicians in the world. Other people envied them, and sometimes borrowed them—as when *Forbidden Planet* hired them to animate the Id-beast. Disney himself had some admirable traits. He was said to be often abrasive, and as a businessman he has been called rapacious. But there was a gentle side to the man who gave us *Snow White* and *The Three Little Pigs,* and an idealistic one—no one but Disney would have dared *Fantasia.*

Immortalist circles cherish the belief (officially denied) that when Disney died he had left instructions for his body to be frozen, ready to be thawed out and returned to life as soon as medical science had learned how to repair it. If this is true, there ought to be trouble in store. His successors are not idealists. *The Black Hole* is as cynical a bit of film as you are ever likely to see. It is full of borrowings and self-borrowings. The cute robots are obligatory ever since *Star Wars,* of course, but *The Black Hole*'s Vincent looks a lot like Disney's earlier Johnny Fedora. The monstrous robot Maximilian, in his apocalyptic final scene, is the spitting image of Disney's Devil in *A Night on Bald Mountain.* Even the technical effects are dumb. The Disney conception of a meteorite swarm looks like rolling orange medicine balls—which is what they were. The Disney conception of the intense gravity around a black hole is that it makes you shudder and shake. There is a line of dialogue early in the film that epitomizes it. One member of the interstellar ships says (more or less) to another, "Say, just what are we doing out here anyway?" And the other replies, "Why, we're searching for habitable life." If this were so, the cast would, of course, have had to be ticks, fleas or pinworms. And for all the acting we get out of any of them, perhaps they were.

According to pre-release publicity, the stars of the films were given scripts with the ending deleted, so that no one, not even they, would know what the climax was to be before the film was released. A more likely explanation is that the producers didn't have an ending. There is none in the film. What there is is a series of catastrophe scenes and light-show montages reminiscent of, but not as good as, the end of *2001* and large sections of *Fantasia*.

Both *Moonraker* and *The Black Hole* advertised that they had retained real genuine scientists to make sure every concept was impeccably correct. *The Black Hole* even flew one five thousand miles just to say so on a local radio talk show. The money was not well spent. Both films have great lacks, but neither lacks anything else as much as it lacks intelligence.

When the major promotion started for *Star Trek, The Motion Picture,* there was a reason why clips from the film were not shown in the slide machines in the railroad stations. There weren't any decent clips to show. There was grave doubt, less than half a year before the release date that could not be changed, that there would even be a film good enough to put in the theaters by then.

Star Trek was a hard-luck project from the very beginning. As a network series in prime time, it attracted a fiercely devoted audience. Unfortunately, the audience was numerically small. The show limped through two years and was canceled.

But Gene Roddenberry, the producer and presiding brain behind the series, was not willing to let it go without a fight. He orchestrated a massive mail campaign. A blizzard of indignant letters from viewers dropped on NBC. The network caved in, and put it back on the air for another year. But the ratings were still a disappointment—and that was that.

Then the reruns began.

Two years after the program had "died" it began to show unexpected strength. By 1972, it was being rerun in almost every major city in the United States, sometimes on several stations in a single market. *Star Trek* conventions began to happen. One of them attracted 18,000 people and returned a profit of a quarter of a million dollars to its promoters. Bantam Books hired James Blish to write "novelized" versions of the original television scripts, and the books took off in the market place; some of them sold more than a million copies each. The Paramount executives watched it happen with awe and disbelief. They had not expected it, and it was getting away from them.

Something had to be done. But what?

They tried a Saturday-morning animated version of *Star Trek* for the kiddies. It just lay there. Trekkers were often very young—the convention attendance ranges upward from six or seven years of age, with an average probably in the teens—but they were not mentally impaired, so they didn't watch Saturday-morning television.

The executives then thought about bringing it back on the networks. It wasn't easy. The powers at NBC were as puzzled as the Paramount people about it all, but they had the solid evidence of the ratings to show that *Star Trek* could not compete in the pressure cooker of prime time network TV. Besides, there were difficulties in getting the cast together again. Nimoy was the key, and he was trying to make it on the legitimate stage; Roddenberry was into pilots for two or three other series—willing enough to go back in with *Star Trek,* to be sure, but only if the package was attractive. It was all troublesome and confusing. Something should be done, certainly. But what?

A feature film? Good idea; so Paramount started preparing scripts and lining up talent. The talent was coy. Shatner, Nimoy and all the others had been convinced of their godhood by tens of thousands of Trekkers at dozens of conventions, and each one expected to see that reflected in a pay check. A script was also elusive. First shot went to Roddenberry himself, who created a sort of "generations" story of the old age of the crew, coming back for one last go at the bad guys. Paramount nixed it and went on. It all took time, but as the months passed they had a script at last. Philip Kaufman was signed to direct what he called "essentially a Leonard Nimoy Spock story . . . it was a love story and it was *adult* science fiction" when the axe fell.

A new concept appeared. Some of the Paramount executives held in their hearts a very large dream, no less than a fourth national television network to compete on equal terms with NBC, ABC and CBS. It would not be a true network in the sense of pouring programs into the microwave relays or the co-ax. It would be syndicated, and it would build on the hundreds of large independent stations all over the country who were handicapped in selling commercial time to national advertisers because each of them sold only its own time, while one network salesman on one call could sell fifty or a hundred cities at once. Vital to that dream was a nucleus to build on—a program with so much strength that the independents would count on it, and come into the fold.

Star Trek was it.

But the job was immense. It progressed by fits and starts and setbacks; and after years of trying to put it together the deal still remained obstinately incomplete. So for more than five years the news on *Star Trek* was always the same. On even-numbered months the film was being rushed into production. On odd-numbered months the television series was about to begin to appear.

The Fourth Network dream died hard, but at last it died and Paramount made its bet. It would be a feature film. Only question was, what would the film *be*? Roddenberry wrote a script, and the Paramount people vetoed it. They hired Robert Silverberg to write one, and vetoed that too. At least a dozen writers of one kind or another were put on the payroll for long periods or short to try to come up with the magic idea that would make it all come together. But none of the writers could please; and at last Paramount remembered the scripts it had commissioned for the "Fourth Network" series. It reached back in among them and pulled out the Alan Dean Foster story that had been intended as the lead-off. And that became *Star Trek, The Motion Picture*. Viewers who think that *TMP* seems rather like any random episode from the television series have exactly the right of it.

There exists a novel version of the script, written by Gene Roddenberry, which shows a lot of inventiveness and interesting detail. Very little of it appears in the film. It is not likely that Roddenberry chose to eliminate the scenes, or that Paramount refused to foot the bill. The explanation is almost certainly that the special effects fiasco which almost doomed the film caused them to be dropped, for at almost the last moment Paramount switched special-effects studios and turned everything over to Douglas Trumbull when the original contractor failed to deliver.

Star Trek, The Motion Picture represents Hollywood

indecision at its lunatic worst. What appeared on the screen was no more than a rescue operation, the best compromise that could be reached between what Roddenberry wanted and what cold reality allowed. And yet—what a pleasure to see them all together again!

In 1968 I got a phone call from Gene Roddenberry to ask a favor. A letter was going out to all the *Star Trek* fans who had ever written in to the show, urging them to write NBC and demand the show be kept on for a third year. Would I be willing to sign the letter? Sure, I said; and for about three years after that my mailbox was full. I never saw the letter, but I know two things about it. First, it called on the recipient to write NBC and make his wishes known. Second, it was signed by "Frederik Pohl, editor of *Galaxy, If* and *Analog.*" I was editing *Galaxy* and *If*, all right, but I was not then and have never been editor of *Analog*. Most of the Trekkers understood what was expected of them and complied. A few did not; they somehow got the idea they were supposed to write to *me* about it, and so I kept getting letters addressed to "Frederik Pohl, editor of *Analog*, *If* and *Galaxy*", threatening dire reprisals if I did not at once put *Star Trek* back on the net. The first dozen or so I answered, trying to set things straight. After that I just gave up. . . . And two years later I got a letter from an NBC exec. They had just found out who was behind the *Star Trek* letter blitz, he said, and it was me. He complimented me on my muscle. I didn't know what to say to that, so I never replied.

—FP

FILMOGRAPHY

STAR TREK (Paramount, 1979, U.S.A.) 132 mins.

Producer, Gene Roddenberry; director, Robert Wise; script, Harold Livingston from a story by Alan Dean Foster; production designer, Harold Michelson; editor, Todd Ramsay; special photographic effects, Douglas Trumbull, John Dykstra; music, Jerry Goldsmith; camera, Richard H. Kline.

Cast: William Shatner (Captain Kirk); Leonard Nimoy (Mr. Spock); DeForest Kelley (Dr. McCoy); James Doohan (Scotty); George Takei (Sulu); Majel Barrett (Dr. Chapel); Walter Koenig (Chekov); Nichelle Nichols (Uhura); Persis Khambatta (Ilia); Stephen Collins (Decker); Mark Lenard; Billy Van Zandt.

We were ready to shoot *Star Trek: The Motion Picture*. We had Ken Adam doing the production design, we were ready to come to London. Ralph McQuarrie was living in London working with Ken, and I was finalizing the screenplay with all assurances from Paramount that this was a "go" project.

Paramount at that point hired some guys who decided they would start a fourth television network. Essentially they had all come out of ABC, and (decided) the best way to do that would be to have *Star Trek* as the center of this network. They said there is no future in science-fiction movies. I said, "But there's a friend of mine who's made a movie called *Star Wars* and it's coming out next week." But they told me to cancel it. Suddenly, out of a clear blue sky, they just canceled it. Immediately after giving me carte blanche and guaranteeing it was a "go" movie—they canceled it.

So they turned *Star Trek* back into a television show. A week later *Star Wars* came out.

For about a year they tried to keep *Star Trek* as a television show. Then—after *Close Encounters* etc., and the television network fell apart—they brought the movie back to life again. By then I was busy.

—Philip Kaufman (19)

SOURCES

1. Lucas, George.
2. Burtt, Ben. From a taped interview with the authors, June 1979.
3. Lucas, George.
4. Kurtz, Gary. From a panel discussion at *Seacon,* Brighton, England, September 1979.
5. Harrison, Harry. From a panel discussion at *Seacon,* Brighton, England, September 1979.
6. Kurtz, Gary. From a panel discussion at *Seacon,* Brighton, England, September 1979.
7. Henry, Allan. From *The UFO Handbook.*
8. Hynek, J. Allen. From the epilogue to *Close Encounters of the Third Kind,* Dell, 1980.
9. Spielberg, Stephen. *Close Encounters of the Third Kind,* Dell, 1980.
10. Bradbury, Ray. From a taped interview with the authors, January 1979.
11. Ellison, Harlan. From a taped interview with the authors, January 1979.
12. Burtt, Ben. From a taped interview with the authors, June 1979.
13. Kaufman, Philip. From an interview with Stephen Jones in *Fantasy Media,* June-July 1979.
14. Puzo, Mario. From an interview in *American Film,* May 1979.
15. Goldstone, Patricia. From *Los Angeles Times,* January 14, 1979.
16. From a letter in *Los Angeles Times,* January 14, 1979.
17. Denby, David. From *New York,* June 4, 1979.
18. Valenza, Anji. From *Tightbeam,* May 1980.
19. Kaufman, Philip. From an interview with Stephen Jones in *Fantasy Media,* June-July 1979.

Chapter 8

Toward a More Nearly Perfect
Science Fiction Film

Science-fiction films are usually fun, sometimes very good, once in a while superb. It is worth exploring just how good they might be—how good they some day may in fact be, if we all live long enough and God is kind. To find that out, we need to explore the limitations of the medium as well as its opportunities.

The vocabulary of filmmakers has been steadily enriched almost every year for more than three-quarters of a century. To that first capturing of moving images on a screen have been added the closeup, the montage, animation, color, the zoom lens, the wide screen—even such diversions as Smellavision, Three-D and SenSurround, not to mention all the wizardry of computers and process shots. It is not easy to spell out just what a film can do, particularly in the days of Doug Trumbull. But there are certain built-in constraints.

For one: Film is linear. It moves before your eyes at a constant rate of speed.

If you are reading a novel, you can pause and reflect before going on. You can even turn back a few pages to make sure you have grasped something that was said. You even have the privilege of skipping. If there is an explanation that you find tedious you pass it by—but it is there in case it should turn out that you need to know it later on.

In a film you cannot do any of these things. Whatever you need to grasp for your enjoyment of the film must be grasped on the fly.

Christopher Reeve accepting Hugo award for Superman at 1979 World Science Fiction Convention.
Locus *photograph by Susan Wood*

Two: Because it is linear, it can say only one thing at a time.

There are devices to help ameliorate the problem—for example the montage. Eisenstein's *October*, showing Kerensky orating, intercut with a peacock preening itself, is the archetypal example. Another, rare because it is so clumsy, is the *Strange Interlude* trick of hearing each character's thoughts spoken off camera. But film can only *suggest* "author omniscient" or "first person" narration, it cannot well show them. The technique does not exist to translate so simple a sentence as "He repressed the urge to kiss her" to the screen.

Three: The film can show you what the director wants you to see of a scene. It cannot show you what you might choose to see for yourself.

If *Star Trek, The Motion Picture* were real and you were suddenly transported to the control room of the *Enterprise*, you would have a wealth of smells, textures, vibrations and even tastes. In film you have only light and sound, and they are chosen for you. You cannot walk to one end of the control room to listen to the hum of a communicator, or to the other to browse the titles on a bookshelf. If there is a fly in the room, you can only see it if the director calls for a closeup of the fly. Books do not supply these sensory impressions either, but they encourage you to supply them for yourself. For the duration of a film you can believe you are seeing the *Enterprise.* But for the duration of a book you can believe you are in it.

Finally: Film is literal. Or, if it is not, you know when it is being not.

This is more important in science fiction than in "mundane" films, because so much of science fiction must be faked. Since the days of Kubrick and Trumbull much of it is almost indetectibly done: when it is a matter of space ships, or of drowned cities, or even of blowing up a planet, models serve splendidly—just as they have always done for air raids, tank battles and *The Towering Inferno*. But hardware is not everything. The difficulties lie in the laws of nature, and in the nature of the science-fiction characters. On a space ship in free fall, or on a planet with a different surface gravity than Earth's, the laws of nature produce different effects. Objects fall faster, or slower, or not at all. Liquids pour in peculiar ways. Candles may not burn. This sort of thing can be shown only by great ingenuity and at considerable expense; so, if it is shown at all, it is over-shown. It becomes a spectacle.

And the characters of science fiction need not be human. They need not be shaped like Earthly mammals at all.

But to show a truly alien character on film you must animate him, or fit him as a costume around a human actor, or move him by wires or stop-frame filming; and it all shows. The director can do his best to conceal it, by limiting his lighting or shooting through gauze; but if you have sat through two hours of *2001* or *Close Encounters of the Third Kind*, with every frame in razor-sharp focus, and it all goes swimmy just as the non-humans appear . . . you know why. It is because the director does not want you to see too clearly what is being faked.

For this reason, although science fiction in print is filled with fascinating non-human characters of all shapes and descriptions, there has never been *one* satisfying one on film or television. Except for comedy. (And five hundred years from now, when we do have creatures from other worlds visiting us, think what the Extra-Terrestrial Anti-

Defamation League is going to have to say about all those Wookies and Spocks.)

Beyond the physical limitations of film there are the social ones.

Film is the most collective of the arts. If you think seriously about the way in which films are made—the way in which they **must** be made, given the fact that they are expected to make money—it is hard to see how any good ones ever happen at all. Half a century ago Méliès could create his 500-foot masterpieces with only hired help, and Robert Flaherty could carry a camera around the far places of the Earth and come back with *Man of Aran* or *Nanook of the North.* Not any more.

> The problem generally is that, if the studio decides to make something, it buys the rights and sometimes wants to make it for the wrong reasons. It doesn't analyze what's good about the original, and looks at it as a saleable commodity of one kind or another, and proceeds to change it all except the title. And even the title. And has people on it who have no idea what the original intention was, or even care. . . .
>
> One of the problems in converting some science fiction to the screen is that a lot of the material is interior. It wasn't written in a visual way. It works perfectly on the printed page, but trying to convert it into film is very difficult. Not impossible. Maybe it is impossible in some cases, but in other cases it's really a matter of taking the thought of the original author and trying to be as true to that as possible. Not enough work goes into that phase. It's much easier to go into production and shoot dialogue and cut it together and come up with a finished product.
>
> —Gary Kurtz (1)

It is next to impossible for one person to make a film out of his own financial resources. George Lucas could. Stephen Spielberg probably could. Stanley Kubrick could come close—in fact, he usually has. But who else? Mario Puzo, whose touch has been gold on four straight box-office triumphs, has a pet project of his own; the financing has not come along. George Pal, with a lot of profitable films behind him, had a big loser in *The Seven Faces of Dr. Lao*, and so for the remaining fifteen years of his life he was unable to get backing for any of half a dozen cherished science-fiction and fantasy projects. The loser canceled out all the winners before it.

So, more and more, the big films are committee decisions. And more and more they are "safe" ones.

It was "safe" to make *Star Trek, The Motion Picture*. The balance sheets worked out. Space spectaculars were doing fine. *Star Trek* had its own devoted audience. Paramount reared back and passed a miracle: "Let there be *Star Trek, The Motion Picture*," they said, and, lo, it appeared. The same with *Superman*. The same, almost, with *Buck Rogers* and the same, for slightly different reasons, with *Battlestar Galactica*. No audience for something called *Battlestar Galactica* was known to exist but, as with *Buck*, what did exist was a television contract to amortize the production costs.

In none of this was there, at any time, a particular human desire to make a particular story. In none of this is a human being even visible—except for Gene Roddenberry, and he produced the script the committee gave him.

A committee cannot create a film. It cannot even really create a concept for a film. A committee is lucky if it can agree on buying one that someone else has created.

There are two basic ways in which a producing entity—a

studio, a consortium, sometimes an individual—acquires a story to be made into a film. They start with either a "concept" or a "property".

The "concept" usually originates with a committee decision, in which somebody looks up and says, "Hey, fellows, why don't we make a state-of-the-art sci-fi flick?" This is not usually the result of a burst of creation. It comes from market analysis, from trend-extrapolation studies and mostly from seeing long lines waiting to get into *Star Wars*. So a decision is made. It is not a commitment to the whole operation; it is just a little exploratory surgery. And so a writer is hired to put some words on paper.

In order to get this assignment, he has generally agreed to a "step" contract, so the words he puts on paper may not at first be very numerous—two or three pages, perhaps only a few paragraphs. The step contract provides that he will bring in specimens of words on paper from time to time. Each time he does so he will receive a stipulated sum of money, and the whole question will be reviewed. There are three options at each step: He will be told to go on to the next step; or he will be fired and some other writer will take over; or, third and most likely, that morning's *Variety* will have said the boom is over and the whole idea will be dropped.

The other way is to buy an actual property—say, a published novel.

> Every time a motion picture company buys a book they get cheated. There is no way an author cannot cheat them. There's always one character missing. . . . the author. And the book is partly what it is because the author's there.
>
> —Kurt Vonnegut Jr. (2)

> Two people, Charlton Heston and one other, for
> five years wanted to do *Make Room, Make Room* as
> a film. MGM said, "Aw, no. What's important about
> overpopulation? No one cares about overpopula-
> tion. That's not interesting. Can't do it." So they got a
> screenwriter, and he said: "The world doesn't care
> about overpopulation so, what we'll do, we'll bring in
> cannibalism. They'll eat that up, you know!" So
> MGM did *Soylent Green* because they thought they
> were doing a cannibalism picture.
> —Harry Harrison (3)

This can happen because a recognized agent submits the novel to a studio, and the studio decides it might make money as a film. More frequently it happens because someone connected with the studio somehow hears of the novel and issues instructions to acquire it. Almost any book that sells substantially well, or achieves good reviews, will be eyed for acquisition by any number of film and television types. A few of them are actually bought— well, more or less bought. If the producer is a shoestringer he will try to tie up the property with an option, as cheaply as possible—ideally, for nothing. If he is well enough financed, he will try to buy it. Openly, if he is candid and not too rich; through an intermediary (a lawyer, an agency or even a dummy producing company) if he is a really big one.

In any event, as soon as he has some sort of title to the property he hires a writer to "lick" it. That is, to figure out how to turn the book into a film. And the writer does that in the same way, by means of the same steps of outline, treatment, script and revisions, as if it had begun as his own concept.

That is how most films are born. Of course, it is not how Lucas, Spielberg, Kubrick and a few others do it; but it is how it is done by committee.

From the point of view of the average writer for print all this is distasteful. To him, writing for film is like a *Playboy* centerfold. Nice to dream about. Not real. If he tries his luck in Hollywood he finds that it is all real enough, and it no longer graces his dreams.

The writer of novels and short stories may from time to time have to bow to editorial madness or to publishing constraints, but generally speaking what he produces is what the customer gets. His writing *is* his product. It is all there is of it. All the paraphernalia of editors and bookstores and printing presses are only mechanisms to transmit his words to the reader. The best of writers-for-print, indeed, write primarily to please themselves, trusting to luck that some editor will be pleased enough to pass it along to the audience.

The writer for film is not so fortunate, and if he tries to work that way he will generally starve. The pages that leave his hand are not finished product. They are only another kind of raw material, like the unprocessed film in the camera or the cans of paint that will be splashed onto the sets. You will never, under any circumstances, see on the screen what the writer has written. At most you will only see what some other intelligence—and usually a collective one, at that—has made of it. Sometimes the rendition tries to be faithful, but what it can never be is exact.

There's worse. Seeing your work distorted is not really as bad as seeing it dead. If your child is born without a foot, it is better than having it not born at all; and there are literally hundreds of films every year that are stillborn.

Perhaps most of them deserve to be. When successive teams of writers fail to "lick" a script, it could be because the stupid thing isn't worth bothering with in the first place. But there are endless other possibilities. This script does not get made because the financing fell through. This one, because the producer died. These others because ownership was clouded and the whole project tumbled into a swamp of litigation, or because partners fell out, or because a star had a better offer from someone else, or because a director was killed in a motorcycle crash. Whatever the reason, the script is dead. Permanently. There is no market for unproduced film scripts. The writer cannot even publish them himself and give them away to his friends, because they no longer belong to him.

Some of the best science fiction writers in the world, over the years, have completed major projects that were permanently shelved, or at least withheld from audiences for years or decades. There's the equivalent of a library of a hundred novels, by your favorite writers, which exist only in the form of spiral-bound, plastic-covered shooting scripts. Ray Bradbury's own script for *The Martian Chronicles.* Harlan Ellison's for *I, Robot.* Gene Roddenberry's original *Star Trek* film script. Richard Matheson has half a dozen complete scripts in some studio safe. James Blish, at the peak of his powers, spent a year or more writing film adaptations of his own stories for an independent producer. None has ever been made.

At that, the writer is almost the best off of any of the creative artists involved in film.

The director cannot direct unless somebody hires him to do it. Then what he has to direct is what someone else has written.

As a teenager I developed a hobby of filmmaking, pursuing it as a kind of total craft. It offered me an opportunity to do so many different crafts I was interested in. I liked cinematography. I liked sound. I liked the ability to perform in an imaginary world. As a kid I had a tape recorder—I more or less always had a tape recorder—and I collected sounds.

Then, as I got more professionally involved, I noticed that there were very few young people entering the industry who ever said, "I'm interested in sound." I pursued that as a goal, because there was almost a vacuum there.

There's been a devaluation in sound in Hollywood in the last twenty years, because of economic considerations as well as other factors. Hollywood has really shown less of an interest in the sound track than it used to. This is because of schedules being accelerated, and the people making films just being less interested in sound. The role of the sound editor is always left to the last minute. The sound track by its very nature is one of the last stages before a film is done. The work takes place at the end of the chain of filmmaking. The time is really minimal. Producers finish their films and, I think as an afterthought, say, "Oh, we've got to have a sound track, too." And so people will be put on to just desperately work around the clock to sort of fill things in. They just barely get done the necessary technical things, and never have

any time to do anything creative—although they could. When I first looked at the industry I was surprised how little time, money and interest was spent on sound. People never talked about sound as something that could enhance their stories. It was just a technical thing.

When talking pictures first started, all of a sudden there were all these new technicians—"sound men". For a brief time they had the expression "sound is king" because, for a while, it dictated the whole process. As the equipment became more reliable and portable, and as the process was better understood, its relative importance shrank quite a bit. I'd say the creative use of sound in the '30s and '40s was far superior to what we were getting, say, ten or twelve years ago.

I'd love to do a movie with no English dialogue and no music. No music in the ordinary sense. Just sound. It could be done, and it would be quite an interesting kind of film. But it's very unlikely. One always has radical ideas, but when you're dealing with a commercial film medium there are lots of people to please before you get your idea tried out.

—Ben Burtt, Jr. (4)

> If a story interests me sufficiently to spend two to three years making a film, then I believe it will interest many others as well. If a film is good, it won't fail to find a proper audience, unless others in the industry—distributors, exhibitors—make some fatal error in selling it.
>
> —Stanley Kubrick (5)

Actors are worse off still. They read the lines someone else has written; and the way they read them is the way the director tells them to. Oh, now and then a Titan in either area can get a script changed, or a director replaced, but that is not the way to bet it. The final decision is not with writer, director or star; it is the money that gives the orders.

And yet, you know, they do it—they all do it. There is hardly a human being who has any hope of success in writing, directing or acting who does not willingly submit himself to all of the frustrations and caprices of the films.

It isn't just the money, though that can be spectacular. It's the excitement—the glamor—above all it is the audiences, ten million or even a hundred million at a time.

And what is it that keeps the audiences coming back?

It is the wonder of film. Three-quarters of a century old and still a wonder. There is a quality of splendor in some moments of science-fiction film that are not duplicated in the print literature.

It's a pity that science fiction films can't be perfect—the best writers, interpreted by the greatest directors and the finest cast exactly as intended, with utterly convincing special effects. But we can settle for second best—since even that, dear God, is still magnificent enough.

SOURCES

1. Kurtz, Gary. From a panel discussion at *Seacon,* Brighton, England, 1979.
2. Vonnegut, Kurt, Jr. From an interview in *CrittiFan,* Valby, Denmark, October 1978.
3. Harrison, Harry. From a panel discussion at *Seacon*, Brighton, England, September 1979.
4. Burtt, Ben, Jr. From a taped interview with the authors, June 1979.
5. Kubrick, Stanley. From an interview with John Hofses in *Soho News,* May 28, 1980.

APPENDIX

Effex in Esseff

The special effects in science-fiction films generate more discussion than anything else in them. It is not just that the effects let us see marvelous pictures, visible manifestations of somebody's fantastic imagination. The process itself strikes a responsive chord. In fact, sophisticated film technology is so seductive that special effects can make a success of a film that lacks almost everything else. Audiences watch new sf flicks as they do a conjuring show, and with the same emotions. The fascination is not only what they are looking at, but how it was done.

The producers of sf films are keenly aware of this, and so more often than not it is the special effects that determine the script of the film, rather than a script requiring certain effects. Screenwriters—maybe all writers—bemoan this new peril to artistic creation, but it isn't really all that new. Like so much to do with the science-fiction film, the subordination of the story to effects began with Méliès.

Another source of worry about special effects is the perception that their importance is a calculated ploy of the major studios (like the star system, or owning theater chains) to retain their dominance of the film marketplace. In this view, the majors encourage emphasis on special effects because only they can afford the equipment and people necessary to create them. They would be competitively less well off if the value of a science fiction film (or any other film) depended more on ideas and creativity, because ideas and creativity are harder to monopolize. But in the long run special effects are important for one real reason: Because audiences make them important. They are what fill the theaters.

When the average movie-goer remarks about the great special effects in, say, *Star Wars,* he is very likely thinking of the scenes of the fighters attacking the Death Star, or of the *Millenium Falcon* jumping to light speed. These are true special effects, all right. But they are only one kind— "special optical effects"—of the three major varieties.

Another sort of "special effects" is mechanical effects performed at the time of shooting a scene. The way the tools fly around Roy Neary's truck in   Close Encounters of the Third Kind is a fine example of "special mechanical effects". So is the rigging of small explosive charges, to simulate blaster hits, in *Star Wars.*

The third sub-area of special effects, "special audio effects", is really just emerging now. It was recognized in 1976 by the giving of a special Academy Award to Ben Burtt Jr. for the alien and robot sounds he created for *Star Wars.* Burtt did not invent the concept. Sound technicians as far back as *King Kong* and even the Weissmuller-O'Sullivan *Tarzan* movies strung soundtracks together, or reversed them, to get an animal roar or an ape-man's yell, and every radio station had its "sound effects" room full of tin sheets and coconut shells. With Burtt, as much in the new *Invasion of the Body Snatchers* and *The Empire Strikes Back* as in *Star Wars* itself, special audio effects came of age.

Of these three distinct areas of special effects, the visual (or optical) special effects are by far the most spectacular—and the most difficult to understand.

The techniques involved in producing optical special effects today are extraordinarily complicated, painstaking and detailed; the easy way, or at any rate the least difficult way, to begin to understand them is to go back to the times when they were simple. Let us avoid getting bogged down in the question "Who was first?" by starting at an arbitrary point: with two Englishmen, G. A. Smith and Robert Paul Williams.

G. A. Smith began his career as a portrait photographer in Brighton, England. Around the middle of the 1890s he built a movie camera and began to make films. They are not very memorable; what his reputation as a pioneer comes from is his 1897 patent on "double exposure" as a special effects technique. It would be interesting to know just how much money he realized from that patent; enforcing it would have been just about impossible.

Robert Paul Williams, at about the same period, was the inventor who, with H. G. Wells, applied for a patent on a "Time Machine". It was not meant to travel in time, only to look as though it were. The Machine was a booth, more or less like the machine Wells described in his novel, on the walls of which films were projected to give the occupant the illusion of time travel. Williams's experience with special effects was gained through teaching himself how to create them for the films for this booth; by 1905, in his film *The Motorist,* Williams in many ways surpassed what even Méliès would do years later. (1)

But Méliès is the name that dominates the field. Whatever Smith and Williams contributed, they were eclipsed by the reputation of Georges Méliès.

The story of how Méliès began his exploration of special effects has been often told. Méliès was shooting on a busy

Paris street. The film jammed. He corrected the jam without moving the camera and continued shooting. When he projected the film, a bus that had been in the frame when the jam occurred was miraculously and instantaneously transformed into a hearse. Méliès realized at once what a marvel that would be for audiences, and used the trick, in endless variations, throughout his filmmaking career. For example, the scene in *A Trip to the Moon,* where the Selenites tumble in the air and disappear, was done in this way; the camera was stopped as they were in mid-flight, and started again when the set was empty.

Méliès was able to achieve the sort of spectacular effects that would later take elaborate matte techniques simply through double exposure. In his film *The Man with the Rubber Head,* we see exactly what the title promises: Apparently a man has an inflatable head, that expands and contracts repeatedly until at last it is pumped up so huge that it bursts. This is all double exposure. First Méliès dressed his actor all in black, leaving only the head exposed, and stood him in front of a black backdrop. Then he ran the camera while the actor stood there, dollying it in and out to change the size of the head's image on the film. The film was rewound, and a set constructed containing a fake torso in the proper position for the already exposed film of the head. The film was run a second time to photograph the set and torso on the untouched emulsion; when developed, the illusion was there. It is not really a very good illusion, by modern standards, because part of the background is visible through the head. But audiences of that day knew little of even still photography, much less cinematography. They loved it. Méliès's success was attained through just such simple photographic tricks, added to the stage effects he had learned as a magician.

Before very long audiences got used to the effects in Méliès's films. They quickly became as bored by them as once they had been enchanted—a process that did not stop with Méliès. All through the history of the field, new techniques of special optical effects have been developed because audiences demanded more astonishing and more believable spectacles. Under this pressure, most of the principles of the field were discovered during the silent days. *Alien* and *The Empire Strikes Back* look staggeringly more impressive than, say, *Metropolis* or *Things to Come,* but not because of very many fundamental new processes. The principles are only slightly changed from those available in the 1920s; what makes them so sense-saturatingly pictorial is largely due to the greater precision with which the effects can be attained—and the greater speed, and therefore economy, which makes them feasible.

For example, the technique for showing flying rocketships by photographing models was pioneered by Charles Urban before World War I. By then, Méliès-style space flight, against full-size painted flats, left audiences cold. In Urban's film *Airship Destroyer* he hung miniature models on wires to make a sequence in which flying torpedos blow up invading aircraft to save the city.

The glass shot or glass matte, a technique for combining a painted background with live action, was first used by Norman O. Dawn in his 1907 film, *The Missions of California.* For this, a sheet of glass is interposed between lens and actors. The background is painted on the glass. It is a clumsy and time-consuming process. The camera must be kept in place while the background is being painted, and it is difficult to keep all parts of the picture in focus. But it was popular in the early days because it required only the simplest equipment. It's never used now.

But Dawn's other contribution is still with us: the in-camera matte. The "matte", as before, is a painted piece of glass; "in-camera" doesn't mean exactly *in* the camera, but in a frame mounted in front of the camera and called a "matte box". You set up your camera and look through the lens. You paint out the part of the shot to be removed with black paint. You then prepare another sheet of glass in reverse: black where the first was clear, clear where the first was black. You put the first sheet in and shoot your live action; rewind the film; put the other sheet in and shoot a painted backdrop, or even another live scene. When you develop the film you have a composite shot without further processing.

The matte must be extremely accurately made and positioned to avoid "plus" and "minus" areas—parts of the frame that were exposed during both runs, or not exposed at all. Even today, pluses and minuses occur—not blatantly, perhaps, but that is what accounts for the "pasted on" look actors have in some sf films.

Progress in special effects often happens in quantum jumps, sparked by the needs of some one important film. *Metropolis* was one such film.

Metropolis made the best use of composite shots of any film ever made until that time. A believable composite shot must have both two (or more) shots which fit together in terms of style, lighting and mood and also an undetectable way of putting them together. *Metropolis* excelled on both counts. A lot of thoughtful planning went into the full-scale and miniature sets created by art directors Otto Hunte, Rich Kettlehut and Karl Volbrecht, styling them so that they would combine harmoniously. And the elements were combined by the best state-of-the-art procedure available, the "Shuftan process". In fact, the effects for *Metropolis* were done by Shuftan himself.

In the Shuftan process, a large mirror, set at an angle of 45° to the optical axis of the camera, is placed between camera and set. The miniature set is placed at right angles, off to one side. For the portions of the frame where the full-scale set, directly before the camera, is to be seen, the silvering is scraped off the mirror, leaving the glass clear. Where the silvering is left on, the reflection of the miniature set is seen instead.

This technique has many of the drawbacks of a glass shot—notably laboriousness, which translated into part of the reason why *Metropolis* was the most expensive film ever made in Germany up to that time. But it yielded the highest quality composite then available, unblemished by background graininess or matte lines.

By the time of the early talkies most of the basic processes were known, but there was a continual evolution of technique. *Just Imagine* marked one advance—almost the first that was from American studios and filmmakers. The miniature model of the 1980 New York City cost a quarter of a million dollars. It may not yet have been surpassed in intricacy, though there have been many since that were more believable. *Just Imagine* used models in motion, instead of mere static backdrops, but the film's major claim to technological fame is that it was the first to employ moving rear projection. This technique requires a complicated mechanical linkage between camera and rear projector, so that both will have their shutters open at the same time; it was not a perfected process, and the backgrounds look shaky today. But they were remarkable for the time.

The "mechanical" effects technicians came into a whole new repertory when Kenneth Strickfaden created *Frankenstein.* The electrical displays, though they owed something to *Just Imagine* and even earlier films, were startlingly effective—so much so that they have been a cliche of horror films ever since.

In 1933 another effect that had been used before, but without creating much stir, triumphed at last in a commercial example. The artist was Willis O'Brien, who had first experimented with stop-action techniques in shorts and silents, like *The Lost World.* Now, in *King Kong*, he made them sing. The monster ape was not one ape but six, and the one which did most of the damage in the film was only eighteen inches tall. (The reason for having six was partly so that several of the laborious stop-action sequences could be filmed simultaneously.) Kong was constructed on steel armatures, complete with ball-socket joints, covered with rubber flesh and rabbit-skin fur. (There were also two larger partial Kongs, a bust and a dissected arm and foot.)

Until you have seen it done, it is hard to believe what plodding labor goes into make a stop-action sequence of a film. Kong's every move had to be charted in advance, each motion or gesture broken down into increments representing the distances the ape's parts would move in each frame. Kong would be put into position and a single frame exposed; moved, and another frame exposed; moved again, and so on. (A film the length of *King Kong* contains about 150,000 frames!)

Kong presented a special problem, because he was hairy. Hair is the enemy of the stopaction animator, because any disturbance of fur while the ape is being moved shows up instantly as a change in texture. O'Brien lavished care on these sequences, but even so the change in texture is visible if you know where to look. (The place to look is in the parts of the model which are away from the action. The moving parts don't show it because the illusion is too strong.)

Along with his stop-action model work, O'Brien completed his achievement of realism in *King Kong* by pioneering miniature rear projection. To see how the two techniques came together, let's look more closely at one particular sequence, the provocative scene in which Kong strips Fay Wray's clothes off. (The scene was cut from the film before its original release, but has been restored in many of the prints now in circulation.)

Fay Wray was dressed in breakaway clothes, placed in front of a neutral background and the camera was rolled. Invisible wires pulled her clothes off, piece by piece. This film was developed and a print was made.

A separate set was made to the miniature size of the Kong model; where Fay Wray was to appear, a small screen made of surgical rubber was placed. (O'Brien had to use surgical rubber because the usual screen materials were far too coarse-grained for this delicate work. It is not stated what kind of "surgical rubber" was employed.) The rubber dried out quickly under the lights and had to be replaced frequently.

Then Frame One of the Wray footage was projected on the screen, and Kong was placed in his initial position. A frame of this scene was shot. Frame by frame, the Wray film was projected on the rubber, and the Kong model was moved to synchronize with it. The sequence was a triumph of O'Brien's ingenious stop-action animation, achieved at great expense in time and labor. And then the censors snipped it out of the release print.

There was not much progress either in science-fiction films or in special effects in the 1940s—the world was busy with other concerns. Rear projection continued to dominate film technique, as the bread-and-butter alternative to expensive location shooting. But in the 1950s the sf film was reborn, and special effects development was reborn.

In the wake of the V-2s, the emphasis was all on space. The first major film to deal with spaceflight realistically was George Pal's *Destination Moon* and, being the first, Pal had to create his effects from scratch.

For the takeoff sequence the film had to show the actors undergoing the massive gee forces of acceleration. Transparent membranes were attached to the actors' faces, attached to wires and pulled taut from behind: the faces were stretched downward. The actors lay in couches whose backs dropped away during the shot, giving the illusion that they were pressed down into them.

The interior ship set had to be made of steel, since it required structural integrity so that it could be rotated into any attitude, in order to hang the actors from wires for the look of weightlessness. Outside the ship, the weightless effect sent Pal back to his experience in puppetry: the actors were stuffed into suits padded with wool to look pressurized, and hung from wires like marionettes. The steel wires unfortunately reflected light, and so a man was detailed to repaint them black every time the cameras stopped. Their movements were controlled by a corps of puppeteers.

There is no scene in nature on the face of the Earth that quite duplicates the endless black and star studded look of space. Imitating it still plagues filmmakers; Pal's solution, adequate for the time but a long way from perfect, was to hang a black velvet drop pierced with holes for automobile headlight bulbs to shine through.

Not all the great sf films of the Fifties showed much sophistication in special effects. *The Day the Earth Stood Still* offered only a rudimentary, and barely credible sequence of the flying saucer approaching Washington before remaining steadfastly earthbound for all the rest of the story. The only intriguing special-effects scene is the one showing Klaatu's seamless saucer growing a door. This was simply done. The door was cut into the hull and the seams filled with putty painted silver. Careful lighting concealed the putty; when the door was needed to open, stagehands pushed it from behind.

While the matte technique made it possible to combine miniatures and real action on the same scene, up until the 1950s the matte was stationary and not very convincing. *The Incredible Shrinking Man* used a new and better technique called the "traveling matte".

There are many ways of doing this, but the purpose is always to change the matte shape as the thing being matted out moves. In *TISM* the film was in black and white and the technique still quite new; much of the film suffers that pasted-on look of early matting.

The process is also useful for color film, and far better examples have since turned up, notably in Ray Harryhausen's *The Seventh Voyage of Sinbad* and the Dino de Laurentiis *King Kong.*

Let us suppose you want to shoot a scene showing your actor in front of a large, but imaginary, building. One way to do this is to construct the building in full size, place your actor on the scene and shoot: highly expensive and slow. The method typical of early films (and of most stage productions) is to paint the building as a backdrop, or as a slide which is projected on a screen: simple, but not visually satisfying. The traveling matte is a better answer. You can readily accomplish everything you want by means of what is called the "blue screen" process.

The first step is to film your actor doing whatever the script tells him to do, in front of a monochromatic blue screen. You film in color, but you print onto black and white film with an emulsion that is insensitive to blue. When developed, you have a black and white image of your star, surrounded by clear film. You make a high-contrast reversal print of this film, which is "Matte A". You then make a negative print of Matte A, which yields a silhouette of a clear actor surrounded by opaque black film; this is "Matte B".

Now you produce your background—the imaginary building—either as a model or a painting of some sort, and photograph it on color film; and now you take the two scenes to the optical printer to be combined.

An optical printer is basically a camera linked to a projector. Fresh color print stock is placed in the camera side of the printer. The background scene and Matte A are put into the projector side, and the film is exposed. It is then rewound; Matte B and the foreground scene (the live actor) are put in the projector, and it is exposed again.

The defect of this system is that what you wind up with is

a print of a print. It is hard to control color values and graininess, which is why, in old monster films, you can always tell when the monster is going to appear; the colors get muddy and the film shows grain. (2)

While Ray Harryhausen was continuing to increase the sophistication of the technique he inherited from O'Brien, the Japanese were going a whole other way. There was not much subtlety in *Godzilla*, either in terms of plot or effects. Instead of going the laborious stop-action route, Godzilla was actually a man (Tomoyuki Tanaka) in a rubber suit. The monster's movements were filmed in slow motion, and the believability of the film depended wholly on the painstaking detail of the miniature sets through which he walked. Although the effects were crude compared to what was being done then in Europe and America, not to mention later developments, the non-stop action made this film series one of the most profitable in motion picture history—proving that sophistication isn't everything at the box office.

Forbidden Planet is, of course, a landmark in the science-fiction film, but its awe inspiring qualities stem more from breathtaking production design than from any one special effect. (Unless you count Robby the Robot as a special effect.) The saucer scenes were live-action shots of several different sized model saucers, suspended by wire from a track and filmed in front of a star field similar to *Destination Moon*'s. Almost every trick available was used for one process shot or another, including rear projection (in the scene where the Id beast melts through the laboratory door to attack Morbius) and matte process (where Morbius takes Adams to tour the Krell ventilation shafts.)

The best work that I've done for films has been things that have never even gotten on film. Projects where somebody has some money and a rough idea for a film, and they say, "Let's get together and figure out if it's feasible." And I do some drawings, and they say, "That looks great," and they give me the script. I comment on the script, and they comment on the drawings, and we kind of get things together. And then, if we get far enough, we go and build us a monster. Somebody gives me a couple of hundred dollars for materials, and I build a prototype. But the rest of the money hasn't showed up yet, and it's kind of like it's on spec. That's the low end of the spectrum in putting together a film.

—John Lackey (3)

The lion-like Id beast, seen only when it was hit by disintegrator beams, was animated by Joshua Medor, on loan from the Disney studios.

Very little new occurred in special effects in the near-decade following *Forbidden Planet*. At Disney, blue screen was being replaced by sulfur screen; Ray Harryhausen continued to improve his method of model animation; all the processes were fine-tuned. But there were few breakthroughs . . . until Stanley Kubrick made *2001: A Space Odyssey*.

It would take a whole book to cover the special-effects techniques used in *2001*. They were not merely improvements on existing processes. Kubrick, Pederson, Trumbull et al almost started from the ground up and reinvented the techniques of special effects to make the film. The most notable effects come from three basic categories of technical achievement: front projection; composite space shots; and slit-scan photography. Let's take them one at a time.

"Front projection" is easy enough to understand in principle. The first question you might ask is, why bother? After all, projecting a scene on a translucent screen from the back had been around for a long time. True; but among other drawbacks, the diffusion of the translucent screen emphasized graininess and dulled the outlines. It is seldom hard to see when a background is rear-projected.

Then why not go to front projection right away? Ah, but there are problems. First, if you project your scene on the backdrop, you are projecting it on your actors too. This covers them with images of an African veldt, and unless you look through the projector lens itself, you can see white patches on the screen behind them where their bodies have shadowed the projection. You can compensate for the images cast on the bodies of the actors by lighting them brightly from another source—but the extra light washes out the image projected on the screen, and you are no better off than before.

However, Kubrick had something available that had not been around for very long: a new and highly reflective screen material developed by the 3M Corporation, consisting of plastic beads bonded to fabric. Each bead acted as a tiny lens. The effect was of a highly directional and very intense reflector, somewhat similar to the layer of reflective cells in the eye of a cat. With the very high albedo screen, the problem of images on the actors simply did not matter—they were not visible. Remained the problem of parallax. The camera lens and the projector lens had to be in the same optical axis. That was accomplished by mounting the projector at right angles to the camera line, and interposing a semisilvered mirror set at a 45° angle to the line of sight.

In *2001* front projection was used in the opening Dawn of Man sequence. A unit was sent to Africa to take 8 x 10 color transparencies of the landscapes. Back in England, a foreground set was constructed in front of a 40' x 90' screen of the 3M material. The projector threw the transparency images against the 45° mirror and then onto the screen; the camera shot through the same mirror, and the illusion was complete—for the camera, the audiences and everybody but the actors, who couldn't see the image on the screen at all because of its directional reflectivity.

The "composite space shots" presented severe problems to a perfectionist like Kubrick. Matte techniques were the obvious way to handle them. But we have already mentioned the problem of making a film of a film, and Kubrick was sensitive to this. His intention was to give the whole of *2001* a "first generation" look—not easily done with color film.

Color film is made of three separate emulsions, red, blue and green, in three layers. It is standard practice to make a set of color separations of every color film—that is, three separate prints, in black and white, made through red, blue and green filters. This is necessary for any film that one wants to keep, because the dyes in the color prints decay in a relatively short time, while the filmmaker wants to keep his film around forever. The black-and-white prints, with stable silver emulsions, decay very slowly; so, years after release, when all existing color prints of a film are showing their age, you bring out the separations, print them through their respective filters onto color stock and, lo and behold, you have a perfect new color print of your film.

Kubrick did this as a matter of course to preserve his films, like everyone else. But he also did it to avoid the color shifts and other undesirable effects that accompany multigenerational (i.e., shooting film of other films) special effects techniques.

Let's take a simple shot, say of *Discovery* passing across a screen ablaze with stars. Kubrick did it by holding the model stationary and moving the camera, on a track that gave the proper movement. He shot each movement three times, exactly reproducing the track of the camera, all in black and white film, but once each with red, blue and green filters on the lens.

It would have been comforting to develop the negatives

to see that everything was all right; but Kubrick's rule was to hold all the special-effects negatives undeveloped, so that they could all be developed at the same time, under the same conditions, to make sure the color values were identical for each.

Next step was to photograph a star field. So that the stars would not show through the spacecraft, a matte was needed. In 2001, the mattes were produced by "rotoscoping", a process in which the outline of the ship was hand-traced, frame by frame. Then, at the processing stage, all three color separations of all the elements, ship, matte and star field, were combined to produce a film with black blacks and true color.

Remember, this was about the simplest possible scene. When the shots contained a number of elements—say, the Discovery, the background, perhaps a pod and one of the astronauts—it became even more complicated. Now you know why 2001 took so long to make.

"Slit-scan" shows up in the "trip" sequence near the end of 2001. As in most special effects, the principle is simple, the execution is not. "Slit-scan" is controlled streak photography.

Suppose you put a piece of artwork on an animation stand —which is simply a camera and easel setup, whose relative movements can be precisely controlled. Light the artwork. Open the camera shutter. Then, while the shutter is still open, move the artwork slightly. The image will be slightly streaked—and, when shown at the usual rate of a projected film, will give a more lifelike illusion of motion than the usual stop-action hard-edged shot. For 2001 the animation stand was computer controlled, and the motion of the artwork relative to the camera was varied from

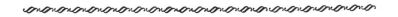

In visual effects, films have gotten to the point where the kind of effects they want to do are very expensive. I hate to seem worldly about it, but it's true. With computer-controlled cameras, etc., suddenly you've had a surge forward in what can be done, but it's also meant a very expensive kind of process. Basically there's conservatism created by the amount of money involved. We can imagine what we'd like to do on film, but we're always surprised at how long it takes. It's like scientific research. You can imagine having five hundred creatures riding across a desert on five hundred other creatures, but to actually do that for a film might take several years to figure out, and a large amount of money. Now the equipment is not manageable, on the time-scale and the money-scale, to allow one or two persons to do special effects.

—Ben Burtt, Jr. (4)

frame to frame; the illusion was excellent, as everyone who has seen the film can see for himself.

By the time of the big blockbuster sf films that ended the decade of the 1970s, filmmakers had become almost obsessive in their attempt to film the never-seen, and eclectic in their methods of doing it. Some of the newest high-powered technology was seen—and some of the oldest.

When Dino DeLaurentiis brought *King Kong* back to the screen, there was some sharp (if unintended) comedy in one of the lines, as Jeff Bridges, looking at the devastation on Skull Island and arguing with a skeptic, says, "What did you think knocked down those trees, some guy in an ape suit?" That's exactly what it was. The *Kong* publicity releases were full of technological drumbeating about the full-size working robot Kong that had been built for astronomical money. Trouble was it didn't work. Every time they started it up, dozens of gallons of hydraulic fluid squirted out of its gut. The mechanical Kong made it to the screen only in the Yankee Stadium sequence, and there only in part. For all the rest of this super-lavish, top-of-the-line production, the special effect was exactly the same as in the old *Godzilla*: an actor named Rick Baker, dressed in a monkey suit, moving through fantastically good miniature sets. The mini-Kong was placed in the full-sized scenes by a new type of blue-screen process that could tolerate Kong's fuzzy body and Jessica Lange's blonde hair without breaking up; the rest was Rick Baker, a "special effect" as old as the morality plays of the Middle Ages.

On the other hand, the very newest in special effects was in—of course!—*Star Wars*. And, of course, what put *Star War*'s technology so far in advance of, say, *2001*'s was the computer. George Lucas put together a special effects team headed by John Dykstra, and they created a computer-controlled camera mount which they dubbed the "dykstraflex".

Before the dykstraflex, all special effects shots had to be done with a stationary camera—or, as in *2001*, with a moving camera on a track, but a stationary subject. There was no other way, because it was impossible to reproduce in the model shooting stage the movements of camera and subject when the live-action footage was shot. This had not been much of a hindrance for filmmakers when the film grammar did not include moving camera shots anyway. However, largely due to the influence of European directors, it has become usual to shoot scenes in a small number of extended, moving-camera shots, rather than the traditional long shot, medium shot, close up pattern that had been universal in Hollywood since the birth of the industry. Now, with the dykstraflex, even special effects can be shot with a moving camera.

The dykstraflex is a camera mount which records all the pans, tilts, zooms and other movements that a camera makes during a particular shot, storing the information digitally on magnetic computer tape. The tape is saved until it is time to shoot model work to combine with the live action; then it is played back, and the camera automatically reproduces the exact moves of shooting the original live action. In this way, when live and model shots are composited, they match exactly.

Perhaps the greatest hits of the original *Star Wars* were that stellar comedy duo, R2D2 and C3PO; the technology was not very advanced above Robby the Robot from *Forbidden Planet*, for the first film. But by the time of the

I'm convinced the most important part of the (sound) process is the sound creator, and the selection of the original raw material. What you go out and record, or what you manufacture.

I always like to place the emphasis on finding sounds. I don't like to place too much on the laboratory aspects, endless processing and analyzing and synthesizing in the studio. I'd much rather spend my time going out into the world with a simple tape recorder and a microphone. In the '40s you could tell which studio made a film by the sound effects. Each studio had its own library of sounds. I collect new ones. By doing that, you not only survey your environment but you also learn, because you're going out and documenting the relationship between sound and emotion. When your goal is to have an effect on the audience, why not go out and see where the emotional association begins? What are the sounds we listen to as we grow up and go to work every day? That's the inventory of sounds that you've got to deal with.

Sound should never call attention to itself. You have to decide sort of in the way a musician does. You reach an emotional goal by using material that people will respond to.

You could develop, say, an alien language just by tapping on a desk with some sort of binary code. You could actually communicate with it, but if you did that in a film, one, people wouldn't recognize it as a language, two, it'd be boring.

—Ben Burtt, Jr. (4)

sequel, *The Empire Strikes Back*, the robots were quite sophisticated devices; where once they had been able to totter only a few steps, now they could walk for miles. Beyond that, the greatest change in technology between the two films lay in Lucas's conversion to Ray Harryhausen-style model animation. This is shown to excellent effect in the Taun-taun sequences, along with elaborate mechanical effects, as in the battle with the walking tanks.

But *Star Wars*'s most special of effects were meant for the ear, not the eye. Ben Burtt Jr. became the prototype of a new breed of special effects artist, and the dialogue he created for the robots and alien creatures won him a special Academy Award.

Gary Kurtz and friend at Science Fiction World Convention, 1977. Photograph by Jay Kay Klein

Movie sound technology has suddenly been looked at with a new viewpoint. There are a number of young people entering it that want to do something new with it. They see all sorts of computers being used to process sound, and they get excited. But when you actually try to put it to application you come up against all sorts of difficulties, of adapting it to the present movie system.

I would say it's the beginnings of what might be a revolution. I wouldn't say a revolution yet. In order to have a revolution you have to get the theaters to change their sound system.

People are vaguely aware that 70mm is better sound than a regular movie, and some people are vaguely aware that the Dolby system might offer them a better sound track. It's a slow process, because they have been going to movies for years to see the normal optical sound track. They accept movies as being that way. But they might go to a rock concert and expect a totally different thing—loud sound, a spectacular display. If you had the quality of a motion picture sound track at a rock concert people would riot.

The real obstacle is getting the motion-picture and theater industries to convert from their old, antiquated system, because it would be an expense to do so. There are a lot of frustrated sound people around, because the studio can do a lot of special things with sound but the people will never hear it.

—Ben Burtt, Jr. (4)

What Burtt represents is a new recognition of the value of sound, and the creation of a special sound effects separate from sound editing in general. This new emphasis has been encouraged, if not made possible, by the widespread adoption of such high-fidelity stereo systems as Dolby, as well as by the sophisticated recording techniques available on phonograph records. Together with John Williams's creative scores for both films, the Lucas trademark is as much audible as visual.

Fully as catholic in its methods, *Superman* too showed great resourcefulness in special effects—even using a midget to play Christopher Reeves in some of the flying scenes. *Alien, Star Trek, The Motion Picture* and many others had interesting variations—even *The Black Hole* had technical interest, if not much other. But if we are to pick one particular motion picture to celebrate because of its special effects, perhaps it should be none of these. Perhaps the one that imposed the greatest demands on its crews, and met them in the most spectacularly impressive ways, was *Close Encounters of the Third Kind.*

In creating the effects for *CE3K, 2001* graduate Douglas Trumbull had ten years of technological advances to add to his already impressive repertory. Trumbull and his associates took note of the dykstraflex and created a camera mount more flexible still, as long as a new way to matte in their spacecraft. This was necessary for *CE3K*'s spaceships because, unlike those in almost any other science-fiction film, they are seen in operation not in empty space, but in the fuzzy atmosphere of the Earth. So Trumbull sought a diffuse image for his spacecraft; he shot the models in a controlled smoke environment, and to matte these fuzzed images into the live action he developed a variable density matte technique.

Some of the most technologically demanding shots in *CE3K* do not look like special effects at all. For example, the night exterior shots of Jillian and Barry look as though they had been filmed on location, with very fast film. Unfortunately, film fast enough to capture a shot like this does not exist. Trumbull photographed them out of many elements, like any of the saucer shots, using composite techniques.

But the most impressive thing about *CE3K* is not any single aspect of its special effects, but the way in which they are combined, mechanical effects and lighting, combined with optical and sound, to create a whole film experience. At one time during the filming Spielberg was using almost every Titan arc light in Hollywood to show the effect of the alien lights on the landscape. He spared no effort; and it shows.

CLOSE ENCOUNTERS OF THE THIRD KIND (Columbia/EMI, 1977) Carey Guffey goes out to see what's making the bright lights and disappears.

It's the attitude, really, about special effects. You can have all the money in the world, and still have a bad shot go through and into the finished picture. It's really a matter of looking at it objectively and saying, "No, we can't include this in the picture. It's better to leave it out." On the other hand, the filmmaker sometimes gets seduced into saying, "Well, it's *almost* good enough. No one will notice." It's very hard to know. You've seen the shot so many times that you know *every* detail—and, for you, *nothing* works, always, when you see your own work. Every special-effects shot has some problem. It's only the audience, that doesn't know how much trouble it was to get that, that can see it objectively.

—Gary Kurtz (5)

What we try to do in *Star Wars* is develop new special-effects shots that don't necessarily give you a much better result, but do it quicker and at less cost. We're hopeful now that, as a result of the introduction of some of the computer technology, some of the effects that took a tremendous amount of time before can be done much more quickly. The tradition was, from *2001*, that it took many, many years to do space shots. Well, what Stanley had to work with in *2001* was very limited resources, even though he had quite a bit of funds. The computer technology hadn't been developed enough so that he could take advantage of it. We were able to take advantage of that, and it went on to the camera that was built for *Close Encounters*, and some other work beyond *Close Encounters*, and now we're at the second level of technology.

—Gary Kurtz (5)

(In the 1978 version of *Invasion of the Body Snatchers*) we had originally talked about some kind of lighter-than-air spores coming down and so forth. When I really got down to doing that sequence I got more fascinated with this organic matter—this space seaweed or whatever that stuff is that comes. As we were doing it I became kind of struck with the feeling that, "My God, those things look like the pictures of UFOs that you see!" These kind of elongated shapes. And the idea struck me that maybe that's what UFOs are. People always see these things. They photograph them, and then when they get to those locations the things are gone. And as Veronica Cartwright says in the movie, "Why do we always expect them to come in Mother Ships?" What if they were just a pulsating life-form that came from seed, that came through rain storms, sank into the earth, sprouted and became . . . Robert Duvall?

I finally found a substance (to represent them) back of an art store in San Francisco. Just one jar of something that I had found there earlier. I had shot part of the film—where the things land, and there's this clear gel hanging on the pods, and the stuff that's on the leaves that grows tendrils; and when I got back to the art store for more it was as though that substance had never existed. There was no record of it! Some woman had come in and bought the other jar. They had to finally break it down and recreate it so we could do the rest. Very strange. It was the pods. They tried to cover their tracks—I know you're out there!

—Philip Kaufman (6)

What next for special effects?

We have not touched on some of the side alleys that have been explored—SmellaVision and SenSurround and the various forms of 3-D; nor have we looked very deeply into those special electronic techniques that are used so widely in television, although it seems likely that they will appear more and more often in feature films as well. It is even possible that someone will find a way to apply holography to films, although the abortive experiments so far, like *Logan's Run*, have been dismal failures.

What seems clear is that anything a writer can describe and a director can imagine, a special-effects technician will find a way to show on the screen; and today, with the computer, the laser and marvelously ingenious optics available to any producer with the price, it can be shown convincingly, spectacularly—and beautifully.

—FP IV

SOURCES

1. Brosan, John. *Movie Magic: The Story of the Special Effects,* Plume Books, New York, 1976.
2. Rovin, Jeff. *From the Land Beyond Beyond,* Berkley-Windhover Books, New York, 1977.
3. Lackey, John. From a radio interview with the authors on KPFK, Los Angeles, January 1979.
4. Burtt, Ben, Jr. From a taped interview with the authors, June 1979.
5. Kurtz, Gary. From a panel discussion at *Seacon,* Brighton, England, September 1979.
6. Kaufman, Philip. From an interview with Stephen Jones in *Fantasy Media,* June-July 1979.